libraries

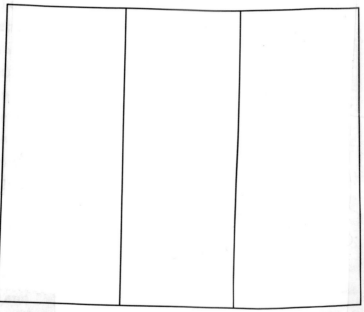

Ti
ur
be
(H
he
th
al
he

of
m
le
Lo
bo
Bu
Tl
la
ur

THE HAPPINESS DICTIONARY

DR TIM LOMAS

piatkus

PIATKUS

First published in Great Britain in 2018 by Piatkus

1 3 5 7 9 10 8 6 4 2

A CIP catalogue record for this book
is available from the British Library.

ISBN 978-0-349-41719-6

Typeset in Stone Serif by M Rules
Printed and bound in Great Britain by
Clays Ltd, St Ives plc

Papers used by Piatkus are from well-managed forests
and other responsible sources.

MIX
Paper from
responsible sources
FSC® C104740

Piatkus
An imprint of
Little, Brown Book Group
Carmelite House
50 Victoria Embankment
London EC4Y 0DZ

An Hachette UK Company
www.hachette.co.uk

www.improvementzone.co.uk

To Kate, and to my family

Contents

Chapter Four: Connection 99

Chapter Five: Appreciation 125

Acknowledgements

I'd like to thank some special people who have made this book possible: my incomparable wife, Kate, love of my life, who fills my world with sunshine and happiness; my wonderful family, for whom I'm so grateful; my fantastic agent, Esmond Harmsworth; Zoe Bohm, Anna Steadman, Jillian Stewart, Jo Wickham and all the great team at Piatkus; Emilia Lahti, who inspired the lexicography itself; and everyone who has contributed to the project with generous suggestions, advice and enthusiasm. Truly, this book is the work of many minds, and I am ever grateful to those who have helped make it happen. With that, let's begin...

Preface

What does the word 'happiness' mean to you? The serenity of lying in your partner's arms? That slightly guilty pleasure of indulging in a rich chocolate cake? The giddy liberation of leaving work on a Friday afternoon and embarking upon a longed-for holiday? The joy of seeing your child take her first steps, or say his first word? That moment when life seems totally perfect, and you wish you could stop the clock there for ever? Perhaps all these things . . . and more!

The trouble with happiness is not that it means nothing, but that it means *too much*. We use the word to cover a universe of positive feelings, from trivial hedonic sensations to our most profound experiences. Consequently, it risks becoming washed out and devalued, cheapened by easy repetition. The experiences themselves may even be diminished, eliding together in one amorphous, homogeneous melange. If happiness covers everything from light-hearted revelry to the deepest fulfilment, we may lose the ability to differentiate. All good things become the same shade of bright but slightly jaded yellow.

Moreover, our limited vocabulary means many wonderful experiences can elude our grasp. Have you ever experienced a sensation you couldn't quite describe, because there is no

English word for it? Without the ability to put a label to it, you may struggle to register the feeling at all. It might hover vaguely for a moment at the fringes of your consciousness, before swiftly dissipating, like a dream upon waking. As such, remembering and understanding it may prove difficult. For such reasons did Wittgenstein argue that the limits of our language define the boundaries of our world.[1]

However, all is not lost. We are not imprisoned by our native language. Even if English has not created a word for a specific phenomenon, *another language might have done so*. These are known as 'untranslatable' words, although that label is a little misleading. They aren't *literally* untranslatable: a sense of their meaning can usually be conveyed in a few words, or at least a couple of sentences. Rather, untranslatability means the term lacks an exact equivalent in another language; in our case, English. Excitingly, as we discover these words, the boundaries of our world expand accordingly.

For instance, I've had a personal interest in Buddhism for nearly twenty years, and as such have encountered many untranslatable words in languages such as Sanskrit. These range from *karma* (an illuminating theory of ethical causality) to *nirvāṇa* (the tantalising possibility of total liberation from suffering). I've reflected deeply on these strange, initially unfamiliar terms, and have even tried to explore them experientially through meditation. *Nirvāṇa* may remain a distant and elusive goal, but my sense of the limits of human possibility has broadened dramatically.

Such is the power of untranslatable words. Their potential is manifold. To begin with, they allow us to conceptualise familiar feelings, such as happiness, with greater clarity by helping us to sift it into fine-grained elements. They may also give voice to sensations we've hazily experienced, but previously lacked the ability to vocalise. They can even lead us to new experiences we hadn't known were possible, such as the far horizons of *nirvāṇa*. Truly, untranslatable words are portals to new worlds.

This book will introduce you to a dazzling array of these words, sourced from around the world. Together, they cover wellbeing in all its magnificent detail – from pleasure and contentment to wisdom and spirituality. I hope to take you on an exciting, mind-expanding journey during which we shall explore the length and breadth of this most vital terrain. As we proceed, I will encourage you not only to revel in the richness of these words, but to consider respectfully 'borrowing' them for use in your own life.

Borrowing words

I'll wager that you've used at least one non-English word in the last twenty-four hours. English is a veritable cornucopia of borrowed words. That term itself is one, deriving from the Latin *cornu copiae*, a mythical 'horn of plenty'.[2] The term 'borrow' might raise a quizzical eyebrow here, since it's not as if these words get 'returned' to their rightful owners at some point, like a dog-eared library book. Indeed, many such words are no longer perceived as being of foreign origin at all. Nevertheless, borrowing is the standard terminology for this process, with the terms in question generally known as 'loanwords'.[3]

'Zero', for instance – a cornerstone of science and mathematics – is Arabic in origin, as we shall see in Chapter 7. And 'tea', that staple of English society, was borrowed from Chinese, via

Dutch. In fact, estimates suggest that some 41 per cent of the 600,000 or so entries in the *Oxford English Dictionary* are borrowed words! These include around 25 per cent from French, 8 per cent from Latin, 3.5 per cent from Old Norse, and 2 per cent from Greek, together with a multitude of loanwords from scores of other languages.[4] For example, in addition to 'zero', Arabic alone has provided dozens of words, from 'algebra' to 'alcohol', 'sofa' to 'spinach'.

Indeed, from one perspective, English itself is entirely borrowed. It is a West Germanic language, brought to the British Isles in the fifth century by the invasions of the Angles, Saxons and Jutes.[5] The dominance of these tribes meant that the existing tongues of post-Roman Britain – mainly Latin and Brittonic – were swiftly superseded. The dramatic arrival of the new 'Anglo-Saxon' lexicon effectively reset the dial, linguistically speaking, constituting the start of 'Old English'.

A further revolution occurred with the Norman invasion of 1066, after which the upper echelons of English society embraced their conquerors' French language and inaugurated the era of Middle English. Eventually, English regained its dominance, but by then the lexicon had been swelled by numerous French words, covering all manner of phenomena that had not been articulated in Anglo-Saxon. Moreover, French itself had borrowed liberally from other languages, particularly Latin and Arabic, which in turn had their own influences, especially the formidable inventiveness of classical Greek.

By this point, English was a veritable melting pot, alchemising terms from multiple countries. The borrowing escalated further after 1500, which marked the start of Modern English. Trade routes opened in the first stirrings of globalisation, and enquiring minds of the Enlightenment gained direct access to texts from around the world. Consequently, English was able to borrow from just about everywhere, particularly Greek and Latin. It even got creative, combining notions from multiple sources. For example, when a word was needed for John Logie Baird's latest invention, the Latin *vīsiō* was attached to the Greek stem *tȇle* to describe the mysterious 'far seeing' afforded by television.

While these waves of borrowing are fascinating in themselves, of even greater interest is the question: *why* are certain words borrowed? Broadly speaking, there are two main reasons. The first relates to situations when there is already a perfectly good native term for the phenomenon in question. In such cases, a fancy foreign word might be employed in the hope of accruing cultural prestige or establishing intellectual authority. Think of an auditor who insists on using the Latin term *per annum* rather than 'each year' when checking through a company's accounts. Such borrowing provides an interesting insight into human nature, but it falls outside the remit of this book.

Rather, we are concerned with the second reason for borrowing words: namely, 'loanwords by necessity'.[6] In such cases, there is a 'semantic gap' because the recipient language lacks a suitable word for the referent in question.[7] Hence, we scrabble for an effective means to articulate what we mean. We invoke clumsy strings of words, and might even resort to flailing gestures or strange sounds. But then we learn that another language has already coined a word for the phenomenon – the *mot juste* that expresses it perfectly. We gratefully latch on to it, giving voice to what we were previously unable to articulate.

You're no doubt familiar with the German term *Schadenfreude* – malicious pleasure at the misfortune of others. Or, more benignly, the evocative *Wanderlust* – the irrepressible longing to roam, to explore the world. Such words pique our curiosity. They appear to reveal something about the culture that created them – as if Germans are especially susceptible to such complex emotions. However, it should be remembered that both have been imported into English. So English speakers must have had at least a passing familiarity with these feelings, even though they lacked the precise words to articulate them. As such, they struck an immediate chord of recognition. 'That's it!' our forebears must have exclaimed. 'That's *exactly* how I feel! How handy to have a word for it.' In this way, words are borrowed, filling our lexical gaps.

Consequently, our emotional landscape is enriched. We are empowered to give voice to feelings that previously remained unexpressed. Some words immediately – and very *satisfyingly* – seem intimate and familiar. They exquisitely capture vague sensations that we have not previously known how to put into words. Indeed, *Wanderlust* chimed deeply with me when I first encountered it. Other words introduce us to exciting new possibilities we never even suspected existed, such as the mysterious idea of *nirvāṇa*, which has so intrigued me in my engagement with Buddhism.

Excitingly, a whole world of wonderful words is just waiting to be discovered. This lexicon is the beating heart of this book. Before we start our adventure, though, I'd like to explain how this project came about, and dwell a little further on why I believe it is so important.

Positive cross-cultural lexicography

I'm a researcher in positive psychology, a relatively recent discipline that focuses on wellbeing. It's a wonderful field, exploring everything that makes life bright and beautiful, from gratitude and hope to love and spirituality. But it has its issues, as do most endeavours. Perhaps its biggest flaw is that it's relatively Western-centric. Although the field now boasts dedicated researchers around the world, it first emerged and took shape in the West, by which I mean principally North America (where it was inaugurated in 1998 by Martin Seligman and his colleagues), Western Europe and Australasia.

The key problem with this Western-centricity is that it runs the risk of formulating a partial and biased understanding of wellbeing, one shaped by its cultural context. Positive psychology – and psychology in general – is mainly structured around the contours of the English language, and driven by the ideas, worldviews and priorities of Western societies. As such, psychology has largely bypassed the experiences and insights developed by non-Western and non-English-speaking cultures.

However, this is beginning to change. Academic psychology is increasingly breaking out of its Western shell and engaging with the rest of the world's cultures, driven forward by scholars from all nations. I want to make a contribution to this emergent spirit of cross-cultural enquiry.

I started to appreciate the value of learning from other cultures when I visited China, aged nineteen, to teach English before starting university. There I encountered a wealth of mysterious concepts, practices and traditions that were utterly unfamiliar to me but seemed of immense consequence – Taoism,

Confucianism and Buddhism, to name but three. These bodies of wisdom were barely even mentioned in my textbooks when I entered university to study psychology, yet I had a gnawing suspicion that, despite their antiquity, they possessed insights into the human mind that far surpassed those of contemporary science.

I was not alone in thinking that Western psychology had much to learn from Buddhism. Indeed, I soon encountered a groundswell of scholars investigating the Buddhist-derived practice of mindfulness. Eventually – after several years working as a musician and a psychiatric nursing assistant – I joined their ranks, undertaking a PhD that focused on the impact of meditation on men's mental health.[8] Thereafter, I pursued a career as a lecturer in positive psychology and continued to search Buddhism for jewels that might enhance the field. This led to even greater appreciation of the benefits of cross-cultural study.

In July 2015, I joined colleagues at an international positive psychology conference. As I meandered around the lectures, I chanced upon a captivating presentation by a Finnish researcher, Emilia Lahti. The topic was *sisu* – a form of extraordinary courage and determination, especially in the face of adversity.[9] Lahti argued that this personal resource lies at the heart of Finnish culture, enabling the nation and its people to survive and overcome myriad challenges. However, while it is specifically associated with the Finns, Lahti suggested that it may be inherent within *everyone* – a psychological resource that is common to all humanity, if only we could learn to harness it.

On my return to England, my mum asked how the conference had gone. We were chatting animatedly about *sisu* when it occurred to us that most languages probably have similarly intriguing ideas that lack precise English equivalents. Now, I'm not a linguist by training, so the notion of untranslatability – and the research that already existed into this topic – was unknown to me at that point. Still, I knew we were on to something. Moreover, given my experiences with Buddhism, I instinctively felt that such words would have much to offer psychology, not to mention English-speaking cultures more broadly.

Before long, I resolved to assemble as many of these words as possible, with a specific focus on wellbeing, given my affiliation to positive psychology. I had no idea if this plan was a foolhardy wild-goose chase, but it captivated me. In this way, I found myself embarking on a quest to collate a lexicon of untranslatable words relating to wellbeing.

I dreamed of establishing a crowd-sourced platform on which people from around the world could offer words from their languages. However, I didn't have a website, or any way of attracting attention to the project. Hence, I realised I would need to kick-start it on my own. I dived enthusiastically into the many colourful websites and blogs that are devoted to the subject, and pored over relevant academic articles and books. These early forays yielded a modest return of 216 words. I analysed them thematically – grouping words that seemed conceptually related – and in January 2016 published the results in the flagship journal of my field, the *Journal of Positive Psychology*.[10]

To my delight, the article generated a fair amount of interest. By then, I had created a website to host the burgeoning list of words (www.drtimlomas.com/lexicography), and this started to receive a stream of helpful suggestions and feedback. I also continued with my own explorations. I would often encounter a new word, then fall into a rabbit hole as the original term drew my attention to a related one, and another, and another. Before long, the lexicon had blossomed to nearly a thousand words.

Soon, the exciting possibility of bringing these words together in a book was becoming a reality and I found myself typing the words you're reading now. I'm thrilled to have this opportunity to delve into many of these fascinating words in the sort of detail they deserve. First, though, I'd like to offer a little theoretical context in the hope of clarifying their value and significance. To that end, I shall introduce a metaphor for the power of language in general: namely, cartography, the drawing of maps.

Experiential cartography

Language is a map that allows us to understand and navigate a path through our experiential world. By 'experiential world', I mean not only the external world of places and spaces, sights and sounds, but our secret, inner world of thoughts and feelings, dreams and desires. In philosophical circles, these inner phenomena are known collectively as qualia.[11] Taken together, these inner and outer landscapes constitute our experiential world. And language is our metaphorical map of it. Indeed, language shares several features in common with actual maps.

First, there is the 'boundary principle'. Both maps and languages carve up the world's dizzying complexity into a series of sectors, separated by boundaries. Just as maps divide our planet into countries and regions, languages segment our experiential world into cognitively digestible pieces by identifying objects (via nouns and pronouns), processes (verbs), qualities (adjectives and adverbs), relationships (prepositions and conjunctions) and communicative acts (interjections).

Crucially, this process of boundary creation is somewhat arbitrary, and largely a matter of social convention.[12] For instance, we have deemed it useful to distinguish between children, adolescents and adults, whereas previous generations generally recognised only children and adults.[13] The new category of adolescents is thus both useful and a matter of social agreement. I do not mean *mere* agreement, unmoored from objectivity or truth. After all, adolescents *do* differ from both children and adults on account of certain age-related characteristics. Nevertheless, our segmenting of this age spectrum depends on convention.

One aspect of the boundary principle is absolutely central to this book: different languages impose subtly different boundaries upon the world. This fact has profound and exciting consequences, and it lies at the heart of this lexicographic project, so I shall return to it shortly. First, though, we need to discuss two further parallels between languages and maps.

The next is that both possess 'scalable granularity'.[14] Consider Google Maps. As you zoom in on an area, the level of detail remains fairly constant. Begin with the planet in its entirety: features that span hundreds of miles, such as the contours of a coastline, are rendered visually in millimetres. Yet you can then swoop down vertiginously until a single house fills the screen. Now objects that are merely centimetres in actual scale – say, a pair of shoes lying outside the front door – are similarly rendered in millimetres.

A similar principle applies with language, which can

likewise carve up the world in increasingly fine-grained detail. The process of zooming in on these details is the very essence of learning. Think back to your childhood and your first few months of school. On entering the classroom for the first time, your impressionable young mind will have been assailed by a barrage of daunting new words: 'science', 'language', 'art' and so on. While all of these surely sounded impressive, their meaning was largely a mystery. If you were to represent them on a global map, each would be a vast yet opaque continent, entirely untroubled by detail. But as your educational journey continued, you slowly learned to identify individual countries within those continents. You gradually realised that 'science' harbours biology, chemistry and physics, while 'art' encompasses sculpture, painting, photography, music and so on.

With time, guided by your personal passions, you were able to zoom in even further. A fondness for music, for instance, may have led you to segment this vast region into numerous individual styles, differentiating classical from calypso, rock from reggae. You dive in further, inspired by a burgeoning interest in classical music to learn the violin. After several months of screeching, you cautiously join an orchestra. Soon, for you, symphonic music becomes a terrain of astonishing granularity. You know your Mozart from your Liszt, your *allegro* from your *andante*. Your linguistic map becomes ever more nuanced.

This process similarly accompanies the cultivation of a palate for fine wine, an eye for great paintings, or a mind for the labyrinths of philosophy. It enhances not only our knowledge of these realms but, even more excitingly, our *experience* of them. Our refined maps allow us to see more clearly, hear more keenly, taste more sensitively, understand more deeply and appreciate more fully. Most pertinently for us here, the process of zooming in can even augment our experience of happiness.

We're all familiar with the idea that people differ in terms of their intellectual capacity, as measured, for instance, by IQ tests. Well, we also vary in emotional granularity: that is, in our ability to experience and conceptualise subtly different emotions.[15] A person with low granularity might label a broad swathe of positive sensations simply as 'happiness'. Conversely, someone with high granularity will be able to segment this umbrella term into numerous individual components – such as joy and bliss – which they will understand as similar but distinct emotions.

However, don't worry if you fear you may be towards the lower end of the granularity spectrum. Crucially, emotional granularity is not a fixed trait. It can be trained and developed, just as you can hone your appreciation of music or fine wine. Indeed, therapeutic exercises have been devised to help children expand their knowledge of emotion words, with demonstrable positive effects on their wellbeing and academic performance.[16]

One of this book's principal aims is to guide you towards greater granularity. As you proceed through the chapters, your map of the experiential world will become ever more detailed and nuanced. En route, we shall visit no fewer than nine different domains of wellbeing – contentment, pleasure, love, connection, aesthetic appreciation, ambivalence, understanding, spirituality and character. Each chapter is structured around a number of key words, each of which illuminates a specific area of that particular domain. Collectively, these terms reveal the domain's full, glorious richness.

This brings us to the third and final parallel between maps and words: the 'guidance principle'. Both maps and language are indispensable guides to our world. The former allow us to navigate a path through our immediate surroundings with great accuracy, and also invite us to venture into new territory. Similarly, language helps us to orient ourselves to where we are now and increase our understanding of what we are *currently* experiencing.

To appreciate this point, consider the phenomenon of alexithymia: the inability to recognise or verbalise emotions.[17] Someone who is alexithymic may experience nervous excitement, guilty pleasure or indeed any other emotion, but these sensations may leave them confused or bewildered. By contrast, someone with highly developed emotional differentiation will know precisely what they are experiencing at any given time. It's as if the second person has a detailed map of their life course and location while the first has only a vague sketch.

Moreover, just as maps tempt us to visit new lands, words encourage us to investigate unfamiliar zones of experience. For example, I've been entranced by Buddhism ever since my first visit to China, as I alluded to above. While there, my young, naive mind was mystified by dauntingly strange words like *Buddha* and *nirvāṇa*. I had no idea what they meant at the time, and to this day they remain opaque. But they prompted me to explore the unglimpsed experiential peaks they signified and pursue new states of mind by following a Buddhist path.

You will have noticed that *Buddha* and *nirvāṇa* are not English words. Yet we have come to use them for want of adequate translations. This point brings us back to the heart of this book. Most other cultures possess terms for which we lack suitable equivalents: untranslatable words. As we shall see, many of these words are incredibly illuminating, partly because different languages map the world in fascinatingly different ways.

Divergent maps

For a wealth of reasons – from climate to tradition – the world's cultures have found it useful to carve up the world linguistically in their own unique fashions. This is known as the 'linguistic relativity hypothesis', or alternatively as the 'Sapir–Whorf' principle, after the anthropologist Edward Sapir[18] and his student Benjamin Lee Whorf.[19] As Whorf memorably put it: 'We dissect nature along lines laid out by our native languages ... The world is presented as a kaleidoscopic flux of impressions which has to be organized ... largely by the linguistic systems in our minds.'[20]

This hypothesis is exemplified by the apocryphal notion that 'Eskimos' – a broad term that can be used, albeit contentiously, to refer collectively to many of the indigenous peoples of the northern circumpolar region[21] – have dozens of different words for snow. This claim is so well trodden that it will surely trigger either a nod of recognition or a sigh of weary scepticism, depending on your perspective. For that very reason, it's worth exploring further in order to shed some light on the notion of divergent linguistic maps.

The subject was first brought to wider attention by Franz Boas, Sapir's mentor. In passing, he noted that the Inuit have discrete words for four different types of snow: *aput* (snow on the ground); *gana* (falling snow); *piqsirpoq* (drifting snow); and *qimuqsuq* (a snow drift).[22] Subsequently, Whorf upped the ante to seven terms, but this was not nearly enough for some, who went on to cite four hundred or so different words.[23] Such was the runaway linguistic inflation that the whole topic has been dismissed as a 'hoax'.[24] However, the issue is rather more nuanced and complex than that.

Its veracity hinges on what we mean by a 'word'. Eskimo–Aleut languages – the overarching category to which the various individual tongues belong – are agglutinative. That is, complex words are created by combining morphemes. For example, the West Greenlandic word for ice – *siku* – gives rise to several compounds, including *sikuliaq* (pack ice), *sikuaq* (new ice) and *sikurluk* (melting ice). In such languages, it is possible to create a near infinity of such words simply by combining various morphemes.

So, do Eskimo–Aleut languages have greater lexical complexity than English with respect to snow? Technically, no, because English has access to a powerful armoury of descriptors in the form of adjectives. Yet, in practice, English is far poorer in this area. Hypothetical possibilities aside, a lexicon's scope is ultimately determined by its usage. Although Eskimo–Aleut and English speakers have roughly equal capacity to speak about snow with great specificity – the former through agglutination, the latter through the use of adjectives – most English speakers have little reason to call upon that ability. Eskimo culture has evolved in a physical environment that is utterly dominated by snow in a way that most English-speaking cultures are not. As such, Eskimo–Aleut languages contain many more words in common usage (as opposed to hypothetical phrases) that relate to snow – perhaps as many as a thousand distinct lexemes, by some estimates.[25]

The question is: why do they need so many words for snow? Essentially, snow is a significant enough phenomenon within the Arctic Circle to warrant considerable granularity. By contrast, given that it usually snows only a few days each year in the regions where English developed, why would we bother with such detail? One principal word will do, along with a handful of other nouns (such as sleet) and adjectives to convey more precise meaning.

But just think of how many words and phrases we have coined for a much more familiar form of precipitation in the UK: rain. There must be dozens of them. That's because rain is enough of a presence here – and occurs in sufficient variety – that the effort to differentiate between its myriad forms seems justified. If I'm setting out for a Sunday walk, I may be reassured to hear it's merely spitting, or heartened by the promise of a passing shower. However, dark reports of a downpour or even a deluge will send me scurrying back inside to the cosy warmth of home.

So, what is the *significance* of these words? First, it's useful to make fine-grained distinctions about phenomena that are particularly salient, whether you are an Inuit judging the snow's suitability for sledging, or an Englishman deliberating whether to persevere with his stroll. More importantly, though, knowledge of the perfect word for a given circumstance may enable you to *see* more, *understand* more and *experience* more.

As a Londoner, imagine if I were whisked away to a remote Arctic community. My hosts and I would look out on precisely the same frozen landscape, but I would see nothing but undifferentiated snow. I would struggle to register how fast it was falling, the size of the crystals, how it was settling on the ground. In comparison to the locals, I would be blind to all of these nuances and dozens more besides. Think of a classically trained pianist and a three-year-old child sitting side by side and listening to a Mozart symphony. The same sound waves would hit their ears, but what a difference in interpretation! The pianist would appreciate every intricate detail of the performance, while the toddler would hear a mere muddle of noise.

To return to our cartographic metaphor, I would have only a rudimentary linguistic map to guide me through the snow. Crucially, though, the story doesn't end there: our maps are not engraved in stone. Indeed, they are wonderfully dynamic and exquisitely amenable to refinement. After a month or two in the Arctic, I would start to pick up some of the local lexicon, learning untranslatable concepts I had never encountered in English. In doing so, my linguistic map of this experiential world would become more detailed. Moreover, I would not only develop a more fine-grained understanding of snow but I would also gain insights into other aspects of Eskimo life, from the locals' religious beliefs to their culinary practices. In short, I would enrich my linguistic map by studying theirs, and 'borrowing' as many useful elements as I could remember.

OK, this is a rather unusual example. However, its underlying principles are anything but. As we saw above, borrowing words from other cultures is central to all language development and something we do all the time. My hope is that you will enrich your understanding and experience of happiness by borrowing from the great library of ideas that are presented in the pages that follow.

The journey ahead

So, I'd like to invite you on an exciting journey in which we shall explore the myriad realms of wellbeing through the subtle, transformative power of untranslatable words. Over the course of the next nine chapters I shall guide you through a beautiful landscape which contains the best our experiential world has to offer. Each chapter explores a specific dimension of happiness via key words that articulate its nuances in fine detail.

We begin by focusing on the sensation of happiness itself, seeking to cultivate a more granular appreciation of its subtleties, from the tranquillity of contentment (Chapter 1) to the more intense peaks of pleasure (Chapter 2). We then turn to what is arguably the main source of happiness – relationships – including the intense bonds of love (Chapter 3) and the more general networks of connection (Chapter 4). Next, we explore what links happiness to aesthetic appreciation (Chapter 5) and ambivalent states of mind (Chapter 6). Finally, we investigate three well-worn pathways to happiness, all of which pertain to personal development: namely, understanding (Chapter 7), spirituality (Chapter 8) and character (Chapter 9).

Before we set out, however, a caveat is necessary. Naturally, I endeavour to do justice to each and every word, but it would be impossible to explore all 124 entries in full and intimate detail – their etymology, usage, diverse interpretations and so on. To give some idea of the scale of such a task, a number of authors have already written full-length books on just one of the words that feature here: the Danish concept of *hygge*. Indeed, no fewer than nine titles were published on this subject – in English – in 2016 alone![26] My intention is rather different: I have deliberately sacrificed a little depth to facilitate a comparative analysis, with each word painted in broad brush strokes. As such, and given that translation is a fiendishly difficult undertaking, my descriptions may not satisfy every speaker of the language to which a given word belongs. Nevertheless, I have striven to catch the spirit of each word,[27] albeit in a limited and partial way. Moreover, I have sought to verify my descriptions not only with reliable scholarly sources but, where possible, with a bilingual speaker of the language in question. As such, while my descriptions may not be canonical or infallible, I have done my best to make them as accurate as possible.

Bearing this in mind, I hope this project will help to fan the flames of cross-cultural appreciation in psychology by providing glimpses into the unique ways and wisdom of the world's diverse cultures. In so doing, the conceptual map of psychology may be augmented and graced by new concepts from which it has hitherto been veiled. More radically, I hope this lexicon will enrich your own personal world and expand your emotional horizons. The book will introduce you to a universe of ideas, sourced from numerous cultures and languages. I invite you to engage with these words in a spirit of respect and appreciation for the cultures that created them, and perhaps even try to use some of them in your daily life. To that end, the book concludes with a glossary of terms and a rough pronunciation guide.

Together, these words have the potential to expand your sense of what it means to be happy and flourish. Some will give voice to feelings that have been hazily familiar but unarticulated. Others may lead you into new realms of experience and allow you to glimpse beautiful possibilities that had previously been obscured. Either way, an exciting journey awaits.

CHAPTER ONE

Contentment

This book delves deep into happiness – its colours and textures, its dynamics and mechanics, its causes and manifestations. And we start by exploring the feeling itself, its emotional tone.

In academic psychology, feelings and emotions relating to happiness – those that are pleasant and enjoyable in some way – are categorised under the umbrella term 'positive affect'. But a world of variation is concealed by this colourless, bland label. Consider the vast chasms of significance and intensity that separate the mild enjoyment of an ice cream from the bliss of being entwined in the arms of your soulmate for the very first time. Or the difference in satisfaction between making a decent cup of coffee on a Sunday morning and seeing your child graduate from university after years of struggle. These are all positive feelings, but they're hardly comparable with one another!

Therefore, as you might expect, psychologists have sought

to differentiate between various types of positive affect. For instance, Paul Ekman, one of the most influential emotion theorists, suggests that there are five basic emotions – anger, disgust, fear, sadness and enjoyment – with the latter essentially constituting positive affect.[1] His recent 'Atlas of Emotions' project[2] then deconstructs enjoyment into twelve discrete types, from least to most intense: sensory pleasure; rejoicing; compassion/joy; amusement; *Schadenfreude*; relief; pride; *fiero*; *naches*; wonder; excitement; and ecstasy.

As useful as this schema is, however, we can go further and identify many more grades of positive affect. By exploring untranslatable words, we can discover subtle variations in emotional experience that have not been identified in English. Indeed, Ekman himself includes three such words in his spectrum. The Italian notion of *fiero* – which we shall discuss in more detail later in this chapter – captures the affirmative pleasure of meeting a challenge that has stretched one's capabilities. Meanwhile, the Yiddish term *naches* describes the unique pride we feel when someone we love does well. Finally, there's the infamous *Schadenfreude*. Although technically a form of pleasure, it is malicious and ultimately detrimental to wellbeing,[3] so it does not merit further discussion here!

In addition to *fiero* and *naches*, there are many other enjoyment words which allow us to delve into positive affect in finer-grained detail. We shall explore them throughout the course of this chapter and the next, which focus on contentment and pleasure, respectively. Viewed as a spectrum of arousal, these categories cleave positive affect in two – from the low-intensity tranquillity of contentment to the vibrant energy of pleasure. If happiness is a beautiful landscape, contentment represents its lush pastures, wherein we wander peacefully at our leisure. By contrast, pleasure constitutes its jagged mountain peaks: exciting to ascend, but more fleeting in nature. That said, variations in happiness are not only about the level of arousal, as if merely turning up the volume. Many more factors introduce subtlety into the proceedings, such as the *meaning* of our experiences. As such, even feelings of comparable arousal can differ greatly in their weight and depth.

With that in mind, let's start breathing in the cool, clear air of contentment.

Ataraxia

Lucid tranquillity, peace of mind, calmness

'The happy man is content with his present lot,' wrote Seneca to his brother in 58 CE, 'no matter what it is.'[4] His fellow-philosopher Epictetus took this line of thought to its extreme when he claimed that it was possible to be 'sick and yet happy, in peril and yet happy, dying and yet happy, in exile and happy, in disgrace and happy'.[5] What strange kind of happiness is this?

It goes by the name of Stoicism, which may ring some bells. This was the label given to the Athenian school of philosophy, founded by Zeno of Citium, to which these great thinkers belonged. It derives from Zeno's habit of conducting his esoteric enquiries underneath a *stoá* – a portico or porch. Nowadays, stoicism often implies resignation to fate, bravely tolerating one's suffering. By contrast, the original Stoics believed a form of happiness was always possible, whatever the circumstances. Their word for this state of mind was *ataraxia*.

This is a good place to start our enquiry into contentment: at the very base of the arousal spectrum, just above the absolute zero of total passivity. For *ataraxia* implies lucid tranquillity and imperturbability, serene detachment from the vicissitudes of fate and circumstance.[6]

One might object that this state is either inhuman or impossible to achieve. These charges do have a ring of truth. After all, with respect to the first, etymologically, tranquillity is closely related to tranquillisation. Arguably, to be fully human, one should be *moved* by life – delight in its joys and lament its sorrows. Yet accounts of the Stoics do not describe an emotionless band of cold, unfeeling automatons. They knew the warmth of love and the heartache of pain. For them, *ataraxia* was essentially a radical form of *acceptance*. This wasn't grudging acquiescence but a gracious willingness to be with whatever was happening, including their emotions. They might be in pain or sorrow, but they were seemingly able to accept such feelings rather than resist them, which modern research suggests is generally futile anyway.[7]

This brings us to the second objection. Serene detachment sounds all very well, but surely it is beyond the reach of most of us? Not according to the Stoics. These bold thinkers placed great faith in the power of the will to eradicate desire and render themselves at peace with life.

Intriguingly, at around the same time but thousands of miles away, another group of philosophical pioneers were exploring a similar kind of tranquil detachment. Even more revolutionarily, they were also developing mental practices to facilitate it.

Sati

Mindful awareness of the present moment

A couple of hundred years before Zeno's deliberations beneath the *stoá*, Gautama Siddhārtha – an itinerant monk in what is now Nepal – made the following proclamation: 'A *bhikkhu* [monk], gone to the forest, to the foot of a tree, or to an empty place, sits down, bends in his legs crosswise on his lap, keeps his body erect, and arouses mindfulness in the object of meditation, namely, the breath which is in front of him. Mindful, he breathes in, and mindful, he breathes out.'[8]

Today, Siddhārtha is better known by his honorific – *Buddha*, or Awakened One – for he founded the great religion we now call Buddhism. The instructions outlined above open one of its foundational teachings, the *Satipaṭṭhāna sutta*. *Paṭṭhāna* is a Pāli word meaning to set forth and establish something valuable, and a *sutta* is a teaching or aphorism. Hence, in this case, a state of mind known as *sati* is established through the Buddha's teaching.

What, then, is *sati*? Like many words, it is polysemous – it has multiple meanings. Moreover, these varied meanings are not fixed; they have subtly shifted across time and space. Before the concept was harnessed by the Buddha, *sati* was associated with memory and recollection. However, he deployed it in a fascinating, new way to describe clear and calm awareness. Still, the link with recollection was subtly preserved, in that *sati* involves remembering to focus on 'what is otherwise too easily forgotten: the present moment'.[9]

This state of mind was presented as central to the Buddhist path and achieving the ultimate aim of liberation from suffering. But, as mentioned above, what was especially revolutionary was that the Buddha developed or promulgated a number of techniques – now known collectively as meditation – to help cultivate the mental state of *sati*. Hence, the detailed instructions in the *sutta*. We shall explore these techniques further in Chapter 8, where we look at spirituality. However, *sati* merits an introduction here, as it is an exemplary form of calm contentment.

Indeed, the whole world is waking up to its power. For, as you might have guessed, *sati* is the basis for mindfulness, which has recently become almost ubiquitous in the West. Some critics have suggested that the term 'mindfulness' – which was how *sati* was rendered by the pioneering Buddhist scholar T.W. Rhys Davids in the early twentieth century[10] – does not quite capture the true spirit of the original Pāli term. They argue that it seems a little too cognitive and cerebral and loses *sati*'s warm, affective qualities, such as compassion.[11] After all, not all cultures rigidly differentiate emotion and thought as we do in English. Instead, they (and modern scientific research) regard them as inseparable.[12] For instance, the Pāli (and Sanskrit) term *citta* means 'heart–mind', as do cognates in other Eastern languages.

Nevertheless, contemporary conceptualisations of mindfulness do still chime with the Buddha's *sutta*. For instance, Jon Kabat-Zinn defines it as 'the awareness that arises through paying attention on purpose, in the present moment, and nonjudgmentally to the unfolding of experience moment by moment'.[13] He was pivotal in introducing mindfulness to the West when he launched his pioneering 'Mindfulness-Based Stress Reduction' intervention in the late 1970s.[14] Since then, empirical trials have consistently shown that this precious form of calm, relaxed awareness greatly benefits mental health.[15]

This Western embrace of *sati* shows the immense value of engaging with untranslatable words. And many other jewels await discovery.

Dhyāna

Intense, focused attention and absorption

Buddhism alone is festooned with such gems, and they are sprinkled liberally throughout this book. Partly this is due to my deep interest in this tradition, but it also reflects Buddhism's wealth of relevant insights. In fact, we might mention another immediately. For, among its many riches, Buddhism has numerous concepts, in addition to *sati*, that describe states of calm contentment. However, these are not wholly synonymous; rather, each of them conveys subtle nuances of feeling.

Buddhist meditators – indeed, all contemplatives – are essentially highly skilled 'psychonauts'. Through prolonged introspection, they explore the inner world in great depth, generating wonderfully detailed maps of their interior terrain. Some regions may be familiar to most people, irrespective of whether they practise meditation themselves. For instance, most of us have probably experienced some form of *sati* at one time or another.[16] However, other areas are rather more remote and rarely visited. One such forbidding place is known in Sanskrit as *dhyāna*.

This is sometimes translated simply as 'meditation', but it

tends to have far subtler definitions in Buddhist texts. Whereas *sati* is an open, expansive awareness, *dhyāna* is a profoundly concentrated act of attention in which one focuses solely on a contemplative target for extended periods of time. The target may be internal – such as one's own breathing – or external, like a flickering candle flame. Once a practitioner has managed to achieve the requisite level of focus – which is no easy task – the result is a state of pure stillness. The mind becomes a deep lake, utterly undisturbed and crystal clear.

Yet remarkably, there are progressively deeper stages of *dhyāna*. Initially, one's attention is wholly fixed on the meditative object to the exclusion of all other sensory information. This is said to induce a tranquil abiding which is extremely pleasurable, almost blissful. Gradually, though, the attentiveness becomes even more focused, until the practitioner finally reaches a point where the very experience of being a person ebbs away. All thoughts and feelings of oneself disappear in a process of radical self-transcendence, leaving just pure awareness. As they slip from view, the meditator enters increasingly profound states of equanimity and peace.

Collectively, the stages of *dhyāna* are known as *samādhi*, which is sometimes translated simply as 'concentration' or 'one-pointed' attention. However, these rather opaque terms fail to convey the deep significance of *samādhi*. Like *dhyāna*, it represents a state of deep, absorptive tranquillity that is pivotal to achieving the ultimate goal of liberation from suffering. This luminous goal itself goes by the name *nirvāṇa*, which we shall explore further in the next chapter. First, though, we have many other forms of contentment to savour, beginning with a pearl from the deep wisdom of Taoism.

Wú wéi

Natural, spontaneous, effortless action

Imagine yourself walking along the pavement on a summer's evening. A few steps ahead is a woman, evidently making her way home from work, holding a loose sheaf of papers. Suddenly, a sheet slips from her grasp and glides to the floor at your feet. You bend down to pick it up, jog to the woman's side, and hand it back to her. She's grateful for this mundane act of assistance.

Now let's rewind to just before you reached down for the paper. The action was instinctive, effortless. There was no deliberation, no premeditation, no moral calculation. You didn't weigh up the pros and cons of picking it up. You didn't even think about it. It just happened, with easy, natural spontaneity. It was an example of *wú wéi*.

The term derives from Taoism, a Chinese philosophy and way of life whose origins lie in unrecorded antiquity. We shall draw upon its wisdom at numerous points throughout this book. Suffice to say here that it centres on the ineffable notion of the *Tao*. Introducing this idea – which we shall discuss in more depth in Chapter 7 – is rather daunting, for the *Tao* encompasses *everything*. It is not only the creative power which brought the universe into being but every aspect of that universe.[17] Clearly, this cannot be encapsulated in one neat, simple definition. It smashes through all human concepts and limitations.

Nevertheless, Taoism's central message is that we can either align ourselves with the *Tao* – the patterns and rhythms of life – or resist it. The former leads to contentment and peace, the latter to suffering and hardship. Taoism offers many metaphors for this process. For instance, imagine two sailors at sea: the skilled yachtsman works with the currents and harnesses the dynamic power of the wind, while the novice tries to fight against the tide and misreads the breeze. Or think of two butchers carving a piece of meat: one cleaves it effortlessly at the joints, while the other laboriously hacks straight through flesh and bone.

Extend these metaphors to your own life. On a good day, you feel the wind at your back, carried along by the currents. You tackle every task effortlessly, dealing with them as naturally as a leaf falling to the ground. This is *wú wéi*. The literal translation of the term is non-action or non-doing, but this does not imply inert passivity or immobility. Rather, it means that actions are accomplished without strain or struggle, without any attempt to challenge the immutable laws of the universe. Every action should be fluid and uncontrived, like bending down to pick up that piece of paper and hand it back to the owner. The correct path is taken effortlessly. We are in sync with the rhythms of the universe, with the unique requirements of each specific moment in time.

Life feels like this when we are at our best. We are perfectly content because there is no fighting against the world. It's just us and life aligned in harmony and unfolding in synchrony. Which brings us to *zanshin*.

Zanshin

Relaxed mental alertness

One of the most famous poems in English literature – Rudyard Kipling's 'If' – begins with the timeless lines: 'If you can keep your head while all about you / Are losing theirs ...' His suggestion is that imperturbability is integral to a noble character, and indeed a happy life. Perhaps you've experienced such moments on occasions, where you are a still, clear point of calm amidst a whirling storm. Pausing quietly in a frantic train station, say, while frenzied commuters dash by relentlessly. Stepping back momentarily from a drunken dancefloor, and marvelling in detachment at the Dionysan energy. Standing tall near a pack of kids who are scooting around with riotous delight. It can certainly be gratifying, or at least stabilising, to retain one's composure when everyone else descends into chaos. But can such comportment be cultivated?

Indeed it can. A key lesson from *wú wéi* is that psychological stillness can be practised even in the midst of intense action. From our earlier discussion of *sati* and *dhyāna*, you might suppose that these states of meditative tranquillity are attainable only in the seclusion of a remote monastery, immersed in silent meditation for hours on end. But in spiritual traditions like Buddhism, the goal is not escapism from the world, a retreat into the chambers of the mind. Rather, practitioners should aim to carry the beneficent qualities they have cultivated through meditation – calmness, clarity, compassion and so on – into the world, 'entering the marketplace with bliss-bestowing hands'.[18]

From this perspective, there is no real distinction between

formal meditation and one's normal routine. That's why Buddhists and other contemplatives are said to *practise* meditation. It's the same as any other skill. Sitting in a dusty classroom conjugating French verbs is not an end in itself; it is a means to explore the delights of France and converse with its people. Likewise, meditation is about perfecting how to behave when one is *not* sitting cross-legged in a silent room. It involves honing a number of skills – *sati*, say – so that these run like golden threads throughout all of our daily activities.

This ideal of maintaining meditative calmness in the midst of action was brought to fruition in the school of Buddhism known as Zen. This emerged after the monk Bodhidhárma imported Buddhism to China around 520 CE, according to legend, whereupon it mingled with Taoism to produce a more 'grounded' religion that was infused with the spirit of *wú wéi*. Many Chinese converts reportedly had little interest in the abstract metaphysics that some of the Indian schools had developed over the preceding centuries. Devotees were usually not expected to master esoteric ontological schemas. Instead, they received ostensibly simple instructions to give their full, undivided attention to whatever they were doing (although in practice that can be fiendishly difficult, as any meditator will know). As one proverb – attributed to Ummon, abbot of Shaozhou (862–949) – put it, 'In walking, just walk. In sitting, just sit. Above all, don't wobble!'[19]

In the late twelfth century, this form of Buddhism migrated across the South China Sea to Japan, where it acquired the name Zen – the local pronunciation of *chán* – which in turn was the Chinese rendering of *dhyāna*. The imported religion swiftly infused Japanese culture as devotees displayed their meditative clarity and spiritual insight through a wide variety of artistic and athletic practices, ranging from the sedate rhythms of the tea ceremony – or *chadō* (the 'way of tea') – to the controlled intensity of martial arts, known collectively as *budō* (the 'way of war'). The latter exemplifies the ideal of maintaining meditative serenity amid even the most frenetic activity.

Accordingly, Japanese Buddhists coined several terms to describe this state, including *zanshin*. Like the Eskimo–Aleut languages, Japanese is agglutinative. Thus, *zan* – 'remnants' or 'that which endures'[20] – is combined with *shin* or 'heart–mind' (as per the Pāli term *citta*). As such, *zanshin* evokes the quality of 'remaining heart–mind': maintaining relaxed mental and emotional alertness, especially in the face of danger or chaos. Clearly, this would be a useful attribute in a medieval martial arts encounter, but any harassed parent or rush-hour commuter would surely benefit from cultivating it, too. And the same could be said for embracing the spirit of *Gelassenheit*.

Gelassenheit

Serene self-surrender and acquiescence

In the 1930s, an American theologian named Reinhold Niebuhr composed a short prayer. By the end of the century, it had become one of the most well-known verses in the world, a source of solace and strength to millions. You may know it as the 'Serenity Prayer':

> *God, grant me the serenity*
> *To accept the things I cannot change;*
> *Courage to change the things I can;*
> *And wisdom to know the difference.*

With this inspiring message, our gaze sweeps from East to West, to the fecund lexicality of German, the source of so many intriguing words. For the spirit of this prayer is perfectly captured by the term *Gelassenheit*.

Even *Gelassenheit*'s grammatical structure is interesting: a noun, created from an adjective (*gelassen*), which in turn derives from a verb (*lassen*). The verb has several subtly different definitions, including to allow, let, leave behind, cease and quit.[21] Adding the prefix *ge* turns it into an adjective which is often used to describe a person who is calm, cool, dispassionate. Finally, through the addition of the suffix *heit*, we arrive at a noun which equates to calmness, coolness, contentment or even serenity. However, *Gelassenheit* has other meanings, too. In religious contexts, for example, it captures the powerful yet serene act of accepting the will of God, as in Niebuhr's prayer. Similarly, Martin Heidegger equated it with *nichtwollen* (non-willing) – not straining against fate and the currents of life.[22] In that sense, it echoes both *ataraxia* and *wú wéi*.

Moreover, yielding to a 'higher authority' – whether God or destiny – can be a powerful antidote to the hubristic, self-aggrandising individualism that often bedevils modern society. For this reason, *Gelassenheit* has been described as *the* central value of the Amish community, for whom humility is paramount.[23]

However, acceptance is not reliant on religious belief.

Nor must it be laden with overtones of passivity. Those who cultivate acceptance can still be dynamic and bold; they can have the 'courage to change the things I can', as the prayer intones. But they also recognise that much of life lies outside their control. This doesn't equate to pessimistic fatalism – as if everything is preordained. It's more an acknowledgement that causal chains are always in motion, inevitably influencing future events. *Qué será será* – what will be will be.

So, whichever forces we credit with shaping our destiny – God, fate, the laws of physics – *Gelassenheit* captures the salvational impact of making peace with them. This is not always easy, of course. The desire to control the future is a universal human trait, and indeed a precious, life-enhancing quality. But greater contentment invariably follows greater acceptance.

In light of this, how should we cultivate acceptance? We might begin by making time for *selah*.

Selah

A quiet, reflective pause

A curious word occurs repeatedly in the Bible: *selah*. It is usually transliterated straight from the Hebrew, rather than translated. But what does it signify?

Perhaps some clues can be found in its etymology. It has been linked to the verbs 'to praise', 'to lift up' and, most commonly, 'to pause'. The last of these seems most tenable, given the biblical context in which it usually occurs: namely, as a liturgical instruction. Scholars have suggested it may be a divisional marker or an instruction to singers to rest for a moment before beginning the next verse of a hymn.

Yet, this may be no mere musical motif. Rather, it may be a gentle invitation to take a *reflective* pause and dwell contemplatively upon the previous verse so that its message reverberates and sinks in. Such moments of reflection ease the path to contentment, not only in religious contexts, but in all aspects of life, in good times as well as bad. The occasional reflective interlude allows true appreciation of episodes of joy or wonder. Similarly, it can help us to absorb the full significance of a solemn or momentous occasion. Moreover, in a crisis, our tendency to react instinctively in a way we may later regret can be tempered by a strategic retreat from the emotional heat. Act in haste, repent at leisure, as the proverb says.

Likewise, reflective pauses are built into mindfulness. The standard contemporary advice is that each meditation should last at least twenty minutes. However, a key element in many courses is the 'three-minute breathing space', effectively a micro-meditation that can be done anywhere, at any time: on a crowded underground train, before a big meeting, even *during* the meeting. In short, whenever you need a time-out.

We all benefit from these reflective pauses, even though we sometimes need to be reminded – or given permission – to take them. Either way, the end result is invariably gratitude and contentment.

And on that note, we might benefit from an even longer pause.

Morgenfrisk

Morning freshness following a good night's sleep

You've had a dreadful week at work – all interminable meetings and punishing deadlines, getting by on the bare minimum of rest, dragging yourself towards the weekend like a marathon runner stumbling towards the finishing line. You make it to Friday evening, slink inside cool, crisp sheets before eleven, and fall asleep in an instant. Mercifully, you have no plans for Saturday. You regain consciousness some twelve hours later, awakening to sunlight and birdsong. *Everything* feels different. You are transformed. Grouchy frustration and cynical misanthropy have been replaced by sparkling enthusiasm, brimming with faith in other people and life's possibilities. You feel as if you can achieve anything, and maybe you will on this radiant morning.

Few things are more rejuvenating than a good night's sleep, or indeed as important to your wellbeing. Feeling well rested constitutes a truly *visceral* experience of contentment. It's as if every fibre of your being is luxuriating in gentle, satiated, soothing satisfaction. Sadly, though, many of us are compelled to live in a state of near-continual tiredness, running on empty for long stretches of time. Yet, strangely, we often underestimate the value of sleep, and even make a virtue of being sleep-deprived, as if this signifies dynamism and success. For this reason, Ariana Huffington sought to initiate a 'sleep revolution' by encouraging the world's hyperactive caffeine addicts to get some proper rest.[24]

We need a word to celebrate the unparalleled redemptive power of sleep. And we have one: *morgenfrisk*, a Danish term that translates literally as 'morning fresh'. The words have their roots in the proto-Germanic *murgana* and *friskaz*, from which we also get the term 'frisky'. Similarly evocative of morning sprightliness is the Swedish *daggfrisk* – 'dew fresh' – which captures the pure, clean sensation of waking up fully rested against the backdrop of the dawn chorus and the first rays of sunlight.

Yet, we often need gentle persuasion to abandon our frenzied busyness. Hence, numerous cultures have learned the value of scheduling a rejuvenating snooze during daylight hours. This is practised across the Mediterranean world, from the Spanish *siesta* (derived from the Latin *hora sexta*, namely the 'sixth hour' after dawn) to the Italian *riposo* and *meriggiare* (which relate to resting around noon, ideally in the shade).[25] Interestingly, then, these traditional rest periods are particularly prevalent in balmy climates, highlighting the intimate connection between environment, culture and language.

And a similar connection is evident in Scandinavians' responses to the cold, dark Nordic winter.

Hygge

A deep sense of warmth, comfort and contentment

Of all the untranslatable items in these pages, few are as widely known as *hygge*. Yet, a few short years ago, its delights were scarcely known outside of Scandinavia. Then, suddenly, it was everywhere. No fewer than nine English-language books featured the word in their titles in 2016 alone,[26] as well as countless articles in newspapers and magazines. Inevitably, it was one of the *Oxford English Dictionary*'s words of the year.[27]

Books such as *Hygge: The Danish Art of Living Well*[28] usually present it as the key to the enviably high levels of contentment that Denmark – and the other Nordic nations – enjoy. These countries invariably feature at or near the top of happiness-ranking tables. For instance, the United Nations' 2017 *World Happiness Report* – which ranks countries according to self-reported, subjective assessments of personal wellbeing – was headed by Norway, followed by Denmark, Iceland, Switzerland, Finland, the Netherlands, Canada, New Zealand, Australia and Sweden.[29]

Of course, Nordic happiness does not rest *solely* on *hygge*. For instance, these countries' strong social connections and egalitarianism should not be disregarded (as we explore in Chapter 4). Nevertheless, *hygge* doubtless has an important role to play, even if its significance has been exaggerated by companies that are eager to cash in on the craze and boost their sales of candles, cocoa and thick woollen socks.

But what exactly is it? Well, there is certainly an element of cosiness to *hygge*. You may be picturing a group of stereotypical blond-haired, blue-eyed Danes, snuggling together under soft blankets next to a flickering wood fire, bathed in candlelight. In that respect, the term reflects its roots in the Old Norse *hugga*, meaning 'to comfort' (and possibly the origin of the English word 'hug'[30]). So, to an extent, *hygge* speaks to an existential sense of feeling protected from the vicissitudes of life. This understanding is strengthened by the observation that the antonym – *uhygge* – translates as 'frightening' or 'sinister', rather than merely 'uncomfortable'.[31]

However, the picture is complicated by the fact that *hygge* is also used in many other scenarios, some of which could never be described as 'cosy' – chatting amiably with a friend over coffee, a tender kiss, cycling on a bright spring morning.[32] So perhaps *hygge* implies feeling warmth 'in one's heart', irrespective of whether the physical environment is snugly.[33] In such precious moments, all seems right with the world. We feel safe and at ease, caring and cared for. If blankets, warm socks and candles can generate these sensations, so much the better! But *hygge* may be found in any number of alternative situations . . . as long as we know what to look for.

Sometimes, though, only the comfort and security of home will do.

Gemütlichkeit

Comfort, cosiness, homeliness

Picture your worst ever commute. The trains are on strike, perhaps, so you wearily trudge through a relentless, icy downpour, soaked to the skin, shivering in your bones. Eventually, you spy the lights of home flickering in the distance. Crossing the threshold, you feel a surge of warmth and relief. You are enveloped by your loving family, who bring you warm clothes and hot food as you settle down in front of a roaring log fire. Is there a word to describe how you feel at that precise moment? How would you convey the inimitable sensation of finally being *home*?

Far more than a pile of bricks and mortar, home is the existential centre of our world. Thus, closely related to the cosy warmth of *hygge* is the often under-appreciated feeling of being at home. This lack of appreciation – at least in the English-speaking world – is reflected by the fact that terms such as 'homely' and 'homeliness' are usually synonymous with plainness or commonness, rather than anything desirable.

By contrast, German speakers seem to have a better grasp of the true value of feeling at home, given their wide range of delicately textured terms on the subject. Particularly nuanced is the noun *Gemütlichkeit*, which stems from the adjective *gemütlich*, which in turn elaborates upon the noun *Gemüt*. Although *Gemütlichkeit* can be translated simply as 'cosiness', it also encompasses 'warmth', 'friendliness' and 'good cheer' – all of which might be associated with the welcome embrace of the familial hearth on a cold night.

The root – *Gemüt* – is equally multilayered, as discussed in the fascinating *Dictionary of Untranslatables: A Philosophical Lexicon*.[34] Philosophers have deployed it to signify a gamut of vital human properties – from mind and mood to heart and soul – without it being reducible to a single definition.[35] It has even been used to encapsulate 'the whole inner world of man'.[36] Its grammatical elaboration into *Gemütlichkeit* therefore implies that these precious inner qualities are embodied in a particular situation or place.[37]

For me, that is precisely the sensation of feeling at home: content, self-contained, at one with an environment that is suffused with warmth and love. This experience is also reflected in other German terms, such as *Geborgenheit* and *Heimlich*, which evoke additional nuances. The former can mean 'safe' or 'sheltered'[38] or even 'hidden',[39] conveying protection or security, whereas the latter means 'homely' in the positive sense of comforting familiarity rather than plainness. As such, especially when considered together, these terms celebrate the deep contentment of feeling at home.

Of course, contentment is not always linked to a roaring fire and a comfortable pair of slippers.

Fiero

Justified pride in one's achievements

Many things have the capacity to befuddle me: IKEA assembly instructions, changing parts on my car, following a recipe correctly. Two hours into preparing one of Jamie Oliver's '30-minute meals', I'll be juggling half a dozen pots and pans, dripping with sweat, wondering whether the ingredients will ever coalesce into something approximating the picture in the book. But I like to give it a go! I may not be a cordon bleu chef – far from it – but it's not about creating the perfect meal. After all, if I were interested in nothing but flavour, I'd simply order a tasty takeaway. Rather, it's about putting my heart into a new task, pushing my limits, trying to achieve something I've not done before. And if I succeed, I experience the deep reward of *fiero*.

Paul Ekman describes this sensation as the 'enjoyment felt when you have met a challenge that stretched your capabilities'.[40] This captures the essence of *fiero*: realising your potential rather than achieving a perfect outcome. If Jamie Oliver presented his customers with one of my dishes, he'd be run out of town. Yet, if I toil away with one of his recipes and make something even vaguely edible, I feel a genuine sense of achievement, knowing I've done my best.

This definition of *fiero* is subtly different from how the term tends to be used in Italy. There, it is usually synonymous with the more pejorative 'pride' or even 'arrogance'. But words are shape-shifters, assuming different forms as they enter new realms, and academia has certainly found Ekman's adapted definition useful.[41] In such ways do words take flight and start to lead new lives, diverging from their original roots.

Ekman evidently views *fiero* as justifiable pride rather than arrogance. But that begs the question: why didn't he simply use the English term? Perhaps because 'pride' has complicated and even dark implications, given that it is traditionally regarded as one of the 'seven deadly sins'.[42] Moreover, pride can often be unjustified. *Fiero* is very different from the unearned vanity of someone who happens to be rich or beautiful due to an accident of birth. It's the pride of the struggling student who has just passed their exams, the hard-working teacher who guided them there, and the parent who raised a decent child, despite all of life's challenges. It's the pride of the doctor who saves a patient's life, the construction worker who built the operating theatre, the cleaner who keeps it spotless.

Whatever path your life takes, you can savour the *fiero* that comes from putting your heart and soul into a worthwhile endeavour and succeeding against the odds. The Danes call this sense of satisfaction *arbejdsglaede* ('work joy'), while the Germans know it as *Erfolgserlebnis* ('success experience'). More broadly, such experiences may bring us the gratification of *sukha*.

Sukha

Pleasure, ease, satisfaction

We've already discussed the contentment that comes with feeling fresh and well rested (*morgenfrisk*), cosy and intimate (*hygge*), safe and secure (*gemütlichkeit*) and successful and accomplished (*fiero*). But is there one umbrella term that binds together all of these various forms of personal satisfaction? Indeed there is: *sukha*.

According to the legendary Oxford don Monier Monier-Williams – author of a pioneering Sanskrit–English dictionary in 1899[43] – this term derives from *su* ('good') and *kha* ('aperture'). Initially, then, it was used to describe a well-made axle that enabled a cart to trundle along smoothly. Once this definition was established, the same term was employed to signal general wellbeing. *Sukha* is the sensation that all is right with the world: you are comfortable, at ease, wanting for nothing.[44] Essentially, the wheels of your life are turning well, and you are rolling along nicely. In contemporary psychology, this form of satisfaction is known as 'hedonic' or 'subjective' wellbeing.[45] It entails generous helpings of positive affect, together with the satisfied judgement that life is pretty good, all things considered.[46]

Unfortunately, most of the world's great religions agree that this kind of untroubled, effortless ease is all too rare. In fact, Buddhism teaches that existence is usually characterised by the direct antonym of *sukha* – *duḥkha*. This is sometimes translated – rather forcefully – as 'suffering'. Yet, while Buddhism accepts that many people do feel deep sorrow and pain, the Buddha did not portray life as necessarily a perpetual tale of woe. He was more keen to point out that human existence is rarely, if ever, *perfect*. In that sense, a better translation of *duḥkha* might be 'dissatisfaction' or 'unease'. All too often, regardless of how well life is going, we see a cloud on the horizon.

Think of starting a hard-won holiday after months of toil. You finally find yourself on a golden beach under an azure sky, throw down your towel, and lie back blissfully on the warm sand. And it really is blissful ... for a few minutes. But then your mind starts racing. The sun is wonderful, but is it perhaps a little too intense? You don't want to burn on your first day. A few grains of sand have worked their way into the small of your back and they're getting itchy. You feel like an ice-cream, but that would entail packing up your stuff and losing your prime spot on the beach. Then you remember the urgent email that arrived in your inbox just before you left the office yesterday. Who will deal with that? And so it goes on – one petty annoyance after another. I'll wager this sounds all too familiar. No matter how hard we try to run our lives like a well-oiled axle, some piece of grit usually finds its way into the works, however small, and niggles away at our contentment.

Psychologists call this phenomenon the 'hedonic tread-mill'.[47] We experience life as a blend of satisfaction and irritation. If we manage to address the irritations, our mood improves ... for a while. But before long equilibrium is re-established as new annoyances start to appear. A pauper curses his luck and dreams of winning the lottery. Then his numbers come up and he moves into a shiny new mansion – all his problems are solved. But in a few months he's complaining that his butler has a bit of an attitude problem and the champagne is too warm.

To overcome this cycle of discontent, Buddhism recommends pursuing forms of happiness that are not contingent on circumstance. Two elements of this process are *sati* and *dhyāna*, as we saw earlier, and we shall explore similar themes later in the book. For now, though, let's continue to focus on the contentment that arises when life does seem perfect.

Xìng fú

Deep, blessed happiness

Recently, I was struck by a curious passage in a book by the eminent economist – and leading expert on happiness – Lord Richard Layard, co-author of the UN's annual *World Happiness Report*.[48] Obviously, I'm wary of finding fault with such a renowned scholar's work. Yet . . .

Perhaps anticipating objections to the viability of making cross-cultural comparisons in levels of wellbeing (as the *World Happiness Report* does), Layard writes, 'One could question whether the word for "happy" (or "satisfied") means the same thing in different languages. If it doesn't, we can learn nothing by comparing different countries.'[49] This seems a reasonable concern, yet Layard swiftly dismisses it, concluding, 'In fact it does.' In other words, he suggests that cultures throughout the world define 'happy' in a single, identical way. But do they?

First, consider that Mandarin Chinese alone has *two* common terms for 'happiness': *xìng fú* and *kuài lè*. These phrases are not synonymous, which highlights the fundamental difficulty of translation. More to the point, they cast doubt on Layard's assumption. After all, when Chinese respondents answer the query 'How happy are you with your life?' – in assessments like the UN survey, for example – their answer will depend on whether the translated question asks them about *xìng fú* or *kuài lè*. Yet these are two discrete emotions, even though the difference between them is often ineffable, even for native speakers.

The two terms' respective etymologies provide a clue to their subtly different meanings. *Kuài lè* combines *kuài* ('quick') with *lè* ('joyful'), lending it a hedonistic quality, implying an immediate hit of euphoria.[50] By contrast, *xìng fú* merges *xìng* ('good luck') with *fú* ('a blessing'). Thus, it represents a deeper form of contentment for which one should feel truly grateful. It could equate to the flood of relief one feels upon entering a cosy room after battling through a blizzard, or the joy of a good night's sleep for an insomniac, or the delight of falling in love after many years of struggle and solitude.[51] It is what we experience when our dreams come true.

In fact, with its connotations of fate, luck and deserved reward, *xìng fú* mirrors the etymological roots of 'happiness' itself. The latter derives from the Old Norse root *happ*, which refers to chance and fortune – to what *happ*ens in the world.[52] As Darrin McMahon explains in his fascinating *Happiness: A History*, this intertwining of happiness and fate reflects the fact that people in early societies had relatively little control over their own lives.[53] Therefore, people who enjoyed good health and happiness also enjoyed good fortune. Indeed, according to the mythological worldviews that prevailed at the time, such beneficiaries were truly blessed by the gods.

In the same spirit, perhaps a better translation for *xìng fú* might be 'blessedness' rather than 'happiness'. And this chimes with our final term in Chapter 1.

Béatitude

Supreme grace and happiness

'Blessed are the poor in spirit, for theirs is the kingdom of heaven.'[54] So begins one of the most famous passages in all literature – the Sermon on the Mount. Delivered by Jesus near the end of his ministry, possibly on the north-west shore of the Sea of Galilee, many theologians regard this oration as the fullest and most poetic expression of his teachings – the 'essence of Christianity'.[55] After exalting those who mourn, those who hunger for righteousness, the meek and the merciful, he asserts: 'Blessed are the pure in heart, for they will see God. Blessed are the peacemakers, for they will be called children of God. Blessed are those who are persecuted for righteousness's sake, for theirs is the kingdom of heaven.'

First, what should we make of that poetically repeated central word – 'blessed'? Just as the Gospel has made its way around the world over the last two millennia, this word is the product of a long migration. In the early Greek versions of the New Testament, the pivotal term was *makários*, which was subsequently framed as *beātitūdō* in Latin and then *béatitude* in French, which in turn entered English as a loanword in the fifteenth century. However, around the same time, *béatitude* was also translated as 'blessed', which itself derives from the Proto-Germanic *blodison* – to consecrate or hallow an object, person or place, originally with blood (as alluded to in its etymology).[56] Hence, in the biblical context, we might say that *béatitude* means being supremely blessed.

Or, equally, it could be translated simply as 'happy'. Therefore, according to McMahon, the Sermon on the Mount could also be rendered: '*Happy* are the pure in heart, for they will see God.'[57] Of course, this is more than mere satisfaction; it is 'perfect' happiness.[58] Here we strike against the limitations of language, and the fact that the word 'happiness' encompasses so many emotional states – from the banal to the sublime. Perhaps 'blessed' is preferable, after all. As Thomas Carlyle put it, 'There is something higher than happiness, and that is blessedness.'[59]

Whatever we call this beneficent state of wellbeing, Jesus' message was revolutionary. Prevailing ideas on happiness positioned it as elusive and ephemeral – beyond the reach of most, attainable only for those few with the power and good fortune to be able to arrange their lives in an agreeable manner. We saw this perspective reflected earlier in *sukha* and *xìng fú*, both of which rely on circumstances being just right. By dramatic contrast, Jesus promised perfect happiness for the marginalised and the oppressed, the poor and the persecuted. Even more radically, he assured these people that they were *more* blessed than the rich and powerful.

This awesome promise was not quite equivalent to the self-empowerment of the Stoics, with their ideal of *ataraxia*, because Jesus left his followers in no doubt that they remained at the mercy of God. Nevertheless, it was a redemptive idea which irrevocably shook and shaped the established world. Hence, it is an appropriate experiential peak with which to conclude this chapter. Before we move on, though, let's recap, as we've covered a lot of ground.

Summary

After this first leg of our journey, you may be feeling slightly breathless, your mind buzzing with new ideas and possibilities. So where have we been? Essentially, we've proceeded along a spectrum of intensity and warmth, beginning with more peaceful and equanimous forms of contentment before advancing towards more vivid varieties. Thus, we started with the Stoic tranquillity of *ataraxia*, followed by the mindful awareness of *sati* and the focused absorption of *dhyāna*. Next we saw that meditative stillness can be achieved even in the midst of action, hence the effortless spontaneity of *wú wéi* and the relaxed alertness of *zanshin*. Relatedly, we encountered the serene self-surrender of *Gelassenheit* and the quiet, reflective pause afforded by *selah*.

Then we began turning up the dial of satisfaction. *Morgenfrisk* spoke to the visceral contentment of feeling well rested, *hygge* evoked deep warmth and security, *Gemütlichkeit* conveyed the cosy comforts of home, and *fiero* expressed the justified pride we can find in our own achievements. Finally, we embraced three forms of vibrant happiness: the ease of *sukha*, the deep blessing of *xìng fú*, and the supreme grace of *béatitude*.

Now, we move on to even more energised forms of happiness in the vivacious allure of pleasure.

CHAPTER TWO

Pleasure

Our travels continue through the sunny uplands of 'positive affect' – the realm of the pleasant and pleasing. In psychology, such emotions are commonly arrayed along a spectrum of arousal. Like a shimmering rainbow, this encompasses everything from the deep violet calm of contentment – which we covered in Chapter 1 – to the more lustrous red vibrancy of pleasure.

In the metaphorical landscape of happiness, contentment is the lush rolling pastures that we roam peacefully, at our leisure. By contrast, pleasure constitutes the soaring mountain peaks. We ascend them giddily, enthused by the intoxication of adventure, drawn on by the promise of a captivating view. These wild forays may be more exciting than the calm repose of the foothills, but they are invariably more fleeting. After all, mountaineers do not settle on the conquered peaks; instead, they return home to the stability of the valleys. In the same way, the rush of pleasure tends to swiftly dissipate as its neu-rochemical messengers ebb away. Maybe that's as it should be. After all, the idea of being permanently stimulated by pleasure is unsettling in a way that gentle contentment is not. Life's richness lies in its dynamic and varied textures.

That said, the sensations we shall encounter in this chap-ter are not *mere* pleasures. Positive psychology often regards pleasure somewhat disparagingly as superficial hedonism. A distinction is drawn between *hedonic* happiness (also known as 'subjective wellbeing')[1] and *eudaimonic* happiness (or 'psy-chological wellbeing').[2] The latter – which we shall explore in depth in the final chapter – has its origins in classical Greece, where philosophers used it to describe 'higher' forms of happiness that were attainable only by living a virtuous life. Accordingly, here we see the early critiques of hedonism also being formulated. For instance, Aristotle despairingly regarded most of humanity as 'slavish in their tastes' and living a 'life suitable to beasts'.[3] By contrast, he felt that 'serious things are better than laughable things' and argued that a life devoted to truth and beauty was qualitatively deeper and more worth-while. To an extent, this attitude persists to this day, with many scholars championing eudaimonic happiness over more hedonistic variants, emphasising the importance of personal development, strong relationships, self-acceptance and attain-ing goals.[4]

However, some critics are beginning to question the wisdom of treating *hedonia* and *eudaimonia* as two distinct forms of happiness.[5] After all, many experiences are heightened as a result of a complex intermingling of the two. Kissing, for example, can generally be a pleasurable experience, but there is a world of difference between a drunken snog with a random stranger and the first tender embrace with one's soulmate. The former may be pleasant enough, but the latter is the stuff of dreams, suffused with mystery and meaning.

In other words, not all pleasures are the same. Something that feels good can also contain hidden depths. Bear this in mind as we sample a banquet of delights, beginning with the revelry of the *craic*.

Craic

Fun, revelry, good times

Early in 2017, the January gloom was enlivened by media excitement about a new 'Professor of Fun', at the University of Cambridge no less.[6] It made for an eye-catching headline, but why was such an appointment even deemed newsworthy? The articles soon laid their cards on the table: fun isn't a serious topic for academic study, and certainly not for an Oxbridge don. It's so frivolous and fanciful!

But this perspective itself is revealing. Why do we regard fun so disparagingly? Could it be a lingering hangover from St Paul's insistence that adults should turn their minds to 'serious' subjects and leave fun to the children. This has certainly been the prevailing attitude throughout academia. Of the hundreds of thousands of psychology papers published over the last century or so, barely a handful are devoted solely to fun.[7] But maybe that's about to change, given that fun now has its very own professor.

Moreover, academics are increasingly appreciative of the value of play in children's cognitive, emotional and social development.[8] Indeed, Cambridge asked for an expert in educational psychology in the advert for its new professorship. But these activities matter to adults, too. We devote the majority of our precious free time to play and fun in the form of our pastimes, sports and hobbies. Sure, it's possible to analyse salsa dancing or singing in the local choir in functional terms, as good ways to meet people. But ultimately we engage in such activities, and dozens of others, because they're fun, exciting, unpredictable, full of merriment. In short, they're a good laugh.

All these notions are encapsulated in the vibrant Gaelic noun *craic*, which is increasingly employed far beyond the shores of Ireland. For instance, should you enter an Irish-themed pub in Sydney or Chicago, you're liable to see a sign exhorting you to 'enjoy the *craic*'. Indeed, the concept has proved an effective means of marketing Ireland to potential visitors.[9] This strategy makes perfect sense given that many a tourist has been charmed by long, hazy evenings in warm, welcoming pubs, entranced by their spontaneous, soulful jamming sessions and friendly chatter.

The word itself is relatively recent – and surprisingly Anglo-centric, apparently – in origin. It is thought to have been adapted from the English term 'crack' (which is still used to denote news or gossip, particularly in Scotland and northern England) no earlier than the mid-twentieth century.[10] Yet over the past seventy years it has become intimately linked to Gaelic culture and the Irish people's well-earned reputation for geniality and merry-making ... even though 'What's the *craic*?' can also mean simply 'What's going on?' in Dublin as well as Glasgow.

But wherever you're from, most of us would surely like to enjoy some good *craic*. And on that note, we might also want our festivities to be enlivened by benevolent mirth and laughter.

Pretoogjes

The twinkling eyes of benign humour

Of all the world's delightful Christmas traditions, few are as endearingly naff as the corny jokes secreted in crackers. Everyone groans at the terrible puns and contorted word-play, but the day wouldn't be the same without them. Moreover, personally, I find it quite helpful to have a little prompting in that regard. In most situations, I have at best what the French call *l'esprit de l'escalier* – 'staircase wit'. If I do think of a witty rejoinder, it usually pops into my mind a couple of minutes too late – just as I'm on the way down the stairs after a party perhaps.

It's not that I don't love comedy. I'm in awe of the John Cleeses of this world and their ability to bring laughter into our lives. Indeed, academia is starting to appreciate the value of humour, for example in terms of its physiological impact upon stress hormones.[11] 'Comedy interventions' and 'humour skills programmes' are even being trialled as complementary therapies for those sufferering with illness,[12] with promising results.

Hence, this chapter would be incomplete without touching on the joys of laughter, as embodied in the wonderful Dutch term *pretoogjes*. Translatable as 'fun eyes', it captures the twinkling expression of someone who engages in good-humoured mischief. Technically, this is known as a 'micro-expression' – a minute, barely perceptible sign, often involving the eyes, that conveys valuable information about a person's emotional state.[13]

Of related interest here is the complex playfulness of

'mischief' itself. This word first appeared in the English language in the thirteenth century, when it was adapted from the French *meschief,* meaning misfortune, harm or even evil. It was not until centuries later that it assumed the more playful connotations it enjoys today: japes, high jinks and all other forms of practical jokery. But mischief is not necessarily mere foolishness or prankishness – it has long played an important role in many cultures. For instance, historically, one person given free rein to speak truth to power was the court jester or fool, concealing his pointed criticism of the king under a veneer of levity.[14]

Or take the strange mysteries of Halloween or the Mexican *Día de Muertos*. Both of these annual traditions are dedicated to remembering the dead (with Halloween a contraction of All Hallows' Eve, the day before the liturgical feast that honours the saints), yet they are not sombre, funereal affairs. Instead, they are mysteriously, powerfully festive, infused with the eerie joy of the carnivalesque. Think of the mischief-making of Halloween – from the capriciousness of trick-or-treat to the dark pageantry of costume parties.

Some people have suggested that these festivals are so popular because they provide a rare opportunity to affirm life and celebrate existence in the face of the encroaching shadow of death,[15] with their mischief and laughter being powerfully redemptive.

And the same could be said of breaking bread, especially with loves ones.

Sobremesa

Communing around the table

Few human activities are so universally celebrated as eating and drinking. Yet, at the same time, few practices are so wonderfully varied. Walk down most high streets in Britain, and every few yards you will find some delicacy from a different corner of the world – from the indulgent richness of mozzarella-laden pizza to the fresh, crisp taste of sushi. Too many delights, not enough time!

The manifold pleasures of food can be filed under the general label of 'Epicureanism'. A loanword of sorts, it derives from the third-century (BCE) philosopher Epikouros. Although most of his writings have been lost to time, with only a few surviving fragments, he has been hugely influential. He was, for instance, a key proponent of the idea that the universe is composed of atoms – from the Greek *ātomos*, meaning 'indivisible' or 'uncuttable' – an insight that modern science confirmed over two millennia later (even if we now know that atoms are divisible). However, he is most closely associated with championing the enjoyment of life. This has resulted in the misconception that he was an unbridled hedonist. In fact, he advocated the humble appreciation of *modest* pleasures – a fine meal with good friends, perhaps – which he saw as the surest route to the aforementioned *ataraxia* (see Chapter 1).[16]

This form of enjoyment is epitomised by the Spanish term *sobremesa*. Literally meaning 'on the table', it describes the culturally vital tradition of sitting with family and/or friends at mealtimes. In addition to consuming food together, this practice entails connecting with one another, particularly once the eating is over.[17] Rather than leaping up as soon as the last bite is wolfed down and fleeing to the seclusion of the TV or the smartphone, *sobremesa* recognises the key social function of breaking bread with your nearest and dearest. Mealtimes are about more than food. They are precious opportunities for weaving together the threads of memory and narrative that create a family, and hence for processing and understanding our lives.

Then, of course, there are terms that extol the appreciation of food itself. The Mediterranean is particularly well endowed in this area, which is hardly surprising given the quality of its produce and various culinary traditions. For instance, as we shall explore in Chapter 5, the French notion of *gourmandise* has given rise to two subtly different English adaptations: the refined 'gourmet', with its connotations of educated connoisseurship; and its coarser cousin 'gourmand', with its more pejorative suggestions of gluttony.[18] Hovering somewhere between these two is the Spanish term *gula*, which expresses the indulgent desire to eat simply for the delicious taste, yet can easily veer towards greed. I suspect that most of us are familiar with that particular fine line.

Finally, after some gustatory indulgence, you may find yourself nodding off. If so, welcome to *abbiocco* – an Italian term for the soporific (and usually pleasant) drowsiness that follows a hearty meal. Likewise, the vivid Dutch verb *uitbuiken* – literally 'outbellying' – conveys the sense of total (and possibly excessive) satiation. It's the perfect description of postprandial Christmas Day, especially in the afterglow of a glass or three of the good stuff.

Utepils

A drink enjoyed outside

Picture the scene: it's been a long, gloomy winter and for months you've been cooped up, yearning for fresh air and the warmth of the sun. And today, gloriously, it feels like spring has arrived. After a day toiling away in the office, gazing longingly at the blue sky outside the window, you're finally given leave to escape. As fast as dignity allows, you dart from the stuffy building and find yourself in your favourite pub garden, an ice-cold glass in your hand. The first sip quenches so many kinds of thirst – physiological, emotional, even existential. What joy! This is the pleasure of an *utepils* – a Norwegian term for a cold beer enjoyed in the sunshine, particularly that first alfresco drink of spring.

Perhaps a colleague joins you just as you're draining your glass. A few drinks later, the two of you might be in the midst of a *pertu* – a Hungarian ritual that traditionally involves drinking with interlocking arms to establish or maintain a friendship (with the term deriving literally from the permission to use the intimate *tu* form of address).[19] Later in the evening, you may even find yourself transported into Dionysian realms and the carnivalesque chaos of *ramé* and *kefi* (see below).

Of course, many of us have bitter experience of the misadventures that can attend the irresponsible consumption of alcohol. Hence, we would probably wish to avoid a *Schnapsidee* – a daft, ridiculous or even downright dangerous plan conceived while under the influence of drink. Should we venture down such a path, the end result may well be a *morkkis* – a useful Finnish term for a psychological or even moral hangover. There are two aspects to this: the chilling memory of one's drunken antics the night before; and, perhaps even worse, the panic one experiences when wondering what one might have done, but can't remember.

Hopefully, though, your enjoyment of a few drinks won't be clouded by such concerns. It might even be energised by a hint of *ramé*.

Ramé

A lively, boisterous social occasion

I can still recall how, at the uncertain age of fifteen, my friend and I diligently packed a couple of rucksacks like good schoolboys and trooped off to the Reading music festival. A couple of hours later, we stumbled wide-eyed into a field of chaos! It was hard not to get carried away. Before long, shirt tatty and torn, I was crowdsurfing like a maniac. By the end of the night, Peter Fonda's rabble-rousing speech from *The Wild Angels* was ringing in my ears, as sampled by headliners Primal Scream: 'We wanna be free to do what we wanna do ... And we wanna have a good time. And that's what we're gonna do. We're gonna have a good time. We're gonna have a party.'

Most people enjoy a good party. Perhaps no other activity is so indelibly associated with fun and carefree pleasure. However, our tastes vary: the majority of folk would probably disdain Fonda's wild hedonism, and I dare say crowdsurfing in a muddy field has limited appeal, too. Fortunately, though, there's no shortage of varied festivities around the world, featuring every conceivable form of 'party'. Those inclined towards more reflective socialising might prefer the Spanish *tertulia* or the French *soirée* – refined gatherings devoted to intelligent conversation and maybe a little light music. After all, one may savour the delights of the mind – the cultivation of knowledge and culture – just as much as the joys of the flesh or the vine.

Such sophisticated activities have a long pedigree. In classical Greece, the great *symposia* were banquets devoted to discussion, music and art (although they were lubricated by hefty quantities of alcohol and could get quite rowdy and debauched). More recently, seventeenth- and eighteenth-century France saw the rise of *salons*: intellectual gatherings that were often orchestrated by a dynamic – and stereotypically rich, intelligent and beautiful – female hostess in her own 'sitting room' (hence the term). These high-minded affairs, which were dedicated to truth and beauty, were pivotal in the development of the Enlightenment.[20]

The Spanish term *fiesta* has rather more vibrant, colourful and even theatrical connotations,[21] but for those who prefer the dial turned up to eleven, there is always the boisterous Balinese concept of *ramé*. The anthropologist Clifford Geertz describes this as a particularly festive, chaotic and lively party,[22] but the term can be used for any social occasion that is especially animated and rowdy. At such moments, it's easy to be carried away by the spirit of *kefi*.

Kefi

Passion, enthusiasm, high spirits

One of the most mysterious figures in the Greek pantheon, Dionysus was the focus of numerous cults stretching back through antiquity. He was emblematic of a wide array of liminal experiences and phenomena – the god of grapes and wine, fertility and rebirth, madness and chaos, ecstasy and spirituality. Accordingly, while some of his devotees were associated with libidinous, hedonistic excess, others were transfixed upon ecstatic self-transcendence.

Invariably, though, Dionysus was evoked in the context of breaking free from the constraints of normal human perception and experience, often with the assistance of trance-inducing intoxicants and activities. According to Nietzsche, this Dionysian quest for liberated consciousness comprised one of the two central aspects of Greek culture.[23] The other was Apollonian – after Apollo, the Greek god of light, truth and beauty – which describes the logic and rationality of the philosophers. Thus, reason may be augmented by the 'divine madness' of Dionysian excess, whereby the rational mind becomes transported into irrationality, with the capacity to reach otherwise inaccessible peaks of illumination.

Few cults worship at the altar of Dionysus today (although a recent article in the unabashedly titled *Modern Drunkard* magazine told of a society in New Orleans known as the Revived Order of Dionysus).[24] Nevertheless, many people still pursue the sorts of experiences that are associated with him: from altered states achieved via psychoactive substances, to self-transcendence through spiritual practices, to Saturday-night revellers drinking themselves into a haze. The latter is particularly common, of course, as people shake off the shackles of the working week, seeking to cut loose and make merry. This type of release is captured by the Greek noun *kefi*, with its heady connotations of enthusiasm, high spirits and even frenzy.[25] It has come to denote a culturally valued emotional state, often heightened by alcohol and evoked by music and dance.[26] But it need not be wild Dionysian self-abandonment. It can be the simple pleasure of briefly abandoning our inhibitions.

Of course, it's not only Greeks who are attuned to the pleasures of music, dance and perhaps a little intoxication. For instance, the expressive Swahili verb *mbuki-mvuki* describes the act of shedding one's clothes to dance in a freer, less inhibited fashion,[27] while the Portuguese term *desbundar* evokes exceeding one's usual limits when making merry. That said, the latter can also suggest a troubling loss of self-control, as might happen during liminal experiences such as 'spirit possession'.[28]

Clearly, then, this is strange, complex territory. It can entail venturing into dark regions that are usually best avoided, while its more benign dimensions provide occasional – and some might say essential – relief from mundane routine and social convention. Thankfully, some states of pleasure are rather more serene and tranquil.

Tarab

Musically induced enchantment or ecstasy

Ten years ago, on a cool summer's evening in Edinburgh, I found myself in a beautiful candlelit church on the corner of Princes Street. Weary from the hustle and bustle of the city's frenetic festival, I settled into a narrow wooden pew, grateful for the free concert that was about to unfold. However, classical music is hardly a great passion of mine, so I was unfamiliar with the pieces listed on the programme. Hence, I was totally unprepared for what followed.

Softly, the pianist launched into a series of delicate, lilting triplets – neither too slow nor too fast, just perfect. Soon a violinist joined her – low at first, then gradually ascending before dropping back, as if hesitant to cross some aural frontier, but then higher still, into the heavens. It was like being led up an infinite spiral staircase. I glanced down at the programme: I was listening to Arvo Pärt's *Spiegel im Spiegel* . . . and experiencing what I've since learned may be called *tarab*. This Arabic term expresses the enchantment and even ecstasy that beautiful music can induce.

This is different territory from the joyous impulsiveness of *kefi*. Here, the emphasis is on captivating absorption – the soaring reverie of the reflective listener. Indeed, in some traditions, notably the esoteric branch of Islam known as Sufism, *tarab* is indelibly associated with the devotees' music, singing and dancing, which are used to facilitate spiritual elevation and self-transcendence,[29] most famously in the case of the 'whirling' of the Mewlewī Order, established by followers of the Persian poet, scholar and mystic Jalāl ad-Dīn Muhammad

Rūmī. Thus, *tarab* is not merely a form of entranced appreciation or even ecstasy; it is imbued with deep spiritual significance. This illustrates the point that it does not always make sense to distinguish between hedonic and eudaimonic happiness, because the two are sometimes inextricably intertwined, and are all the more powerful as a result.[30]

Many traditions have harnessed the transcendent power of the arts in this way. Christianity, for instance, has a long history of devotional singing, through which adherents express and amplify their joy and reverence. Moreover, it has continued to develop new forms of worship in this respect. For example, your local church may host the occasional 'Taizé' service. Developed by a spiritual community within the French town of the same name, such services usually involve meditative singing – or just listening in contemplative silence – in a candlelit church. They can be magical.

Of course, not all captivating experiences are occasioned by music; nor do they require a spiritual context to give them significance. Hence, there are many more general expressions of delight.

Joie de vivre

Exuberant joy of living

Although France is just a short hop over the Channel, it can feel like a world away. Growing up I went there most summers on holiday, and I remember those weeks as some of the happiest times of my young life. It wasn't just the long, sunlit days, the deep blue Mediterranean, the exquisite food and the romantic girls – although they certainly helped. It was more that indefinable *je ne sais quoi* that suffuses the land and its people.

Above all, many of the locals seemed to exude a *joie de vivre* – literally, 'joy of living'. Indeed, it seems entirely appropriate that the word 'joy' is borrowed from our Gallic cousins, given their apparent expertise in cultivating it. And *joie de vivre* takes this characteristic to an even higher plane – no mere passing delight but something far more durable: a lasting disposition rather than a fleeting mood that is vulnerable to the vicissitudes of fate and circumstance. It has even been termed a *Weltanschauung* – an overarching philosophy of life. It is 'joy generalised, a result of many experiences, a sustained and boundless enjoyment of the here and now'.[31] Is there any better way to spend one's days?

It is useful to think of *joie de vivre* as the 'knack of knowing how to live'[32] – a skill that is similarly encapsulated in the phrase *savoir vivre*. This brings us into interesting psychological territory. Notions such as *joie de vivre* are often viewed misleadingly as fixed personality traits: you either have them or you don't. Admittedly, some people do seem blessed with a generally sunny disposition – a *bon vivant* with a zest for living, perhaps – whereas others are more prone to gloominess. Yet all skills – including *joie de vivre* and *savoir vivre* – can be practised and honed. For instance, we can all add to our happiness through means such as cultivating gratitude[33] or learning how to savour the moment.[34]

Whenever I look longingly towards France – with its romance, elegance and two-hour lunches – I can't help thinking they have mastered that 'knack' of knowing how to live. The tradition of long, leisurely lunches – as opposed to wolfing down a sandwich alone at one's desk – isn't so much an individual personality trait as a manifestation of a whole nation's appreciation of good food and companionship, and their steadfast refusal to be rushed. But the good news is that we can all learn to cultivate a similar attitude and bring more *joie de vivre* into our lives.

And if we're fortunate, the dial of pleasure may be turned up even higher.

Njuta

Profound enjoyment and appreciation

As we saw in the Preface, we mentally carve up our experiential world by drawing boundaries and coining words for the resulting regions. Intriguingly, these boundaries may blur and shift over time, yet the labels often remain the same. Consequently, a word can come to represent rather different terrain from that which it originally signified.

An interesting case in point is 'enjoy'. Today, this simply means finding pleasure in a particular activity, or even just a basic interest: for example, I might claim to enjoy reading the newspaper every morning. Yet such a tepid connotation is quite a fall from grace, given the word's heady origins. It entered the English language in the fourteenth century, derived from the French *enjoir* – literally, 'filled with joy'. How majestic! Think of a particular highlight in your life. I remember a feeling of intense love when my wife and I took to the floor for our first dance on our wedding day. Looking back on that moment, I find it hard to conjure up a suitable phrase to convey its full power and perfection. 'Enjoy' barely scratches the surface, whereas '*filled* with joy' at least comes close.

Another option might be *njuta*, although it is rather blandly rendered in most Swedish–English dictionaries simply as 'enjoy'.[35] In actuality this word is far more intense, conveying passion or even lust, albeit not necessarily in a sexual sense (as, for instance, one might speak of lusting after a hot shower). It's best to think of *njuta* as an elevated form of appreciation: the intense delight you feel when seeing a dazzling sunset, perhaps, or the gratitude you experience when unexpectedly treated to a delicious meal. Clearly, this is a very long way from the meagre semantic sustenance of 'enjoy'.

Speaking of words whose intensity has changed in the act of borrowing, this brings us back to the ancient Greeks.

Ékstasis

Euphoric transportation outside oneself

From the intellectual furnace of classical Greece comes an intriguing trio of words, all three of which have long been common currency in English. Strangely though, as with 'enjoy', their original meanings have somewhat faded from view, leaving little more than a semantic residue. All three are thus further examples of the slipperiness of meaning and the shifting nature of concepts as they pass through time and across borders.

This phenomenon is particularly evident in the word 'enthusiasm'. Like 'enjoy', it now has a mealy-mouthed quality, denoting a rather lukewarm form of passion. It may be bright and cheery, but it's hardly the stuff of dreams and legends. Yet the original term *enthousiasmos* combined *en* (in) and *theos* (God) to describe divine inspiration – the sensation of feeling swept away by the otherworldly power of a sacred force.[36] I might be an enthusiastic supporter of my local football team, but they hardly transport me to a divine realm!

Curiously, while 'enthusiasm' and 'enjoy' have been watered down over the centuries, 'euphoria' has gone in the opposite direction. Etymologically, it fuses *eu* ('good', 'pure' or 'beautiful') with *phérein* ('to bear' or 'to carry').[37] Hence, in its original Greek form, it commended a person on their good bearing, whether physically, mentally or morally. For instance, Aristotle used it as a near synonym of *eudaimonia* (see above) – the fruit of a virtuous life.[38] However, since then, the term has passed through a maze of historical and cultural filters. After reaching English in the seventeenth century, it was initially deployed in medical contexts in relation to the amelioration of illness and therefore an increase in the patient's comfort. In this way, it began to imply a positive mental state, one that was not necessarily connected to virtue but was more likely due to the ingestion of medicine. From there, the word started its ascent to the heady affective heights it occupies today as evoking elation or intense happiness, usually in reaction to some highly charged stimulus (such as a psychoactive substance).

Our third word – 'ecstasy' – also has intriguing roots that are often unappreciated today. The Greeks combined *ék* ('outside' or 'beyond') and *stasis* ('stature') to make *ékstasis*. Thus, this word was used to describe people who 'stood outside' themselves in some way. Sometimes this could imply something disturbing, such as insanity or spiritual 'possession'.[39] More benignly, it might evoke an exalted state of rapture or 'mystical union' with God, arising from heartfelt contemplation of the divine,[40] and it was mainly in the latter sense that the term entered English in the fourteenth century.

Nowadays, 'ecstasy' is often used simply to signify an intensely positive emotion. Indeed, in some contexts, such as psychiatry, states of ecstasy might be viewed as *too* positive, *too* intense, artificial or socially inappropriate.[41] Yet, in its more wholesome manifestations, it equates to what Goethe termed *'herrliche Gefühle'* – the 'glorious feelings [that] give us life'.[42] Think of losing yourself in an enthralling piece of music so that all of life's worries start to disappear ... or indeed taking a more physical route to a state of rapture.

Jouissance

Orgasmic delight

Having wended our way from the pleasant foothills of *craic* to the peaks of 'ecstasy' and 'euphoria', there is an impending sense of 'climax', a word which – appropriately enough – derives from the Greek term for a ladder or staircase. Of course, it is also a synonym for one of the most commonly experienced ecstasies: the quicksilver thrill of orgasm. Of all the pathways towards self-transcendence, this may be the most quotidian and accessible.

Its delights are well captured by the French noun *jouissance*, which derives from the rather mundane verb *jouir* – 'to enjoy'.[43] However, while 'enjoy' has slipped its moorings to describe somewhat prosaic forms of satisfaction, *jouissance* has drifted in the other direction. It is now used almost exclusively to denote the sensual heights of *coitus* (from the Latin *coire*, or 'go together'). Unsurprisingly, the French term has attracted considerable interest, not least from the legendary – and rather inaccessible – psychoanalyst Jacques Lacan,[44] who focused on the complex dynamics of sexual climax.

Lacan believed that men and women have a limit to the amount of pleasure they can tolerate, because at these tremulous peaks there is the painful realisation of the inevitable and impending come-down. Therefore, if we transgress beyond this limit – as per *jouissance* – pleasure itself can become painful.[45] We are granted a tantalisingly brief release – an intimation of immortality – but then our ordinary humanness reasserts itself. Our leaden feet re-establish contact with the earth, and we are forced once again to trudge through the mud of our regular thoughts and routines.

Moreover, while the fleeting pleasure of orgasm may be glorious, we should be cautious of its intense power. Indeed, the word's Greek root (*orgasmós*) conveys thermodynamic qualities of heat, expansion, force and impulsivity. George Lakoff and Mark Johnson have perceptively analysed the phenomenology implied by this imagery in their metaphorical model of cognition.[46] Subjective states that are characterised using notions of heat – from the 'heat of passion' to 'hot-headedness' – are invariably unstable and tend to elude conscious control. Such notions are captured in the Russian term *azart*, which describes highly charged excitement and fervour but also recklessness and risk-taking.[47]

So, as with 'ecstasy' and 'euphoria', for all their exuberant intensity, climactic feelings are often viewed as unstable, uncontrollable, even dangerous. But does that mean all forms of heightened pleasure are necessarily unwieldy and tempestuous? Or is it possible to establish a surer footing on some experiential peaks, without a consequential rapid descent through the clouds?

Nirvāṇa

Total liberation from suffering

Like many teenagers in the early 1990s, I was fairly obsessed by Nirvana, whose outcast grunge spirit seemed perfectly tuned to the dynamics of the age. I was intrigued by their name, too. However, beyond thinking it sounded vaguely cool, I had no real idea what it meant.

A few years later, when I travelled to China to teach English, the term captured my attention once again when I found myself irresistibly drawn to Buddhist and Taoist monasteries. As noted in the Preface, there I expanded not only the physical limits of my world but also my conceptual horizons, as I immersed myself in ideas that seemed utterly unfathomable to my Western mind. Among these concepts was the Sanskrit term *nirvāṇa* (*niè pán* in Chinese). As I enquired into its meaning, kindly interlocutors would patiently relate it to liberation, enlightenment and awakening. This left me none the wiser . . . but ever more intrigued. My curiosity escalated as I gazed upon images of the Buddha and his beatific smile, attesting to unsurpassed tranquillity.

It all seemed so otherworldly. Yet, I was told repeatedly that the Buddha was a human being like anyone else, and in theory we could all emulate the psychological breakthrough he had made. But what was this breakthrough? It seemed it was nothing less than the complete and final cessation of *duḥkha* (see Chapter 1) and the consequent attainment of *mokṣa* – total freedom. More esoterically, *nirvāṇa* promises release from *saṃsāra* – the endless cycle of birth, death and rebirth that is inherently pervaded by *duḥkha*. This cycle can be interpreted according to various time-frames: from the successive physical lives implied by theories of reincarnation, to the moment-to-moment manner in which the human self is continually renewed. Thus, leaving aside metaphysical claims of reincarnation, Buddhists believe that anyone might attain *nirvāṇa* in *this* lifetime.

Delving into the mechanics of this process would require an entire book to itself, and even that would just scratch the surface. Nevertheless, it is possible to glimpse some aspects of the concept of *nirvāṇa* simply by focusing on its etymology, namely 'to blow out' or 'extinguish'. This does not imply some cataclysmic process whereby a person suddenly ceases to exist, vanishing in a puff of sacred smoke. Instead, it is the psychological processes which cause or contribute towards suffering that are extinguished. Key among these are craving and attachment, both of which leave us perennially dissatisfied and anxiously trying to improve our situation, even when life is pretty good. If we can manage to replace these with the more positive processes of *sati* and *dhyāna* (see Chapter 1), we may reach the bountiful land of peace and contentment that is *nirvāṇa*. This is not necessarily a permanent state of being, but it is certainly not precarious, in marked contrast to 'ecstasy'. Nor is it dependent on chance or circumstance. Rather, it is an elevated peak from which one may need never descend.

This seems a suitable place to conclude our tour of pleasure. Before moving on, though, let's pause once again to glance back at the route we've taken in this chapter.

Summary

Having left the calm valleys of contentment behind, our path ventured into more dramatic territory as we encountered more energised forms of pleasure. Starting on a light-hearted note, we explored the fun and revelry of *craic* as well as the good-natured mischief and laughter of *pretoogjes*. We then sampled the convivial delights of food and drink with *sobremesa* and *utepils*. Next, our pulses were quickened by the boisterous liveliness of *ramé* and the spirited passion of *kefi* before we soared into more elevated realms with the enchantment of *tarab*.

We then embraced the exuberant joy of living with *joie de vivre* and the profound delight of *njuta*. Finally, moving towards the climax, we saw that it is possible to lose oneself in *ékstasis*, revel in *jouissance* and finally enjoy the total liberation of *nirvāṇa*.

Now that we have luxuriated in pleasure, we can broach that most enduring and vital aspect of human happiness: love.

CHAPTER THREE

Love

I'm going to jump right in and say that loving and being loved may be the single most important factor in our happiness (besides health, perhaps). And I'm not just a hopeless romantic. Rigorous cross-cultural studies into which aspects of life make the greatest contribution to human wellbeing – from income and employment to freedom and opportunity – invariably place personal relationships at or near number one.[1] Indeed, it's tempting to say (or sing), 'All you need is love.' But what *is* love?

At times, the answer seems as obvious as a dazzling bolt of lightning in a thunderstorm. At others, it is frustratingly shadowy, eluding our clumsy efforts to grasp it. Part of the problem is that, like the term 'happiness', 'love' is used for so many different sensations and emotions that it generates a maddening kaleidoscope. My world was shaken when I fell for my dazzling wife-to-be. Struggling to articulate my fevered state, I naturally reached for the word 'love'. Seeing an old couple in the twilight of their lives hobbling by hand in hand and, again, 'love' will flash in my mind. Or I may use it – equally accurately and deliberately – to describe my feelings towards long summer evenings in the park, ice-cream, our dog Daisy or the music of Tom Waits.

Clearly, whatever love may be, it covers a lot of experiential ground. Admittedly, many of our most vital words are polysemous, sheltering an array of meanings. 'Love', though, has been described as 'polysemous in the extreme'.[2] One theorist calls it an 'empire uniting all sorts of feelings, behaviors, and attitudes, sometimes having little in common'.[3] But what an empire it is – a veritable earthly paradise that houses our deepest longings and most precious experiences. The goal of this chapter is to draw a detailed map of that wonderful realm and label it with words and phrases from around the world.

Psychology has already embraced several of these terms. In the 1970s, John Lee created an influential typology of six different 'styles' of love that he identified by exploring the literature of the classical world.[4] However, most of these styles relate to *romantic* relationships. Of course, this category of love is among the most treasured, and we shall cover it in depth below. But what of the other forms? They are no less important, and we should celebrate them. Fortunately, we have access to literally hundreds of untranslatable terms that not only reveal nuances within Lee's six styles but further illuminate love's bountiful variety.

I have organised these evocative words and phrases into fourteen discrete forms, or 'flavours'. I use 'flavours' to avoid implying that we can necessarily pigeon-hole a relationship as exclusively constituting just one of these forms. A romantic partnership, for instance, might blend together several flavours, thereby producing a unique 'taste', and moreover this blend may subtly change over time. Here, I have labelled each 'flavour' with a relevant Greek title, in recognition of classical Greece's particularly rich lexicon of love. The first three are oriented towards experiences, objects and places, rather than people. Hence, we are already in different territory from that charted by Lee. Thereafter, I present words that capture all manner of loving emotions – from passion to compassion, devotion to desire. With that tantalising promise, let's begin.

Meraki

Ardour for one's own actions and creations

What do you love to do? Which activities light up your week and enliven your life? How would you spend your days if work did not demand so much of your time? Star-gazing or salsa-dancing? Surfing or stamp-collecting?

Whatever your personal inclinations, such passions are perfectly captured by the Greek word *meraki*, which evokes 'the care and love someone has for what he/she does'.[5] As a verb, it expresses one's desire or longing for a certain activity. As an adverb, it describes the spirit in which one might undertake that task. Either way, *meraki* is a catch-all term for the love of particular experiences, whatever they may be. Its rejuvenating potency is highlighted in a study which suggests that it forestalls the possibility of becoming bored or disenchanted with a task – and indeed perhaps with life more generally. After all, our passions help give real meaning and purpose to our lives. As one participant put it, '*meraki* has no limits'.[6]

Sheltering beneath this umbrella term are numerous words that relate to *specific* experiences. Greek further excels in this regard, mainly through creative use of the suffix *-philia* (or prefix *philo-*). Originally, this simply referred to a friendly kind of love (as we shall discuss below), but it has since been harnessed to create neologisms for all manner of experiences – from *ambulophilia* (a passion for walking) to *gephyrophilia* (a fondness for crossing bridges). This suffix/prefix does not necessarily imply anything sexual, I hasten to add (even if it does in select cases) – it is essentially just a generic term for attraction or appreciation of some kind.

Indeed, both *ambulophilia* and *gephyrophilia* came to mind recently when I was fortunate enough to visit Florence. Strolling through its beautiful cobblestoned streets in the balmy evening air, crossing the Ponte Vecchio with its lights twinkling on the Arno below, I wouldn't hesitate to describe the experience in the most loving terms. How liberating just to meander and savour the sights and sounds. Naturally, the Italians have an expression for this activity – *passeggiata* – as we shall see in Chapter 5.

Indeed, like beautiful melodies, many of the various forms of love echo allusively throughout this book. *Meraki* itself is intertwined with our next entry because, in our passion for certain activities, we often come to cherish the objects we associate with them.

Érōs

Appreciation of cherished items

As a teenager, I dreamed of owning a cherry sunburst Gibson Les Paul guitar. This craving was inseparable from my parallel longing to be – and I really do mean *be* – Slash from Guns N'

Roses, striding across stadium stages wailing the solo from 'Sweet Child o' Mine'.

My passion for music and its accoutrements is best expressed by the term *érōs*. Of course, these days, this word usually conjures up images of romance, as symbolised by the cherubic Renaissance figure of Cupid, who unites lovers with a twang from his bow and arrow. Yet, in the classical era, while *Érōs* was the Greek god of love, this did not necessarily describe a yearning for other people. Hence, it was not specifically linked to sexual desire, as it tends to be today. Unfortunately, in contemporary discourse, most of the Greek terms that are associated with love – from *philia* to *érōs* – tend to be lazily conflated with romantic love and imbued with sexual desire. Therefore, we need to remind ourselves that far from every form of love is romantic or sexual. A love for music, for instance, can be just as profound and all-consuming as sexual desire.

While *epithymía* captures the essence of carnality (see below), the theologian Paul Tillich argues that *érōs* is a higher form of love, as it is imbued with truth, beauty and goodness.[7] Indeed, Plato and others generally invoked this term in the context of aesthetic appreciation rather than romantic or sensual love. From this perspective, one loves an object because it reflects the perfection of the divine, and this allows one to share in that divinity. As Plato wrote, 'he who loves the beautiful is called a lover because he partakes of it'.[8]

So, here we have our second glorious form of love: a deep appreciation of things, be they physical entities, such as that Les Paul guitar, works of art, like the spectral chords of *Spiegel im Spiegel*, or memories, as in when I reflect on my dad's loving encouragement to join his band on stage for a rendition of 'Stand by Me' when I was a nervous thirteen-year-old. *Érōs* can even denote love for an abstract concept or transcendental principle, such as justice or honour. Either way, it is genuine love and warrants recognition as such. As does the deep affection we develop for particular places.

Chōros

Connection to places

Think of a place that is particularly close to your heart, and all of the people, experiences, sights and sounds that you automatically associate with it. Your home town, perhaps, especially if you now live somewhere else; or possibly where you spent your honeymoon, or a blissful family holiday? Such places are the stages upon which our favourite characters walk, and where our dearest scenes are set. They are where we feel most rooted, most connected.

The love we hold for these places is reflected in the term *chōros*. In classical Greece, this word represented the unique quality of a particular location: the affection it inspires and the meanings it evokes.[9] Recall *Gemütlichkeit* from Chapter 1, for instance – the priceless satisfaction you feel when returning home after an arduous journey. Home is more than a mere building. It's your nest, where you feel safe and secure, hidden from prying eyes and protected from the sharp edges of the outside world. It's a chamber of memories, suffused with the stories and experiences that comprise your life history. All of this contributes to *chōros*.

Understandably, given the vital importance of such rootedness, comparable notions have developed around the world.

The Spanish noun *querencia*, for instance, is used to describe the place where one feels most secure. The term is used in bullfighting, for example, for the area where the bull 'naturally wants to go in the ring', as Ernest Hemingway famously discussed in *Death in the Afternoon*.[10] It can have comparable meanings for humans too, reflecting that 'deep sense of inner well-being that comes from knowing a particular place on the Earth; its daily and seasonal patterns, its fruits and scents, its soils and bird-songs. A place where, whenever you return to it, your soul releases an inner sigh of recognition and realisation.'[11] It is your intimate knowledge of the streets of your home town, the fields and parks where you played as a child, and even your native land's weather. Similar resonances imbue the Māori term *turangawaewae* – literally, 'a place to stand' – which describes that small portion of the planet one calls one's own.[12]

Sadly, many of us have also experienced the other side of this particular coin: the deep longing we feel for certain places when separated from them by fate or circumstance. Chapter 6 includes a batch of evocative terms that describe this sort of yearning. As with all forms of love, *chōros* exists in the absence of its object as well as in its presence.

With that in mind, we turn to the most potent source of love – people – and specifically the friendliness of *philia*.

Philia

Platonic bonds of friendship

Arguably nothing is more important to us than the people we love. Yet, as we have seen, not all bonds of love are romantic, let alone sexual. So, our first form of love for people is the deep affection we feel for our closest friends. Given Greek thinkers' fascination with all forms of love, it is entirely appropriate that this one is named after perhaps the most important philosopher of all – Plato. His reflections on the theme of friendship were so influential that non-sexual relationships with our closest companions are still described in terms of 'platonic' love. However, here we can deploy the term that Plato himself used: *philia.*

We must tread carefully, though. As with 'love' itself, *philia* is a polysemous shape-shifter that is used in multiple and sometimes troubling or perverse ways. For instance, in modern discourse, it can have unfortunate connotations when selectively used as a suffix to denote sexual deviancy. By contrast, in classical Greece, it simply meant 'friendly love', encompassing fondness, appreciation and loyalty. A person could bestow such feelings on just about anything they held dear in a non-romantic way – from personal friends and relatives to a specific town and country. Indeed, we still see this convention in neologisms like 'Francophile', which is used to describe people who love all things French.

Plato's usage was much more precise: he viewed *philia* as a glorious ideal of close friendship – the affinity between two or more people who choose to spend their time together. Today, we have myriad names for such people: 'pals', 'mates', 'buddies', to name but three. We could also speak of *compadre* – a Spanish term of endearment which is loosely translated as 'godfather' (or, literally, as 'co-father'). Similarly, *comrade* (from the Spanish *camarada* – 'roommate') has been widely adopted as an invocation of solidarity, especially within socialist and communist circles.[13]

Most of us cherish the relationships that these terms describe, even if we usually refrain from attaching the label 'love' to them. And that term is even less likely to appear in definitions of our next entry.

Philautia

Self-regard, -respect, -esteem and -compassion

'Mirror mirror, on the wall, who is the fairest of them all?' So asks the self-obsessed Wicked Queen in the fairy-tale of *Snow White* by the Brothers Grimm. Such overweening pride and arrogance is the stuff of legends, right back to the fatal self-absorption of Narcissus, who became so transfixed by his own reflection that he couldn't tear himself away and eventually perished. Modern studies have shown just how damaging this level of self-regard can be to the narcissists themselves and those around them.[14] Yet, at the same time, researchers are discovering the importance of cultivating self-worth, self-esteem and self-compassion.[15]

This gives some idea of the complexity of possibly the strangest form of love: that which we feel for ourselves. It's so complicated because it entails a relationship between two entities that are ostensibly one. As soon as we say, 'I love myself,' we enter a personal hall of mirrors. Most of us would struggle to explain the difference between 'I' and 'myself'. Yet we all understand the phenomenon in question – namely, the deep affection we may feel for ourselves (or alternatively, sadly, may struggle to feel).

We have the word *philautia* to describe this unique, self-reflexive connection, which sits alongside the myriad other terms that employ *philia* as either a prefix or a suffix. Despite their diversity, most of these terms can be grouped within the three non-personal forms of love with which we opened this chapter – for experiences, objects and places – from *acaophilia* (love of itching) to *anthophilia* (love of flowers) to *anglophilia* (love of England). By contrast, *philautia* deserves its own category as it is the unique – and often misunderstood – phenomenon of loving oneself.

As with most aspects of human life, the Greeks were among the first to recognise – or at least to document – the importance of this emotion. Aristotle, for instance, regarded it as the precondition for all other forms of love, given that it is hard to respect and care for others unless we first respect and care for ourselves.[16] However, he also differentiated between the positive and negative aspects of *philautia*. Naturally, he valorised the benevolent self-esteem which develops through the reflective pursuit of virtue, and the desire to improve one's character in order to extend help and affection to others. He certainly did not advocate narcissism, arrogance or egotism.

Fast-forward two millennia, and the French similarly sought to tease apart the parallel strands of self-regard, albeit in a slightly different and complex way. For they coined two words for self-love, both of which may be construed as either admirable or regrettable character traits. First, we have *amour de soi* (literally, 'love of oneself'), as described by Jean-Jacques Rousseau[17] (who, above all else, is credited with distinguishing between the two terms).[18] Such self-regard does not require the ongoing approval of others, which sounds good, in principle. However, precisely because of this, it has the potential to develop into self-absorbed disregard for other people.[19]

Conversely, *amour propre* (literally, 'self-love'), which *does* rely on the validation of others, seems to imply vanity.[20] Yet, the determination to secure approval may result in benevolent behaviour from which everyone benefits.[21] Perhaps, then, the ideal is a combination of the two.

Whichever balance we strike, though, we cannot avoid the strange fact of being in a relationship with ourselves. Moreover, as with all relationships, we surely hope it is a loving one. As do we for the bonds we forge with our family.

Storgē

Nurturing, protective, familial care

Blood is thicker than water, as the proverb says. No matter how close we are to our friends, or how strained our familial relationships may be, an almost unbreakable bond connects us to our kin.

Geneticists argue that we are fundamentally pre-programmed to care most for those who carry similar strands of DNA to our own. Those who prefer more social explanations suggest that we are for ever indebted and tightly connected to whoever cared for us when we entered this world as fragile infants, irrespective of genetic ties. Likewise, when we become protectors or carers ourselves, our concern is likely to be lifelong.

In classical Greece, this deep familial connection, care and affection was termed *storgē*. There is admittedly a fuzzy boundary between *storgē* and *philia* – as there is between many of the 'flavours' here – given that some friendships can be so close that the person is essentially considered kin. Indeed,

John Lee characterised *storgē* as a form of companionate love. Nevertheless, it is useful to differentiate between affection for one's closest friends and the immutable bonds that usually exist between family members. No matter how close two friends may be, the superhuman vigilance with which a mother or father watches over their newborn infant is generally absent from such a relationship. This form of deep, nurturing, protective love is well captured by the Aboriginal Pintupi term *kanyininpa*, which the anthropologist Fred Myers defines as 'an intimate and active relationship between a "holder" and that which is "held"'.[22]

But familial love involves more than concern and protection. It encompasses celebration and joy, too. Think of the blushing pride we feel when a close relative achieves some long-held ambition, as expressed by the Yiddish term *naches* (see Chapter 1). Similarly, there is the innocent pleasure of *cafuné* – a delightful Portuguese word which describes the act of raking your fingers gently through a loved one's hair. Finally, there are numerous expressions of fond playfulness, such as the charming French expression *frimousse*, which complements a cute little face.

And now we step into a very different realm of love as we explore the great and complex terrain of romance.

Epithymía

Sensual or sexual desire and passion

Romance is love in its most archetypal form, the stuff of historical folklore (Antony and Cleopatra), immortal literature

(*Romeo and Juliet*) and personal legend (you and whoever has swept you off your feet). It is the more or less exclusive bond between two people who are 'in love' or simply identify as partners.

However, there are numerous different types of romantic love, and a single relationship usually encompasses several of them. If each type is a flavour, then relationships are a complex and ever-changing brew, each with their own taste. Or to switch metaphors, if each type were a colour, relationships are a rainbow, woven from various hues, as well as from some of the other tones discussed here, such as the friendliness of *philia* and the nurturing care of *storgē*. Different colours may come to prominence at different times, and the relationship will evolve through kaleidoscopic shifts in palette. One way or another, though, most of the colours will likely feature somewhere in the mix.

The first flavour or colour – the spark that ignites the relationship – is often the craving of desire and passion. This is the trembling moment when the *frisson* of connecting with a fellow human being develops into something more embodied and sensual, when one's body yearns to become entwined with another. In classical Greece, such unequivocal passion went by the name *epithymía* (in contrast to the non-sexual appreciation of *érōs*). It derives from *thymós* – often rendered as 'spiritedness' – which in turn came from the Indo-European root *dhu*, a term that evokes 'the swirling of air in a vortex', and therefore implies the tumult of 'uncontrollable desire'.[23]

Other terms from further afield help to trace the contours of this passion. Perhaps you've locked eyes with someone across a crowded room, transfixed by mutual desire. This seductive non-verbal magnetism is reflected in *mamihlapinatapai* – from the Yagán language of Tierra del Fuego. An example of 'lexical density' – packing lots of meaning into a single word – it has been defined as 'looking at each other hoping that either will offer to do something which both parties desire but are unwilling to do'.[24] Then there are the butterflies that flutter deep in your core whenever you interact with – or even merely think of – someone you desire. The Tagalog term *kilig* – literally, 'to shake' – captures this sensual nervousness perfectly. Finally we have the climax of *jouissance* (see Chapter 2) for the ephemeral ecstasy that accompanies the peak of sexual interaction.[25]

Yet, romance is not always passionate. Sometimes it's positively playful.

Paixnidi

Playful affection

In my junior school, we occasionally played kiss chase. We were only ten, but we all abided by the strict rules of the game. The playground was surrounded by buildings whose walls were clad in drainpipes. You merely had to touch one, and no one was allowed to kiss you. So the boys would dash across the playground, from one drainpipe to another, while the girls would try to catch us before we got there. If they managed to intercept us, they'd kiss us. But why were we running? Most of us *wanted* to be kissed, or were at least curious what it would feel like. We had reached that strange age when girls start to become intriguing rather than 'gross'. Yet still we ran, even though we wanted nothing more than to be caught. It was all very confusing, but it does illustrate the playful side of romance.

Of course, romantic games are not the preserve of school-children. Everything from flirting to playing hard to get falls under the auspices of *paixnidi* (or *ludus* in Latin), which trans-lates simply as 'game' or 'play' and which most of us continue to practise in some form or another throughout our lives. For instance, the Tagalog term *gigil* describes the irresistible urge to pinch or squeeze someone because they are loved, cherished or just too damn cute.

However, the playfulness of *paixnidi* should not be conflated with shallowness or superficiality. In some contexts, the word can signify the mysterious dance of life itself, encapsulating important spiritual truths. For example, in Western contempla-tive traditions, *ludus amoris* describes the cosmos as the divine 'play' of God.[26] From this mystical perspective, the Almighty entices, eludes and, ultimately, embraces the spiritual seeker.[27] Meanwhile, in Hinduism, *līlā* depicts a comparable game of cosmic hide-and-seek. Such ideas can expand our cognitive horizons and fill us with the awe-inspiring notion that love pervades the whole universe.

However, given all this talk of games, you have probably realised by now that *paixnidi* can have a darker side, too: manipulative scheming. Indeed, many of the studies that have explored Lee's typology have emphasised this 'gamefulness' rather than the benevolent playfulness described above.[28] This is captured by the Boro verb *onsay* – to 'pretend to love' – and perhaps it is not even love, but a sinister simulacrum. Either way, we should not allow the playfulness of *paixnidi* to transgress into harmful artfulness ... or even more disturbing territory.

Mania

Troubled, tangled or twisted intimacy

John Lee labelled the darkest corner of love's shadowlands *mania*. There are no redeeming features here; no playful side. This is a catch-all term for all the ways in which love can become troubled or twisted. As such, it is the one form of love we would never hope to cultivate. It is included here principally to serve as a warning and show those places on the map that should be avoided. However, its inclusion also highlights the fact that the seemingly simple term 'love' actually encompasses a multiplicity of diverse feelings, and shows the advantage of adopting the lexicographic approach. For analysing untranslatable words allows us to tease apart all of love's various elements, at least conceptually if not experientially. We need to understand that not all forms of passion and romance are beneficent, and words like *mania* serve as signposts, alerting us to danger.

Of course, *mania* is a familiar loanword, denoting madness or obsession. In classical Greece, the *manaie* (plural) were spirits who personified insanity, frenzy and death.[29] In the context of love, *mania* is similarly multifaceted. It captures the noxious jealousy or possessiveness that can torment formerly rational people. It can also convey the extremes of anguish we may feel in relation to our loved ones, when concerned for their safety, perhaps, as in the Spanish term *ansias*. It articulates the intense self-preoccupation that arises from unreciprocated love. And it serves as an umbrella term for all the ways we can be rendered confused, unstable or desperate by what the French call *amour fou* – limitless 'mad love'.

This is not to judge or condemn those who suffer from

mania; most of us have probably tasted that bitter draught at one sorry point or another. It is all too easy to feel insecure in love and find it intermingled with negative emotions like anxiety.[30] Love can be complicated, highly charged and difficult to navigate. It is worth bearing this in mind as we celebrate its gentler forms, including the equanimity of *prâgma*.

Prâgma

Sensible, rational relationship-building

Here, we move from fragile instability to enduring stability, from unbalanced intensity to measured calm. In stark contrast to the maelstrom of *mania* is the placid considerateness of *prâgma*. This is love that is rational, sensible and well thought through. Think of a middle-aged couple with adolescent children. The impassioned fires of *epithymía* may perhaps have cooled, but they are now fondly cooperating to raise a family, run a household, keep the whole show on the road. Is this a lesser form of love?

Prâgma translates literally as 'deed' or 'action'. The type of love it evokes is often regarded rather pejoratively, disparaged as 'empty love',[31] implying an ongoing partnership in which neither party feels either intimacy or passion. However, this fails to capture the nuances of long-term affection. True love encompasses not only the first few months of swooning delirium but also the process of building a life together, forging a bond that does not rest on the passing whims of desire. Eric Fromm appreciated the value of such togetherness. In *The Art of Loving* he warned that most of us place too much emphasis on falling in love and not enough on learning how to 'stand in love'.[32]

There's no denying that some couples stay together unhappily – 'for the sake of the children', say, or to conform to some religious ideal or ethic. But in its fullest sense, *prâgma* exemplifies Fromm's notion of standing in love. It is the deep kinship, loyalty and teamwork we see in couples who have formed a long, stable, successful partnership. This sort of rational, mature love is reflected in the Korean noun *jeong*, which denotes a deep affinity between people. It is also evoked by the French verb *s'apprivoiser* (literally, 'to tame'), which in the context of a deep relationship depicts the mutual process whereby each side learns to trust and accept the other in the knowledge that no love is perfect. It always needs work.

If we are fortunate enough to experience such enduring affection, we may even feel it was ordained by destiny.

Anánkē

Star-crossed destiny

In Plato's Symposium (or *Symposion* in Greek), Aristophanes took to the floor to tell a strange story. At the dawn of history, humans were unified, complete, perfect beings. But then, worried about their increasing power, Zeus – king of the gods – cleaved them into two distinct half-beings. The pair then spent their days on earth looking for their 'other half' – the essential mirror image without whom they would never be complete. Today, we might call that perfect other half our soulmate.

Think of Romeo and Juliet, drawn together by unshakeable fate, transcending bitter sectarian divides. Or Tristan and Isolde, consumed by unforgettable yearning for each other, notwithstanding their marriages to others. Or Jack and Rose, swept up by life-altering passion aboard the *Titanic*. You have probably noticed that all of these familiar tales are tragedies: the all-consuming love leads inexorably to a heartbreaking conclusion. That's precisely what gives these stories their narrative force and renders them so vivid and memorable.

Yet such love is not *inevitably* tragic. Sometimes everything works out for the best. If you're of a certain age, you probably cheered when Ross and Rachel finally got together – for good this time – in the final episode of *Friends*. Maybe you know couples who seem similarly destined to be together. Perhaps you're lucky enough to feel this about your own relationship.

Such star-crossed love could be gathered under the label *anánkē*, a binding force or necessity which the classical Greeks knew could not be resisted. As Simonides wrote, 'Even the Gods don't fight against *anánkē*.'[33] Powerful forces that lie far beyond our control determine when – or whether – we meet our soulmate. This sense of helplessness is captured by the Japanese phrase *koi no yokan* (literally, 'premonition of love'), which articulates the vertiginous feeling you experience when you are *about* to fall for someone, and the certainty that love will follow if you take the plunge. I felt this when I first locked eyes with the woman who is now my wife across a smoky London bar. Then there is the fall itself – the *coup de foudre* (literally, 'lightning bolt') – when the promise and power of love becomes overwhelming.[34] Later, as the relationship starts to take shape, it may be guided by what the Chinese call *yuán fēn* (literally, 'binding force') – irresistible destiny.

This may be the apotheosis of romance, but other forms of love can be just as powerful and transcendent.

Agápē

Compassionate, charitable benevolence

We've explored the love of friends (*philia*), family (*storgē*) and even ourselves (*philautia*), as well as the deep appreciation of experiences (*meraki*), objects (*érōs*) and places (*chōros*), before scaling the heady heights of romantic love, culminating in the star-crossed ardour of *anánkē*. So, is there anywhere else to go? Well, we've yet to mention some of the most elevated forms of love, such as *agápē*.

In the Bible, this is the boundless, unconditional love that God feels for humanity. Yet, as transcendent as that love may be, Jesus did not regard it as the lofty preserve of divine beings. Indeed, he implored his followers to cultivate it in their relations with one another. As such, *agápē* is valorised as the pre-eminent theological virtue. In the words of St Paul, 'So faith, hope, love [*agápē*] abide, these three; but the greatest of these is love.'[35]

You may have heard this verse with the word 'charity' used in place of 'love'. That's because the translators of the King James Bible were strangely reluctant to use the latter term. These days though, most scholars agree that *agápē* is better rendered as 'love'. Specifically, it is a uniquely benevolent, compassionate and, crucially, *non-exclusive* form of love. This sets it apart from the unconditional and selfless love that parents usually feel towards their children specifically, such that they would sacrifice themselves to protect them from harm. By contrast, *agápē* is more a universal love, if you will, directed towards everyone.

Christianity is not alone in celebrating the virtues of *agápē*. Buddhism, for instance, extols this form of love as key among the qualities people should cultivate, to the extent that the tradition has been described as a 'religion of compassion'.[36] This is reflected in the importance of *mettā* – often translated as 'loving-kindness' – among Buddhists, and in the meditation practices that adherents practise to attain it (as we shall see in Chapter 4).[37] Such terms are augmented by other words that highlight the virtues of kindness and hospitality – from *melmastia* in Pashto to *ubuntu* in Zulu, both of which we shall also meet in Chapter 4. First, though, we must consider two final forms of love.

Koinōnía

Sudden, ephemeral sparks of connection

Have you ever felt a sudden lightning bolt of connection with another person, or even a group of people? This is not the swooning sensation of love at first sight – the star-crossed encounter that presages a passionate romance. As we have seen, we have *anánkē* for that feeling. Nor is it the sudden eruption of lust, for which we have *epithymía*; nor the stable, enduring bonds we develop with family and close friends, as per *storgē* and *philia*. Rather, it is that ephemeral moment that is illuminated by a spark of communion.

This could entail fleeting eye contact with a complete stranger – nothing romantic per se, but something significant just seems to pass between the two of you. Maybe you feel the slightest hint of recognition, or suspect that they might hold an answer you have long been seeking. Then again, it might involve an unexpected interaction with a casual acquaintance or colleague, when you suddenly and perceptibly 'click' for the first – and perhaps the only – time. Or the group consciousness of the crowd at a music concert or football match, united in shared focus and emotion.

Such feelings are encapsulated by the term *koinōnía*, which pertains to communal intimacy. In the Bible it is used to describe the 'relationship of faith' between believers and God, and among believers themselves.[38] This isn't exactly the generic embrace of community that members of a church might feel as they go about their daily lives.[39] Rather, think of the sudden efflorescence of the whole congregation during a particularly uplifting gospel service.[40]

Such experiences are not limited to spiritual contexts, as conventionally understood. That said, we may well interpret these episodes as spiritual – whatever their apparent context – for they invariably involve the kind of self-transcendence that lies at the heart of spirituality (see Chapter 8). This sensation is also often characterised by its ephemerality: the swiftness with which it arrives and subsequently disappears (in contrast to the stable longevity of *prâgma*).

And sometimes, this sudden crackle of unanticipated electricity may even seem unearthly, charged with otherworldly power.

Sébomai

Worshipful awe and reverence

There is one place left to look in this exploration of love: to the heavens. As we have seen, *agápē* denotes the benevolent love that Christians (and other religious faithful) believe God extends towards humanity. Now, whatever your thoughts about omnipresent deities, one can appreciate that, in conceiving of a relationship between God and humankind, there is a corresponding form of love directed 'upward' from earth to heaven. Hence, every major religion also promotes the concept of worship, or *sébomai*.

This is love that entails the utmost respect and reverence, not to mention 'fear and trembling', to borrow Søren Kierkegaard's portentous phrase.[41] Hence, it reflects the essentially infinite power asymmetry between humanity and our deities. Here we enter the tremulous realm of awe, which has been defined as a rarefied 'spiritual emotion' that exists only 'in the upper reaches of pleasure and on the boundary of fear'.[42] Yet, while we tremble, in some mysterious sense we are also eternally grateful to the otherworldly power with the potential to transform our lives.

This kind of love is found across cultures and traditions. In Hinduism for instance, the word *bhakti* describes adherents' devotion towards specific spiritual beings and the sacred more generally.[43] Similarly, a revered spiritual teacher is granted the title *guru*, and may even be perceived as an *avatāra* – an incarnation of a particular deity (anglicised as 'avatar').

Yet, this devotional form of love need not be explicitly spiritual. For instance, it can be extended to secular 'idols' – adapted from the Greek word *eidólon*, which originally referred to an image of a deity. In recent times, think of the outpouring of reverence that accompanied the early passing of two musical legends, David Bowie and Prince. Even agnostics and atheists occasionally display this kind of worshipful adulation, be it for footballers, royalty, film stars or any other kind of modern-day god.

Once again, appropriately enough, we are left in awe of the magnificent array of sensations and emotions that all come under the umbrella of that deceptively simple four-letter word: love.

Summary

In this chapter, we began by looking at three impersonal forms of love: the ardour for one's own actions signified by *meraki*; the passion for cherished items denoted by *érōs*; and the connection to places expressed in *chōros*. From there, we turned towards the great variety of love for people: *philia*, which describes platonic bonds of friendship; *philautia*, which relates to expressions of self-regard; and *storgē*, which encompasses the kind of protective care we feel towards our kin.

Next, we ventured into the richly textured terrain of romance: the sexual desire of *epithymía*; the playful (or sometimes manipulative) affection of *paixnidi*; the dangerous intimacy of *mania*; the enduring relationship-building of *prâgma*; and the star-crossed destiny of *anánkē*.

Finally, we explored three transcendent forms of love: the compassion of *agápē*; the ephemeral but powerful connection of *koinōnía*; and the awe of *sébomai*.

Now, we turn our attention to the vitality of connecting with others more generally.

CHAPTER FOUR

Connection

So, love makes the world go round. Our nearest and dearest light up our lives and give us a reason to get up in the morning. Of course, they play the starring roles in the story of our lives. But what about the often-overlooked and largely uncredited background cast: the extras and supporting players who contribute to almost every scene? These are the people with whom we interact every day. We would very rarely say we 'loved' them, outside of particularly generous moments that are graced with *agápē* (see Chapter 3), or even genuinely notice them most of the time. But they have a profound impact on every aspect of our lives, including our happiness, which has an inescapable and poweful social dimension.[1]

Yet, this fact is usually ignored in the West, where people tend to be regarded as individual units, beholden only unto themselves and perhaps a handful of close friends and family members. Any links to or responsibilities for the rest of society are generally downplayed. This perspective was epitomised by Margaret Thatcher's infamous claim that 'there is no such thing as society', followed by her rallying cry of self-interest and self-reliance: 'It's our duty to look after ourselves.' After almost four decades of neoliberalism, is it any surprise that so many Westerners now disregard the importance to wellbeing of connection, solidarity and belonging?

Fear not, though. All is not lost. We can adapt, change, find new ways of being, and untranslatable words have an important role to play in this regard. Through them, we can find happiness in places that we have previously neglected, since many cultures still appreciate the value of collective existence.[2] Several of these are in Scandinavia, which has bucked the individualistic Western trend and enjoys enviably high levels of happiness ... quite possibly in consequence.[3]

Such cultures recognise the power of social networks in shaping our wellbeing and have coined numerous words to describe the phenomenon. If every person is an individual note in the symphony of life, these words allude to the gestalt of melody and harmony. They range from terms that speak to the importance of kindness and compassion to others that celebrate solidarity and communion. Together, they open our eyes to the importance of collective existence.

We begin with a particularly powerful term that crystallises the underlying message of this chapter.

Ubuntu

Kindness arising from common humanity

What does it mean to be kind? 'Kindness' is a subtle term of rare power. It is often overlooked or even belittled, taken for granted as a banality or dismissed as a form of meekness that hinders one's progress in this cut-throat world. Yet, it is actually a revolutionary act of self-transcendence that breaks down the suffocating walls of narrow self-interest. Indeed, from a certain perspective, it is the cornerstone of civilisation itself.

The word's etymology is revealing, as it is related to the notion of kin, or family. Hence, 'kindness' originally referred to the type of affection that is also captured by *storgē*: the care that characterises relations between close relatives or members of a tribe or clan.[4] However, the definition gradually broadened to encompass benevolence that may be bestowed by anyone on anyone, regardless of personal connection.

The full, glorious potential of this form of kindness is exemplified by the term *ubuntu*, a contraction of the Zulu phrase *umuntu ngumunti ngabantu* – 'a person is a person through other people'.[5] *Ubuntu* thus implies, 'I am because *you* are.' This concept, which is fundamental to humanist African philosophy, both valorises and provides some explanation for the importance of kindness. Archbishop Desmond Tutu clarifies: 'It speaks of the fact that my humanity is caught up and inextricably bound up in yours. I am human because I belong. It speaks about wholeness; it speaks about compassion.'[6] *Ubuntu*, then, is an evocation of our shared humanity, to the extent that failing to act with kindness amounts to self-harm wrought upon the common body.

A powerful antidote to Western individualism, *ubuntu* highlights our fundamental interrelatedness. If we can regard our fellow humans in this generous spirit, we will automatically treat them with kindness. After all, *they* are *us*, and so their welfare cannot be separated from our own. Thus, *ubuntu* is this chapter's central motif, a guiding light that is refracted through all of the subsequent terms, not least *mettā*.

Mettā

Friendly loving-kindness

Make yourself comfortable and gently allow your breath to slow down. Take a moment to consider yourself, reading this book, perhaps as part of a quest to find some happiness or peace of mind that has previously eluded you. Some days you might even wonder if you have the strength to continue with the search. But you persevere – bravely, hopefully – for you fully deserve happiness and love.

Now look at yourself as a parent would gaze towards a vulnerable child. Imagine an expression filled with loving-kindness, a blessing of light that bathes you in care and compassion, healing your wounds, giving you the fortitude to carry on. Whisper softly, 'May I be happy. May I be well. May I be free from suffering. May I be free.' Gently repeat the refrain for a few minutes as you dwell in the embrace of positivity, feeling protected and loved.

Now, with your heart still glowing, bring to mind a close friend. You know that they have their own struggles too, and also yearn for happiness. In the same spirit that you wished yourself well, allow your love to flow towards them, wherever they may be. Whisper, 'May *you* be happy. May *you* be well. May *you* be free from suffering. May *you* be free.' Picture yourself as their guardian angel, offering a quiet blessing of hope. Your love and compassion are like rays of light, shining from a beacon.

Next, call to mind someone to whom you are indifferent, perhaps a neighbour you rarely see. Try to imagine their daily battles, their longing for wellbeing. Then extend this to someone you find difficult: a troublesome work colleague, perhaps, or even a politician who stirs animosity within you. In a spirit of tender magnanimity, try to wish them freedom from whatever is troubling them. Finally, extend your circle of compassion outwards to encompass an ever-wider span of people: all of your community, those in distant lands, and ultimately the whole world.

You have just sampled a powerful Buddhist meditation, known as the *mettā bhāvana* in Pāli, which means the cultivation (*bhāvana*) of loving-kindness (*mettā*).[7] *Mettā* is one of four 'divine qualities' that all Buddhists are encouraged to practise, alongside *karuṇā* (compassion), *upekkhā* (equanimity) and *mudita* (sympathetic happiness). These are known as the *brahma-vihārās*, which translates as 'the abodes of Brahma' (Brahma being the creator god in Hindu theology).

At this point, a cynic might ask, '*Mettā* may be lovely for those who receive it, but what's in it for me?' The answer is: 'A great deal!' As with *ubuntu*, Buddhism holds that we are all interconnected, so we treat ourselves well when we care for others. And this is no abstract concept: according to the law of *karma* (see Chapter 9), we actually *feel* good as a result, since ethical actions usually lead to positive mental states. Indeed,

Buddhism is not the only religious tradition to extol *mettā-*like qualities. For instance, Judaism celebrates the practice of *gemilut hasadim* – the 'bestowal' or 'acts' of loving-kindness.[8]

Clearly, then, we would all benefit from cultivating a little more loving-kindness in our lives ... and distributing it with *omoiyari*.

Omoiyari

Altruistic sensitivity and empathic action

Picture yourself walking down the road. Suddenly a little kid comes hurtling towards you on rollerblades. You see him connect with a loose paving stone and crash to the floor in a tangle of limbs. He immediately bursts into tears. There's almost no need to ask how you would react. Human nature impels us to rush over and try to help in some way. We look around anxiously for his parents and help pick him up off the floor. It doesn't matter that he's a stranger: we feel his pain, and it matters to us. Admittedly, we would undoubtedly experience rather more panic and concern if it were our own child. But we certainly understand this kid's suffering on some level, and we are moved to alleviate it.

These reactions are highly significant. Jolted out of our usual self-absorption, our locus of concern suddenly expands to encompass another person. This is nothing less than self-transcendence, which lies at the heart of psychological and spiritual development, as we shall see in Chapter 8.

A triumvirate of loanwords captures the radical shift in concern from oneself to someone else: 'sympathy', 'empathy' and 'compassion'. The first two hail from ancient Greece, combining *páthos* – 'suffering', or simply 'emotion' – with prefixes which denote 'with' and 'in', respectively. 'Compassion' derives from *pati* – the Latin version of *páthos* – plus the prefix 'with'. Thus, all three terms describe sharing another person's suffering, although there are subtle differences between them. 'Empathy' relates to actually feeling what the other person is experiencing, as if we are in pain, too. Conversely, 'sympathy' and 'compassion' mean we feel *for* them: we are not in pain ourselves, but we understand that they are hurting and wish them well. Nevertheless, all three are applicable to our rollerblading scenario, and others like it.

Yet, a crucial element is missing. What of our urge to *do* something? Action is only implicit in these loanwords; it is not inevitable or guaranteed. We may feel sorry for the person, but still do nothing to help. By contrast, remedial behaviour is present in the Japanese term *omoiyari* – 'altruistic sensitivity'[9] – which encompasses an intuitive understanding of someone else's needs *and* consequent action. Thus, it adds an extra dimension of active benevolence to empathy, sympathy and compassion.

Concern for the wellbeing of others can have other dimensions, too.

Muditā

Vicarious, sympathetic happiness

What does it take for us to see the world from someone else's perspective, walk in their shoes, if only for a moment? Under what circumstances do we feel a surge of empathy, sympathy or compassion? The obvious answer is at times of pain or suffering. This is understandable. Crises clamour for our attention. However, on reflection, one realises that it's also eminently possible to share other people's delight and bathe in the rays of their happiness.

Mind you, there is a common misconception that this sort of vicarious pleasure is reserved for family members: parents delighting in their child's encouraging exam results, perhaps. As we saw in Chapter 3, this celebratory sympathy is indeed an important aspect of the familial love of *storgē*, alongside care and concern. And it is beautifully captured by the Yiddish terms *naches* (see Chapter 1) and *kvell* – from a Germanic verb meaning 'to well up' – for that process of feeling and, moreover, expressing joy at someone else's achievements.[10]

However, as we saw earlier, *mudita* – one of Buddhism's four *brahma-vihārās* – is a form of positive sympathy that we can feel for *anyone*, not just close relatives. While *mettā* describes the extension of loving-kindness to others, *mudita* involves rejoicing in their happiness. And it is instinctive. Think of how infectious a smile can be: we are hard-wired to respond in kind. And why not? After all, someone else's success does not necessarily impoverish us. There are plenty of win–win situations, known as *taarradhin* in Arabic.[11] But even if we do lose out due to others' achievements – such as when a colleague secures a promotion instead of us – our disappointment can be tempered by evoking *mudita*. This is one of the reasons why it is so revered in Buddhism: it is an antidote to resentment and a pathway towards peace.

This is because a root cause of our suffering is self-centredness. We have a tendency to get tangled up in spiders' webs of guilt, envy, worry and fear. But *mudita* offers an escape route. No less than *metta* and *omoiyari*, it is a pathway to self-transcendence. We abandon our selfishness and enter a deeper, broader form of 'intersubjective' existence that is far more nourishing and fulfilling.[12] And this process is aided by practising *melmastia*.

Melmastia

Unconditional and unselective hospitality

What would you do if a stranger knocked on your door and asked for food and a room for the night? Many of us wouldn't even hear what they had to say, because we wouldn't open the door. After all, it's all too easy to distrust unfamiliar people, and sometimes with good reason. However, there are some places where unflinching hospitality is an important feature of daily life. The mountains of Afghanistan and north-western Pakistan, for instance, are home to the Pashtuns, who count among their number Malala Yousafzai, the youngest ever Nobel laureate. Over their long history, they have developed an intricate ethical code known as *Pashtunwali*. One of its key tenets is *melmastia*: the moral obligation – and indeed honour – to offer hospitality to any visitor, even an adversary, without expectation of recompense.[13] Beyond merely showing kindness to strangers, this means granting a generous welcome and asylum to anyone who requests it.[14]

Similarly, *manaakitanga* – 'reciprocal hospitality and con-nectivity' – is a cornerstone of Māori culture.[15] It encourages a host and their visitor to work together to find that precious 'common ground upon which an affinity and sense of sharing can begin'.[16] It rests on the notion that, while we all have our differences, we also have much which unites us. If we can tap into that universal kinship, generosity and kindness naturally follow. Meanwhile, visitors to Greece may have been fortunate enough to receive *xenia* – 'guest-friendship' – from one of the locals, while those to Israel might have similarly experienced the Jewish tradition of *hachnasat orchim* – 'welcoming the stranger'.[17]

In one sense, all these terms are synonyms for 'hospitality'. However, this rather emotionless word fails to capture their deep significance in their respective cultures. Beyond alerting us to the value of empathy and compassion, they remind us to care for fellow human beings and so help us overcome our narrow-minded tendency towards individualism. As such, perhaps we should all take a leaf out of these cultures' books. A good place to start would be to invite a neighbour round for a cup of tea or coffee. After all, studies have shown that generosity is a sure path to happiness, so you will benefit just as much as your neighbour.[18]

Moreover, it can be fun to spend a bit of time with other people, bonding over a coffee.

Fika

A sociable coffee break

As the rest of the world continues to gaze enviously towards Scandinavia, with its well-earned reputation for happiness, many attempts have been made to identify the region's 'secret'.

High on the list, as we saw in Chapter 1, is the concept of *hygge*. Rather more modest, but no less intriguing, is the practice of *fika*, which has been presented as the 'Swedish key to happiness at work'.[19]

Its literal definition is quite banal: in essence, it simply refers to a coffee break (as a play on the Swedish word for coffee, *kaffe*). However, that mundane English phrase does not come close to conveying the importance of this twice-daily ritual, which is invariably observed around 10 a.m. and 3 p.m. in many Swedish workplaces. For, as *Fika: The Art of the Swedish Coffee Break*[20] explains, it's not really about coffee at all. While a little caffeine boost is probably appreciated, *fika's* real value lies in providing a couple of precious opportunities to pause and reconnect each day. Workers are able to extricate themselves from the glare of the computer screen or the monotony of the assembly line and socialise with their colleagues, if only briefly. These are like water-cooler moments, but scheduled . . . and therefore keenly anticipated. They have better pastries, too!

In short, *fika* is simply an agreeable custom that brings people together. Many similar traditions have developed around the world. As we saw in Chapter 2, the French adore their *soirées* and *salons*, not to mention an *apéritif.* Literally 'a drink taken before dinner', the latter term is also used to describe the occasion itself – a moment of connection before everyone's attention turns to the invariably delicious food. Meanwhile, other traditions of social connection are freighted with rather more significance as expressions of virtue or moral obligation, such as *melmastia*.

An entire book could be devoted to these practices, all of which might be viewed functionally as 'excuses' to get together. Socialising is too precious to be left to the haphazard whim of circumstance, so we think up reasons to congregate, then develop traditions around those reasons. These customs provide walled gardens of time and space in which we no longer feel alone. Ideally, they can also offer opportunities to enjoy the warm communion of engaging conversation.

Enraonar

Civilised, reasoned, empathetic conversation

In the 1960s, Anatol Rapoport – a Russian mathematical psychologist – devised a set of guidelines that he hoped would facilitate civilised debate. After all, it's tragically easy for differences of opinion to degenerate into callous misrepresentation and bitter rancour. His idea was that you ought to follow some key principles should you find yourself arguing with someone with whom you disagree. First, try to articulate *their* point of view in a way that is so clear, fair and generous that they will graciously thank you for putting it so well! Next, list any points of agreement and acknowledge anything you've learned from them. Only then should you offer some critiques and try to point out where they've gone wrong.

This guidance seems increasingly necessary in today's fractured society. Whether gathered amiably for a *fika* or communing in cyberspace, the way we talk matters. Moreover, Rapoport's rules were not merely an appeal for civility. He also felt they inspired receptivity towards and sympathy for one's arguments, rather than antagonism and mistrust. Vicious slanging matches rarely get either party anywhere, so it's advisable to follow Rapoport's guidelines. Or, more generally, we might aim for the enlightened Catalan ethos of *enraonar*.

Essentially, this means conversing in a civilised, reasoned manner. It does *not* mean po-facedly confining oneself to serious topics and soberly avoiding all levity. There is still plenty of room for laughter, love and lightness of being. *Enraonar* simply reflects the fact that discourse varies significantly in quality, so we should always aim to communicate in 'the best possible manner'.[21] It entails striving to understand and to make oneself understood, speaking clearly and calmly, with precision and coherence. It might even include brightening a discussion with a joke or two ... or whatever it takes to keep the conversation running smoothly. Admittedly, this ideal is not always attainable in the heat of an argument, but it's good to have goals.

Civilised interaction is also reflected in the Persian practice of *ta'ârof*. Although sometimes translated simply as 'politeness', this doesn't really capture the nuanced form of 'ritual courtesy' that is central to this cultural ideal.[22] *Ta'ârof* has even been likened to a 'verbal wrestling match' of civility, particularly with respect to giving and receiving gifts. For instance, a host might repeatedly encourage a guest to accept more food or drink, offers which the guest will repeatedly decline. Eventually, though, the guest will relent.[23] This is no hollow ritual, but a way to make the guest feel welcome while also minimising their imposition on the host. If all social interaction is like a dance, even the most twinkle-toed may benefit from such choreographed steps to guide them.

Ultimately, conducting conversations in the spirit of *enraonar* means wishing the best for the other person, infused with a sense of *ubuntu* or *mettā*. A natural consequence of this is that one takes the time to listen to others' stories and truths.

Dadirri

Deep, respectful, contemplative listening

How often do you ever really *hear* another person? Too often, we give the impression of listening closely while actually preparing a response, then jump in as soon as our interlocutor closes their mouth. On precious occasions, though, we may find the patience and grace to maintain a receptive and attentive silence; just listening without any desire to impose our opinion, offer advice, or steer the conversation towards ourself. In short, letting them speak.

I used to work as a nursing assistant in a psychiatric hospital, where I spent many hours listening to patients. It was a disorientating, humbling, but above all moving experience. In the midst of their suffering, most of the patients just wanted a friendly, compassionate ear to listen to their troubles and bear witness to their stories. I was not a trained psychotherapist, but I tried to emulate the qualities that all good therapists possess, such as empathy and positive regard.[24] I hope that the patients found these rather one-way discussions meaningful. I know I did.

Australian Aboriginal languages have a word for this kind of deep, reflective listening: *dadirri*. Miriam-Rose Ungunmerr-Baumann provides an evocative account of the comfort it can provide: 'When I experience *dadirri*, I am made whole again. I can sit on the riverbank or walk through the trees; even if someone close to me has passed away, I can find my peace in this silent awareness.'[25] Seen in this way, *dadirri* transcends the simple act of listening and signifies an entire contemplative way of life. It entails remaining receptive and attuned to the world around us in a spirit of respect and reverence.[26]

Moreover, as the beautiful evocation above alludes to, this attentiveness and respect are not reserved for human beings. We can enter into communion with nature itself by opening our ears and hearts to the natural world so it may breathe its truths. Given the existential crisis of climate change, such listening skills are becoming ever more vital. Therefore, Western societies can try to learn from cultures that have retained the ability to listen to and respect the earth.

And this goes hand in hand with the recognition that we would all benefit from treating the rest of humanity with a little more respect.

Shalom

Peace, wholeness, harmony

When I was six years old, my parents enrolled me in a youth group called the Woodcraft Folk – a hippyish, socialist, unisex version of the Boy Scouts. Thereafter, my childhood was illuminated by outdoor adventures in the wilderness to the soundtrack of protest songs around the campfire. I remember being particularly intrigued by a chant that centred on the Hebrew word *shalom*.

At the time, we were told that it means 'peace', which is not inaccurate. But it transcends such a simple explanation. It actually derives from a verb meaning to complete or perfect. As such, as a noun, it encompasses a wealth of inspiring definitions – from wholeness and harmony to peace and tranquillity. Moreover, it serves as a deeply meaningful salutation – a heartfelt greeting or farewell. Its Arabic cognate is *salām*, which is often embedded within the phrase *as-salāmu ʿalaykum* – 'peace be unto you'.

Admittedly, in some instances, these phrases might be uttered somewhat automatically, with the underlying sentiment not at the forefront of the speaker's mind, just as English speakers rarely mean 'God be with you' when we say the shortened version – 'goodbye'. However, I suspect that most of those who use the Hebrew and Arabic terms remain conscious of the fact that they are expressing a blessing of peace. If so, what a resonant way to acknowledge other people and to signal your respect for their dignity and value.

Similarly uplifting greetings can be found around the world. The Hawaiian term *aloha* – which again serves as either 'hello' or 'goodbye' – literally means 'breath of life' and so evokes notions of love, spirit and grace. Indeed, much more than a friendly form of address, it denotes an entire way of living that reflects Polynesian culture.[27] As an online guide to Kauai puts it, 'a life of *aloha* is one when the heart is so full it is overflowing with the ability to influence others around you with your spirit'.[28] Meanwhile, yoga devotees will be familiar with the Sanskrit and Hindi term *namaste*, which is often translated as 'I bow to the divine in you'. What a sentiment! It certainly beats 'Alright, mate.'

Martin Buber suggests that greetings such as *shalom*, *aloha* and *namaste* encourage an 'I–thou' perspective in place of the sadly more familiar 'I–it', in which other people are seen as little more than objects that stand in our way.[29] When we adopt an 'I–thou' stance, we acknowledge the other person's full dignity as a human being and accord them all the respect they deserve.

Indeed, when people pull together and look out for one another, they can accomplish more than they would alone.

Talkoot

A voluntary, collective endeavour

As settlers began to fan out across North America in the seventeenth century, one challenge they faced was how to build the
large barns they needed to store produce and shelter livestock.
These buildings had to be erected quickly – before the onset
of the next harsh winter – so the pioneers turned to a practice
that had been forged back in rural England: barn-raising, in
which the whole community came together to erect the frame.
Such projects were generally voluntary, with no expectation of
payment: everyone just helped their neighbours in the knowledge that they could count on reciprocal generosity at some
point in the future. This was community spirit in action.

Similar communal endeavours for the common good can
be found the world over. In Finland, for instance, any 'short,
intensive, collective effort with a tangible goal' is known as a
talkoot.[30] It might involve friends turning up to help you paint
your house, or a group of neighbours keeping the street neat
and tidy. Once again, money rarely changes hands, and the
whole community benefits . . . as does every participant, if only
through the warm glow of altruism.

It's appropriate that there's a Nordic term for this sort of
cheerful collective effort, given the region's enviable levels
of happiness. Of course, its countries are also stable and
affluent, structural factors which surely contribute to their
emotional prosperity, as the World Bank intimates.[31] And yet,
other wealthy countries – such as the USA and the UK – do
not come close to achieving similar levels of life satisfaction.
Indeed, despite Americans' and Britons' burgeoning affluence

over recent decades, their overall wellbeing has seemingly flat-lined – a phenomenon known as the 'Easterlin paradox' (after Richard Easterlin, the economist who first reported it).[32] In itself, then, GDP does not guarantee a flourishing society. So perhaps the rest of the world should try to emulate concepts like *talkoot*?

For most theorists agree that much of Scandinavia's happiness can be explained by its citizens' sense of *togetherness*. For a start, Nordic societies are exceptionally equal. In the USA, for example, the average CEO's salary is 354 times higher than those of the company's workers; in Denmark, the equivalent figure is just 48 times higher.[33] As Richard Wilkinson and Kate Pickett have shown in their groundbreaking book *The Spirit Level*, more equal societies do better on almost every metric, from health and wellbeing to education and crime.[34]

Relatedly, Nordic people generally have higher levels of so-called social capital.[35] This is a measure of the extent to which we trust and feel connected to those around us: the quality and quantity of our friendships; the strength of our support networks, both personal and structural (such as the welfare state); and community cohesion more broadly.[36] Unsurprisingly, high social capital tends to equate to higher levels of wellbeing.[37]

Of course, there's no need to move to Helsinki to enjoy one of the prime manifestations of good social capital – a *talkoot*. You could organise your own, and it will almost certainly be an uplifting experience as your usual self-preoccupations start to dissolve and you come to understand the potential of people power.

Folkelig

The soul, will and power of the people

The notion of 'the people' has a long history. Philosophers in classical Greece realised that when a number of people come together in some way, they cease to be a collection of individuals who continue to behave as they always have. Rather, a powerful group dynamic usually develops. The crowd starts to resemble a living being – with the individual people as its cells – seemingly complete with its own will, motivation and emotions. This process concerned Plato, who held the Athenian collective responsible for the persecution and death of his mentor, Socrates. As a result, he disdained democracy and advocated rule by a highly educated elite.[38]

Nevertheless, this era is notable for Athens' attempts to skilfully harness the 'will of the people'. It saw the first stirrings of *dēmokratíā* – 'democracy' – which entailed channelling the *krátos* ('force' or 'power') of the *dêmos* ('people' or 'citizens'). Indeed, numerous familiar terms can be traced to this uniquely formative period, when many of our ideas relating to how people should live together were first developed. The term *polis* – 'city-state' – for instance, was the root of various influential derivations, such as *politios* – 'of, for, or relating to citizens' – which in turn is the basis for our term 'politics'. Or take the word *doxa*, meaning common belief or practice, which is the basis for 'orthodox', 'heterodox' and so on.[39] Where would we be without this conceptual inheritance from our Greek forebears?

Of course, since classical Greece, many other societies have acknowledged the potency of the people. One particularly evocative iteration is the Danish adjective *folkelig*, which roughly translates as 'folkish'. Note that this does *not* mean 'folksy', with its implications of rural simplicity. Nor is it accurately captured by other common translations, such as 'popular' or 'national'. Rather, its essence is 'of the people'.[40] Hence, it is used to describe the vague yet powerful notion that agency and identity are not the sole preserve of the individual, but can also be aspects of the collective. This doesn't necessarily imply some sort of mystical 'shared consciousness'. It can simply mean that people have the capacity to think, speak and act as a group, with one dominant voice.

That said, undertones of dissent are always possible. After all, as Plato argued, sometimes the people can make mistakes.

Janteloven

The discouragement of individualism

In 1933, Aksel Sandemose published a novel called *A Fugitive Crosses His Tracks*[41] that scandalised Danish society.[42] It describes a fictional community named Jante that is governed by a set of strict laws, known as *Janteloven*. These precepts not only discourage individualism but demand total self-abnegation. The first law, for instance, states chillingly: 'You shall not believe that you are someone.' Essentially, Sandemose took aim – in rather extreme fashion – at what he interpreted as powerful normalising forces at work throughout Scandinavia.

For much of this chapter, we have rightly celebrated the virtues of group solidarity and the power of community spirit. However, it is worth sounding a note of caution. After all, it has

long been recognised that the crowd can go astray, as exemplified by the warning in Exodus 23:2 that 'Thou shalt not follow
a multitude to do evil.' Indeed, even if a crowd's motives are
essentially benign, they can still prove problematic. For, as the
philosopher David Bakan points out, human beings live a dual
existence.[43] On the one hand, we are firmly situated within
social networks, so there is an imperative to fit harmoniously
with the group. Bakan labels this 'communion'. However, we
also exist as individuals who need to express ourselves and
behave in our own unique ways. Bakan calls this 'agency'.

These two modes of existence can be complementary when
our individual interests and ideals align with those of the
group. Yet, sometimes, clashes occur, which can bring us into
conflict with the collective, and possibly result in the erosion
of agency and freedom. When discussing *talkoot*, we saw that
the Nordic nations are lauded for their egalitarianism and
communality, and that this cohesion is a potent factor in their
general happiness. At the same time, though, the concept of
Janteloven reflects the possibility that an emphasis on communion can potentially threaten individual development and
self-expression.[44]

Thus, we must remain wary of abrogating our individuality,
falling prey to 'groupthink' and ceding all responsibility to
others. Following the herd in this manner leads invariably to
inauthenticity, according to existentialist thinkers.[45] Hence,
while we should continue to celebrate community spirit,
notions such as *Janteloven* remind us that each of us must also
protect, cherish and nurture our uniqueness. That said, at their
best, groups help all of us to flourish as individuals.

Saṅgha

A nurturing, spiritual community

Back in 2008, I was thrilled to have the opportunity to focus on one of my principal interests – meditation – in real depth for my PhD, I set myself the task of investigating its impact on men's mental health, and managed to find thirty volunteers who agreed to attend lengthy interviews and participate in some quite annoying cognitive neuroscience tests. The interviews were especially revelatory. As anticipated, most of the participants explained that their meditation practice had helped them to develop their emotional awareness and cope with the stresses of everyday life.[46] Much more surprising though – to me at first – was the significance of the *saṅgha* in their lives.

Concepts from other times and places can sometimes seem remote from and irrelevant to hectic, modern, Western society. The Pāli term *saṅgha* is one such notion. Literally meaning 'assembly', it is used in Buddhism to describe any group of practitioners. For the volunteers in my study, this meant the centre where they practised their meditation and the community that cohered around it. Some of the men attended only occasionally; others lived and worked there full time. But almost all of them emphasised how important it had become for them.

I quickly realised that *saṅgha* is a living, breathing concept with great potential to boost human wellbeing. It is not a relic of the past, nor confined to those Eastern cultures where Buddhism has been practised for centuries. Just as Westerners have recently benefited from engaging with mindfulness, we are also starting to understand the value of the *saṅgha*. For my research showed that this was no mere club, nor simply a convenient physical space where the interviewees gathered to meditate. It was a safe, nurturing environment that enabled them to explore whole new ways of being.

All too often, we feel pressured, or even coerced, into acting in stereotypical ways, including on the basis of our gender. Men frequently encounter the imperative to play the invulnerable tough guy, cajoled by heavily weighted injunctions like 'boys don't cry'. Unfortunately, these masculine norms can be destructive to men themselves, contributing to mental and physical health issues,[47] and to those around them, by encouraging noxious behaviours such as aggression.[48] In sharp contrast, the *saṅgha* promoted alternative gendered norms: men were encouraged to be kind and caring, to forgo alcohol and drugs, and to explore their inner sensitivity and vulnerability.[49]

Most of the participants in my study had chosen to follow this path to a better way of living. But that's not to imply that they had run away: the centre was located in the heart of London, and most of the men had jobs and friends in the 'real world'. Moreover, with the support and guidance of the *saṅgha*, they were determined to show that world that there is an alternative. These were not passive members of a club; they were active members of a dynamic and forward-thinking community of like-minded individuals.

None of this is restricted to Buddhism, mind you. This ideal of *saṅgha* could be used to describe any powerful community that the members create in accordance with a set of principles to help them become the best possible version of themselves. And, if we're fortunate enough to find – or create – our own *saṅgha*, then *simpatía* surely awaits.

Simpatía

Social accord and harmony

At its best, human interaction is like a dance. We move with balletic grace, our movements in perfect synchrony. This doesn't mean that we must rigidly conform to tightly choreographed routines. There is still room for spontaneity. Indeed, our most meaningful encounters tend to feel pristine and fresh, as if springing into life at that precise moment. Yet even – or especially – then, our movements somehow align perfectly with our partner's. We intuit their intentions perfectly, a fraction of a second before they act, and respond accordingly. The dance is fluid, supple, poetry in motion.

Spanish- and Portuguese-speaking cultures might describe this ideal as *simpatía*. Literally meaning 'sympathy', this term evokes that wonderful sensation of interpersonal harmony and accord. One expansive definition describes it as 'the act of participating in the affective states, the joys and sorrows of others; compassion; agreement or fusion of the emotions; communion; natural attraction of one person for another, or for a thing; inclination; the beginning of love'.[50]

As we have seen throughout this chapter (and indeed in the previous one on love), truly connecting with others does not entail total submersion within the collective or the abandonment of one's precious individuality. Rather, it's about striving for *simpatía* and enjoying the feeling of just 'clicking' with fellow human beings. We each play our own melody but contribute to a vast, vibrant, coherent symphony.

This notion of social accord and synchrony has been extolled around the world. For instance, the anthropologist Clifford

Geertz highlighted the significance of the 'metaphysical concept' of *tjotjog* among the people of Java.[51] He defined it as 'to fit, as a key does in a lock', and therefore achieve harmony. The Javanese reportedly use the term when describing everything from agreements between friends, or a well-matched husband and wife, to a perfectly tailored suit, or realisation of a desired goal. Basically, whenever it is invoked, life is going well.

Moreover, this ideal of harmonic interconnectedness sometimes extends beyond social relations and assumes an even deeper existential significance. For example, the Diné people of the south-western United States advocate a principle known as *hózhǫ́*, which revolves around living in balance, peace and harmony with the rest of the world. This is a 'complex wellness philosophy and belief system ... that guide[s] one's thoughts, actions, behaviors, and speech'.[52] In short, it is harmony as a way of life.

Unfortunately, it's all too easy for that harmony to be shattered. The Hopi – who are close neighbours of the Diné – have a word for just such a scenario: *koyaanisqatsi*, which has been translated as 'nature out of balance' or 'time out of joint'. This amounts to an existential state of emergency during which the collective – indeed humanity as a whole – seems determined to follow a dysfunctional and destructive way of life. The dance becomes ragged, the movements jerky and out of sync. We lose touch with our deepest needs as well as the needs of the planet. The end result is ruin.

Tragically, *koyaanisqatsi* often seems an apt description of our current age. Hence, the sooner we start to live by principles such as *hózhǫ́*, the better. At the very least, we can all make the effort to reach out and improve our connections with those around.

Summary

Our story here began with the inspiring motif of *ubuntu*, the kindness that arises from our shared sense of common humanity. We then touched upon three benevolent affective qualities: the loving-kindness of *mettā*; the altruistic sensitivity of *omoiyari*; and the vicarious happiness of *muditā*. Next, we encountered the hospitality of *melmastia* and the subtle joys of *fika*, the not-so-humble Swedish coffee break. Thereafter, we focused on the art of skilful communication, including the civilised conversation of *enraonar*, the contemplative listening of *dadirri* and the salutation of peace and harmony embodied in *shalom*.

Next, we explored the voluntary endeavour that is a *talkoot* and the will of the people as encapsulated by *folkelig*. After a brief aside to warn about the dangers of *Janteloven*, we moved on to the profound benefits that can accrue to members of a *saṅgha* and the social harmony of *simpatía*.

Thus ends our consideration of relationships. Now we turn to the subtle arts of savouring and appreciation.

CHAPTER FIVE

Appreciation

Take a moment to let your gaze roam freely around your surroundings. Alight upon an object or feature that you find pleasing. Whatever your milieu, *something* will catch your eye: the cleanliness of a pure white wall; a careworn pattern on a piece of crockery; even dust motes dancing in a sunbeam. Allow your eyes to linger on it. Really drink it in. Try to appreciate its contours, colours and textures. Revel in the tiny details. How does it feel when you do that?

All too often we are trapped inside our own heads, confined by mental preoccupations, running frantically around a self-created maze of thoughts and obsessions. Of course, sometimes we do need to think things through and harness the power and foresight of our rationality. But it's easy to get drawn into ruminative self-absorption and fall into a downward spiral of negative mood.[1] Hence, any antidote to spirit-sapping introspection is valuable. And one particularly powerful remedy involves *savouring* life and learning to appreciate wherever you are and whatever you're doing. This doesn't only free you from your own thoughts. It can transform your world by making it shine with a beauty that you had never previously perceived or even suspected. Beauty may be in the eye of the beholder, but savouring teaches your eyes to see beauty in unexpected places.

Once again, untranslatable words are useful here because they can serve as signs that declare, 'Hey! This is really worth noticing, even if English speakers haven't realised it yet.' As we explore these subjects further, we will learn to savour them and start to see the world from new perspectives. In the process, we may become more receptive to their *rasa* and *dhvani*.

The Sanskrit term *rasa* refers to the essence – or literally the 'juice' – of something, such as the theme of a work of art and the emotions it evokes. Perhaps you've seen Van Gogh's *The Starry Night*? If so, what does it stir within you? Soft tranquillity enveloped by celestial beauty? Loneliness in the infinity of the cosmos? As you peer more closely, you may become attuned to the picture's *dhvani*. Another Sanskrit term, this translates as 'echo' and encompasses the layers of implied or hidden meaning that are concealed within an object's depths. For instance, does the knowledge that Van Gogh painted this canvas after committing himself to an asylum generate any sort of resonance? What about the fact that he saw this scene through the bars of his cell window and painted it no fewer than twenty-three times during his incarceration?

Analysing art in this way helps us appreciate its full aesthetic power. But we need not reserve such contemplative attentiveness for great paintings. All of life can be viewed through thoughtful and appreciative eyes. As ethereal as Van Gogh's masterpiece may be, what of the veil of stars that envelops us every evening? What stops us from being entranced by our own starry night and perceiving the heavens just as passionately as he did in 1889?

As each day unfolds, we can open ourselves up to the *rasa* and *dhvani* of objects, people, landscapes. In the process, the 'ordinary' – all that we normally take for granted or even overlook completely – might be revealed as extraordinary and poetic.

We begin with the most ubiquitous and generous canvas of all – the natural world.

Fuubutsushi

Phenomena that evoke specific seasons

Imagine it's a sunlit evening in early April, and you're walking home from work. The winter has been long and bleak, but finally it feels as if the earth has turned a corner. The first glimmers of spring are in the air. Over the past five months you've barrelled along this well-worn route, head down, your mind a murky river, teeming with agitated thoughts, worries, self-recrimination, regrets. But not today. For you've been liberated by the fragrance of freshly cut grass drifting on the breeze. This prompts you to look up, whereupon you spot cherry blossom on the gently swaying branches. Before long, you are seeing premonitions of spring everywhere.

Japanese has the perfect word for these signals: *fuubutsushi*. Translated as 'scenery poetry', it denotes anything that evokes a particular season – from those familiar intimations of spring to the lustrous glories of summer, from the auburn hues of autumn to the crisp frost of winter. Then the cycle begins again. Each stanza of this sensory verse may prompt a wistful memory of a previous season, such as a rose blooming in November, or stir anticipation for one that has yet to arrive, such as an unexpectedly balmy current of air in February. Alternatively, it may perfectly reflect the present moment.

Indeed, if we're attentive, it's possible to discern poetic eloquence all around us.

Èit

Quartz placed in streams to sparkle

Words can capture the natural world in all its exquisite detail, as Robert Macfarlane amply demonstrates in his majestic book *Landmarks*.[2] What's more, all of the terms he explores hail from the many tongues and dialects of the British Isles. (Sometimes we overlook the diamond mine in our own back yard!) For example, the magnificently specific Gaelic term *èit* – attributed to the Isle of Lewis – denotes the act of placing pieces of quartz in a fast-flowing stream so that they sparkle in the moonlight and coax salmon from the shadows.

Other cultures have similarly coined words to describe the dazzling play of sunlight as it refracts through the world. Maybe this fascination with light in its myriad forms has its origins in the fact that we ourselves are stardust – our bodies constructed from the atomic remnants of celestial fireworks. Or perhaps our ancestors simply knew that their lives depended on the sun's intensity and the moon's command of the tides. Either way, our minds and hearts are drawn towards the light.

Hence the poetic resonance of the Swedish term *mångata*, which implies that moonlight creates a flickering 'road' on the surface of an expanse of water. With equal delicacy, the modern Turkish phrase *gümüş servi* uses the metaphor of a silver cypress to evoke the same phenomenon.[3] A few hours later, we might be spellbound by dappled rays of sunlight filtering through the leaves of just such a tree. This natural *chiaroscuro* – an Italian term for contrasts of light and shade in works of art – is known by the Japanese as *komorebi*, which implies that the tree is literally 'leaking' light.

Such words serve to amplify nature's wonders by quickening our senses, sharpening our gaze and enhancing our sensitivity. After all, we are bathed in dappled sunlight whenever we walk down a tree-lined avenue in the summertime. It may register, mechanically, on our retinas, but do we really *see* it? Under normal circumstances, probably not. Yet once we are able to describe this routine but beautiful dance of light, we are compelled to pay attention and really drink it in.

That said, although the beauty of nature is all around us, sometimes it pays dividends to seek it out.

Smultronställe

A quiet nature retreat

As a child, I used to spend most summers with my family in a quiet French village that traverses a roaring river, straddling a deep-sided valley which felt truly wild and remote. On occasions, I would feel the call of solitude, and would head out to what the Swedes call a *smultronställe* (literally, 'forest berry patch') – a quiet rural retreat. For me, this was a forgotten place where the river flowed through a nearby forest. I would sit on a large, flat rock and spend an hour or two hidden peacefully from the world.

Of all the words that glorify nature, among the most evocative for me are those that reflect the strange, lonely allure of forests and woods. These places usually have a profound tranquillity, at once ancient and eternal. They are primordial spaces where human beings – with their machinations, noise and destruction – are no more than a distant memory. Far from bright lights and electronic sounds, they are fonts of repose and rejuvenation, as Wilbert Gesler has highlighted in his studies of 'therapeutic landscapes'[4] and 'healing places'.[5]

These attributes are widely recognised, not least in Japan, where the notion of *shinrin-yoku* ('forest bathing') articulates the restorative sensation of soaking up – literally and/or metaphorically – the tranquillity of a natural environment. Japanese doctors even prescribe this form of 'forest medicine' for patients who are suffering from physical and psychological ailments, with impressive results.[6] Similarly, the Finnish term *maadoittuminen* celebrates the notion of 'earthing' or 'grounding' oneself in nature,[7] just as I did when I sat on my rock all those years ago. Sometimes I was sure I could feel the earth's energy recharging my spirit.

Such retreats can be powerful, and even unsettling, especially when undertaken alone. The solitude generates strange internal currents. To this day, whenever I escape into nature, I have a peculiar sense of disappearing – not only from other people's sight, but from the face of the earth and indeed history, as if I never existed. I become no more than a node of consciousness, registering the sights and sounds of the planet, which continues to inhale and exhale with utter indifference to my presence.

This eerie sensation is captured by the German term *Waldeinsamkeit* – the 'forest solitude' that descends when you stand alone amid the trees and feel as if you are the only person left on the planet. The earth seems infinitely older than humankind, let alone a single human lifespan, and one is left in no doubt that it will outlast our species by countless aeons, too. The result can be a heightened appreciation of the non-human majesty of nature.

That said, the experience isn't entirely comfortable. As such, a spell of this kind of solitude can make one yearn for the company of some fellow savourers, with whom you can enjoy the earth's splendours together.

Passeggiata

A leisurely stroll

If you've ever had the good fortune to visit southern Europe in the spring or summertime, you may have marvelled at a magical late-afternoon scene: streams of people wandering along with no destination in mind, simply taking in the warm Mediterranean air. Perhaps you yourself joined them and silently wished that this was part of *your* daily routine.

Acts of appreciation are not restricted to the natural world. At their best, urban environments can also offer numerous opportunities to savour, promenade and drink in the sights and sounds of the good life. Thus, Italians revel in their evening *passeggiata*, while the French celebrate the *flânerie*.

One might argue that the English word 'strolling' conveys something similar. However, this generic label lacks the resonance of the Italian and French terms in their respective cultures. For instance, in her ethnography of an Italian village, Giovanna del Negro describes the *passeggiata* as a vital 'cultural performance' that is freighted with significance and tradition.[8] Similarly, the *flânerie* has long been a vibrant element of French culture, particularly in the nineteenth century when it was intimately associated with impassioned poets and artists gliding through the streets on an elevated plane of existence.[9]

Such practices are not only characterised by their urban settings. Another key aspect of their appeal is their communal nature, for these are colourful, social spectacles in which every participant is both audience and performer. They're all about seeing and being seen. Accompanied by our fellow strollers, we acknowledge one another's enjoyment of the same easy delights. It has to be one of the finest ways to work up an appetite for a long, leisurely dinner ... and to walk off a few of the calories afterwards.

Gourmet

A connoisseur of good food and drink

In March 1986, Rome was the scene of a dramatic act of cultural infiltration when the first McDonald's opened in Italy, bang in the heart of the venerable Piazza di Spagna. While some of the locals were keen to sample the novel delights of the Big Mac, many others were mightily displeased at this perceived affront to the culinary traditions of a nation that is so closely associated with good food and fine dining. One of the leaders of the resistance was Carlo Petrini. In July that year, he and some pals gathered in the cellar of a nearby restaurant and plotted their response – not only against McDonald's, but also everything such institutions symbolised in terms of shifting habits of cooking and eating.

Thus was the 'slow food' movement born. It initially went by the label 'Arcigola'. However, its literal translation – 'society of gluttons' – is rather misleading. The intention was not to promote greed, or *haute cuisine*, or lavish indulgence. Petrini and his friends were simply enthusiastic supporters of good food and everything associated with it. The inadequacy of the English translation reflects the relative paucity of our language, which struggles to differentiate between gluttony and gastronomic appreciation. Other tongues are better equipped. For instance, as we saw in Chapter 2, French has provided two loanwords in this area: 'gourmand' and 'gourmet'. The difference between the two lies in the relative balance of quantity (prized by the former) versus quality (demanded by the latter). Whereas a gourmand tends to be greedy, a gourmet is a connoisseur. Indeed, while most people assume that the two words share the same food-related etymology, the latter actually derives from *groume* ('wine-taster').

Thus, Arcigola was founded in a gourmet rather than a gourmand spirit. However, even these precise loanwords lend themselves to misuse in English, with gourmets frequently associated with three-star Michelin restaurants, pretentious *haute cuisine* and £600 bottles of Château Lafite Rothschild. That is not the ethos of Arcigola at all. Rather, the group simply opposes every aspect of fast food – hence its championing of what it terms 'slow food'.

In contrast to the standard mass-production systems of the global fast-food industry, slow food is about working with nearby producers and using the best ingredients responsibly. Wherever they are based, the movement's supporters understand the importance of the local *terroir*: the ecosystem in which a product is grown and the qualities it possesses as a result. Then, rather than wolfing down their meals in haste, they appreciatively savour the flavours and textures. In addition to being a more pleasurable experience, this is healthier too, since it helps diners to sense when they are full, so they are less likely to overeat.[10] Finally, slow food is also about connection: mealtimes should be enjoyed with our nearest and dearest in a spirit of *sobremesa* (see Chapter 2).

Essentially, the true *gourmet* spirit is learning to savour food and its accompanying joys. And this might well extend to a passion for creating gastronomic delights oneself.

Aficionado

A knowledgeable enthusiast

Last Christmas, my wife and I attended a colleague's annual festive get-together for the first time. These were the stuff of legends, as he had a glowing reputation as an expert home-brewer. That said, based on previous bitter (literally) experience of such endeavours, I wasn't overly excited. If I'm honest, I imagined a keg of barely passable, musty ale. How wrong I was.

On entering the house, we were each handed a menu on which was listed at least twenty varieties, all with lovingly

crafted descriptions that highlighted their unique, subtle flavours. Then the man himself appeared – a tall, genial, Willy
Wonka-type figure who encouraged us to try any and all of his
wares. Every glass I tasted would have done the finest Belgian
Trappist proud. Later, as we marvelled tipsily at his set-up in
the basement – an elaborate array of twisting pipes, kegs and
vats – he explained how he had managed to capture *this* beautiful flavour and *that* majestic taste. No doubt he could turn a
handy profit if he were so inclined. Indeed, plenty of people
were urging him to make brewing his business. But he was
content to remain a teacher and pursue his passion in his spare
time, just for the *meraki* (see Chapter 3).

He was the very embodiment of an *aficionado*, a loanword
that derives from the Spanish verb *aficionar* – 'to inspire affection or enthusiasm'. Thus, it describes someone who is very
appreciative, passionate and knowledgeable about a certain
subject.[11] This is slightly different from 'connoisseur', although
the distinction is rather hazy. Indeed, many *aficionados*, not
least my brewing friend, probably merit both labels. In French,
a *connaisseur* is 'one who knows', with the term denoting
expertise. That said, it has more appreciative undertones than
'expert', which generally implies knowledge but not necessarily
great passion. For instance, most connoisseurs of French wine
love it as a drink in addition to possessing a professional level
of knowledge on the subject.

By contrast, *aficionados* are usually amateurs, although not
in the rather disparaging way in which that term is often used
in English – juxtaposed with 'expert' to imply a lack of skill
or understanding. Rather, the meaning is closer to the original French word *amateur* – from the Latin verb *amare* – 'one
who loves'. In that sense, an amateur will pursue a particular

activity solely for the love of it, not in the expectation of extrinsic rewards, such as money or status.

That is the spirit I saw amid the home-brewed ales and Santa hats. Hopefully you too have a similarly captivating pursuit that brings you – and others – that kind of joy. At the very least, it's great to find something that really *absorbs* us.

Hugfanginn

Enthralled, absorbed, captivated

In May 2008, Chelsea met their bitter rivals Manchester United in the Champions League Final – the pinnacle of European club football. After a chaotic ninety minutes, the score stood at 1–1. Thirty draining minutes of extra-time followed, but the teams remained deadlocked. It had to be penalties. The supporters' hopes and dreams now rested on what was, essentially, a lottery.

I was watching in a bar as Chelsea's captain, John Terry, began the long walk from the centre circle to take his team's fifth penalty. If he scored, Chelsea would win. If he missed, the tension would continue. The television camera focused on his granite features as he readied himself amid torrential rain and the glare of ten thousand flashbulbs. At that moment, I appreciated that sport could be just as powerful as any drama, probably more so. The script was unwritten, the passions fierce, the denouement approaching. The entire stadium was trans-fixed, hushed. Even in our little bar, time seemed suspended. Every eye was on the screen, spellbound. I felt powerless to look away.

Icelandic has a word for such an experience: *hugfanginn* (literally, 'mind-captured'). This reflects the fact that enthralment or fascination is not necessarily voluntary, as scientific studies have shown.[12] We may be transfixed by highly concentrated sources of interest, concern or beauty. Picture a lone figure on stage, illuminated by a single spotlight while all around fades to black. Think of Maria Callas singing 'Ave Maria' at the Met, Jimi Hendrix playing 'Purple Haze' at Woodstock, Marlon Brando on Broadway ... or, indeed, John Terry taking that penalty in Moscow. Which he missed.

That said, captivation does not always involve laser-like focus on a single point. Sometimes a scene is so majestic and expansive that it washes over us like a wave as we gaze diffusely. In Japanese, this is known as *boketto* – staring vacantly into the distance, while all thought or sense of self evaporates. This might be precipitated by an awe-inspiring vista. If you've stood upon a snowy mountain peak, you may know the vertiginous sensation of feeling dwarfed – literally and metaphorically – to the point of non-existence by the sheer scale of it all. Your eyes wander, seemingly at random, in a futile attempt to take in the magnificence of your surroundings. Or *boketto* might arise in gentler fashion. You might be lying back in a deckchair on the beach, lulled by the gently lapping waves, staring idly out to sea. No strained focus, no precise attention. Your mind is wide open, a blank canvas that is gradually filled by a stream of sights and sounds from all around.

In fact, one of the most spellbinding sources of both *hugfanginn* and *boketto* is the mysteries of music.

Harmonía

Concordance, union, agreement

We all have our personal favourites in art and music: the song that makes your heart sing along in delight; the painting that transfixes you every time you see it. But is beauty entirely subjective – just what each of us happens to love for some idiosyncratic reason – or are there deeper principles at work? Humans have been trying to answer this question for at least 2500 years.

Most of us are familiar with the name Pythagoras from interminable maths lessons about triangles. But less widely appreciated is that he was one of history's most profound and influential thinkers. And one of his most revolutionary and intriguing ideas was the strange, mystical notion of the 'harmony of the spheres'.

According to legend, the origins of this concept are rather prosaic. Pythagoras regularly walked past a blacksmith's forge, and became intrigued by the melodious sounds of the hammers striking against the anvils. Unsurprisingly, given his preternatural mental acuity, he soon realised that the pitch varied in accordance with each hammer's size. This observation led him to investigate the harmonic properties of the lyre – a common stringed instrument in ancient Greece. He calculated that each note's pitch was in exact proportion to the length of the string, with intervals between the notes generated by simple numerical ratios. For instance, take a string that produces a C when plucked. Halve its vibrating length by placing your finger at its midpoint and you go up an octave (the same note as the original C, but twelve semitones higher). Shorten it by a third and you get a perfect fifth (the note G);

shorten it by a quarter and you get a fourth (the note F); and so on.

Until that point, music had been regarded as rather unearthly, as is reflected in its etymology. The Greek term *mousiké* means 'of the Moũsai' – known as the Muses in English – a group of nine goddesses who personified divine inspiration for all knowledge and the arts. Yet Pythagoras realised that music's mysteries could be penetrated through the nascent power of mathematics. But the significance of his vision was not limited to the soothing melodies of the lyre. More radically, on the basis of this insight, he developed an esoteric view of the cosmos as a whole.

Essentially, he argued that the planets' orbits followed the same harmonic principles, in the same ratios to one another as notes on a scale. This was the philosophy that came to be known as the 'harmony of the spheres'. In classical Greece, the term *harmonía* did not merely imply that two concurrent notes are well matched, as 'harmony' does today. Rather, it described fundamental concordance and union. Moreover, Pythagoras' philosophy encompassed more than just celestial order and coherence. More esoterically, he claimed that the universe generated faintly audible, divine music, and that sufficiently receptive people could hear it.

Even at the time, the possibility of celestial cosmic melodies was widely disregarded. However, the broader notion that the universe is essentially harmonious and adheres to coherent principles has proved pervasive and enduring. Indeed, amid all of the modern world's trouble and strife, we continue to find redemptive instances of order and harmony: in the earth's annual rejuvenation each spring, perhaps; in the unchanging grandeur of the canopy of stars; or, indeed, in the delights of a Mozart concerto.

This begs the question, what is the secret of order and harmony? One answer lies in the perfection of proportion.

Kairos

The ideal way, proportion, amount or moment

For over two thousand years, painters and architects have known about the 'golden ratio'. This 'irrational' number – that is, one whose decimal values continue into infinity – is usually rounded down to 1.618 and symbolised by the Greek letter Φ (*phi*). It occurs whenever Φ describes *both* the ratio between two quantities *and* the ratio between the larger quantity and the sum of the two. So, imagine a building that is 5 metres high and 3.09 metres wide. If you divide the height by the width, you get 1.618; and you get the same result if you divide the height plus the width by the height.

This number – like other mathematical constants, such as π (3.142...) – recurs throughout nature. Indeed, it's found in all manner of wonders – from seashells to galaxies. For these creations involve spiral-like configurations that appear to be governed by the golden ratio. Google 'seashell golden ratio' and you'll see what I mean. At the centre of the seashell's spiral, picture a tiny rectangle of the proportions described above (which we'll call rectangle 1). Now imagine an identically proportioned but slightly larger rectangle (rectangle 2). The shorter side of rectangle 2 lines up perfectly against the longer side of rectangle 1. And, together, they create an even larger rectangle (rectangle 3), whose proportions also perfectly match 1 and 2. Now imagine a still-larger rectangle (rectangle 4), again with the same proportions, whose shorter edge aligns perfectly with the longer edge of rectangle 3. And so on, and so on. This accumulation of ever-growing rectangles, whose proportions beautifully express the golden ratio, together trace out the contours of the seashell, and likewise the spirals of the galaxy, the blossoming of a flower, even the composition of the 'Mona Lisa'.

Moreover, as the examples above attest, the proportions of the golden ratio are invariably perceived as aesthetically pleasing. It therefore epitomises the notion of *kairos*, a term that describes doing something in just the right manner, to the perfect scale and/or at the most opportune moment. Hence the recurrence of the golden ratio throughout art and architecture, from the columnic façade of the Parthenon in Athens to Michelangelo's ceiling of the Sistine Chapel, both of which are perfect examples of *kairos*.

But you don't need to travel to southern Europe to see the divine proportions of Φ. They are all around us – from civic buildings that draw the eye to paintings that charm the heart. You might even decorate your own home according to this timeless principle. Should you choose to do so, you'll join the ranks of those visionaries who have brought beauty and light into the world by harnessing the power of Φ, not least during the Renaissance.

Leggiadria

Grace, loveliness, elegance

As the thirteenth century drew to a close, an extraordinary phenomenon that would eventually transform Europe and indeed the world flickered into life in northern Italy. The vast treasures of the classical age – philosophy, art, poetry and literature – which had been mostly concealed or lost for many centuries began to filter back into European consciousness. In contrast to the dark pessimism of the Middle Ages, this marked a new celebration of humankind's potential. More precisely, it was a *renewal* of the humanism that had flourished so vividly in ancient Greece. Hence, the new dawn became known as the Renaissance: rebirth.

The next few centuries saw an astonishing (re)awakening of philosophies, ways of thinking and modes of appreciation. There was an incredible blossoming of the arts, as painters and poets embraced a dazzling array of new – or rediscovered – topics, techniques and aesthetic values. Consider, for instance, one of the most celebrated artworks of the age, Sandro Botticelli's *The Birth of Venus*, which he completed around 1486. The subject harks back to the golden ages of Greece and Rome, and to their ideal of a goddess of love – named Aphrodíte by the Greeks and Venus by the Romans. She was venerated by thinkers such as Plato, who viewed her as both an earthly goddess symbolising romantic passion and a heavenly deity who could inspire great intellectual and spiritual love. Earlier, the poet Homer had created the legend of her emerging fully formed from a seashell. It was this vision that Botticelli immortalised in his masterpiece.

It's not only the painting's subject matter that is emblematic of the Renaissance, but its aesthetic too. For Botticelli's goddess is a vision of ethereal beauty who exemplifies *leggiadria* – 'poetry in motion' suffused with grace, loveliness, prettiness and elegance.[13] Indeed, she seems to be on the verge of floating from the shell, as if purer and lighter than air. Moreover, many aspects of the image conform to the mysterious proportions of the golden ratio. To achieve this feat, Botticelli elongated the goddess's torso and neck and set her in a physically impossible pose (since in the real world, she would topple over). In other words, he eschewed the dull restrictions of realism to provide a glimpse of radiant perfection.

Such was the aesthetic genius of the Renaissance. Moreover, its artists didn't only look to the past for inspiration. They were innovators who developed a wide array of techniques and styles – as well as an accompanying lexicon – all in the service of representing truth and beauty. These range from the precision of *disegno* (fine-art drawing) to the hazy elision of *sfumato* (when oils on a canvas shade imperceptibly into one another), and from the dramatic contrast of the *chiaroscuro* (juxtaposition of light and shade) to the illusion of *quadratura* (painting architectural details onto a ceiling to give the impression of three-dimensional space). These were not merely artistic techniques; they were new ways of perceiving and understanding life itself.

Once again, as with *harmonía* and *kairos*, you might observe them in any number of contexts – from the *chiaroscuro* of dappled sunlight to the *sfumato* of elegantly applied make-up. Above all, look out for examples of *leggiadria* as these will surely brighten your day: a gentle smile on a child's face; an unexpected act of kindness; a skateboarder weaving fluidly down the street; a tree swaying softly in the breeze, its leaves fluttering delicately to the ground. There is beauty everywhere.

Although the notion of *leggiadria* wasn't 'invented' in the Renaissance, the artists, architects, writers and poets of that era certainly did us a great service by celebrating it so effusively. Indeed, they not only appraised human existence as never before but also laid the groundwork for subsequent generations of philosophers to delve even deeper.

Gestalt

An overall pattern or configuration

Just as the scenery is shifted in an epic play, the glories of the Renaissance eventually gave way, in the seventeenth century, to the Age of Enlightenment. This was more of an evolution than a revolution. Over the preceding centuries, scholars had lauded the unrivalled intelligence and rationality of humankind. So it was probably inevitable that these qualities would become trained like a laser upon the world around. The ultimate aim was to bring clarity and order to the complexity and chaos of life. The result was an efflorescence of scientific endeavour that eventually created the world that we know today.

This restless pursuit of knowledge – which reanimated the empirical curiosity of earlier eras, particularly classical Greece – gave rise to new perspectives and conceptual schemas that influenced how human beings engaged with the world, and with each other. German-speakers were particularly inventive in this respect, as is reflected in their coining (or redeployment) of words such as *Gestalt* and *Ganzheit*.

Gestalt was originally a simple term for 'form' or 'shape'. However, in the nineteenth century, Christian von Ehrenfels used it to describe the overall configuration of something and, moreover, to convey the notion that the whole can be more than the sum of its parts. He often cited the example of a melody: we do not merely hear the individual notes; we merge them together to create something far greater, existing on another level. Similarly, a face is not merely a collection of separate physiognomic features; it is a whole unto itself. Likewise, *Ganzheit* too suggests unity, completeness and holistic integration.

German philosophers' use of such terms reflected their growing recognition that the world cannot be understood simply by focusing on its individual elements; we also need to consider how all of the components interlock as a totality. These ideas helped shape the new modes of enquiry that started to emerge in the second half of the nineteenth century. For instance, when Wilhelm Wundt established his Institute for Experimental Psychology in 1879 – widely regarded as the inception of the field in the modern era – his work was often termed *'Ganzheit* psychology'. Similarly, artists and critics explored the role of *Gestalt* processes in perception and appreciation. Consequently, painters would strive to achieve harmony among the constituent elements on each canvas. Of course, this had familiar echoes of the past, not least the golden ratio.

And yet, around the same time, some radically different approaches to art and truth were starting to emerge.

Dada

Avant-garde art that rejected convention

In early 1917, the respectable patrons of New York's Society of Independent Artists were most affronted by a certain R. Mutt's submission to their forthcoming exhibition. It was nothing more or less than a shop-bought porcelain urinal, which the artist had titled *Fountain*. The piece – which was actually the work of the French painter and sculptor Marcel Duchamp (although some people now suspect it might really have been created by his friend Baroness Elsa von Freytag-Loringhoven[14]) – was flatly rejected, even though it met all of the submission criteria. The patrons couldn't have known that it would become one of the most important artworks of the twentieth century. Clearly, Duchamp (or the Baroness) had ventured a long way from the elegance of *leggiadria* and the unity of *Gestalt*. Strange new aesthetic currents were brewing.

One might call *Fountain* avant-garde – a generic label for any revolutionary idea or practice. Duchamp himself termed it 'anti-art', so he surely intended to challenge conventions, including the notion that works of art should be pleasing to the eye or indeed have any meaning at all. As incendiary as *Fountain* was, though, he was not alone in adopting this iconoclastic approach. Rather, he was part of a broad multi-generational movement that began with the first stirrings of modernism in the mid-nineteenth century, continued with Picasso's disorientating cubism, and culminated in postmodernism, when rigid adherence to artistic traditions dissolved completely.

One prominent element of the latter phase was Dadaism, a movement which Duchamp helped to inspire and with which he was loosely affiliated. Its nature is partly reflected by its name. According to one story, the Austrian artist Richard Huelsenbeck chose it by plunging a knife at random into a dictionary. The blade landed on *dada* – a French term for 'hobby-horse' or, alternatively, 'meaningless babble'.

Like Duchamp, the Dadaists rejected modern aesthetics, ideologies (such as nationalism and capitalism) and even rationality itself. By defying sense and meaning, they cultivated an air of chaotic nihilism. Yet their movement was also a profound reaction to the cataclysm of the First World War. They loathed the conventions of so-called civilised society because they held them responsible for Europe's degeneration into insanity and barbarity. Viewed from that perspective, Dadaism was no hollow protest. Rather, it was a concerted effort to liberate humanity from destructive patterns of thought that were laying waste to a generation. And, to some extent, it succeeded, because it showed future generations that it was possible to challenge convention and find innovative ways to express and appreciate beauty and value.

These days, few people are moved by the Dadaists' artworks, but their spirit remains inspiring. They told the world that self-appointed guardians of taste shouldn't be allowed to decide what is worthy of our attention and admiration. We can all make bold, free choices about what is or is not beautiful. An old, rusty bike leaning against a wall can be a masterpiece of weathered elegance and perfect proportions. A humble kitchen chair is no less than a triumph of form and function.

Therefore, it is a misconception to view the avant-garde as concerned with nothing but disruption and deconstruction. Indeed, many avant-garde artists explored new forms of value, including radical visions of the sacred. Wassily Kandinsky, for instance, lamented the impoverishment of the human spirit in the modern age, and sought to redress the balance by imbuing his art with profound spirituality, as he explained in *Concerning the Spiritual in Art*.[15] He tried to represent his own journey into the sacred realm through the deep, reflective use of colour and shape, and hoped that his work would encourage others to follow the same path. In short, he saw art as a vehicle for self-transcendence.

This idea may have seemed revolutionary in early twentieth-century Europe. But it has distinct echoes of a distant, and indeed ancient, artistic tradition.

Kanso

Elegant simplicity

According to legend, one day the *haiku* master Bashō saw a frog jumping into a pool of water. The sound reverberated through the poet's perceptual universe and his usual atomistic sense of self – in which he experienced himself as separate from the rest of reality, as most of us tend to do – was suddenly erased. In that instant, he was liberated from conventional thinking.[16]

And how did Bashō choose to record this momentous occasion? Did he write an essay, a treatise, a book? No, he summed it up in a *haiku*:

The old pond.
A frog leaps in;
And a splash.

So far this chapter has mainly focused on the languages of Europe. But lexical nuance in relation to aesthetics is found across the globe, not least in Japan. For that country's scholars and artists have long understood the power of art to express profound philosophical and spiritual concepts.

Zen views discursive prose as a poor vehicle for communicating ineffable spiritual truths. Instead, it advocates 'pointing directly' to those truths through the immediacy of art and imagery.[17] Moreover, it sees the value of adopting this approach in secular contexts. For instance, if you wish to convey the beauty of a rose to someone who has never seen one, is it better to write an essay on the subject or simply show them a photo? However, while acknowledging the limitations of language, Japanese has developed a rich aesthetic lexicon that endeavours to capture, even if imperfectly, the insights that art can generate.

There are some recurring themes amid this richness. One of these is simplicity, as exemplified by Bashō's sparse lines. This ideal is encapsulated in the concept of *kanso*, defined as 'beauty in elegant simplicity'.[18] Practitioners of *kanso* disdain clutter and, indeed, anything that is not essential. As with every aesthetic concept in Zen, the word has a powerful twofold meaning. It can be used to describe a particular work of art that is executed in that clean, simple style, but it also evokes the importance of simplicity itself. Thus, there is inherent harmony between form and concept. Strip away all ornamentation to reach the 'essence of things'.[19] Cut through the dense thicket of discursive thought to come 'face-to-face with the suchness of the world'.[20] Thus, Zen art aims to capture 'reality in its isness'.[21] This might entail painting a rose, rather than trying to describe its beauty in dry and dusty prose. But if words must be used, they should be simple, direct and precise.

This linguistic succinctness reaches its apotheosis in the *haiku*, which condenses experiences and objects to the bare facts, with no superfluity. But these sparse poems are not *merely* simple. They reflect other aesthetic qualities, too. One of these is *datsuzoku*: freedom from habit, routine and the conventional. The aim here is to abandon habitual discursive constructs so that one views the world with absolute, pristine freshness before capturing that freshness in a work of art. Rather than thinking, 'Just another noisy frog,' Bashō truly *experienced* the creature's dive into the water in all its vivid nowness. Then, in the spirit of *shizen* – literally, 'naturalness'; the avoidance of pretence, contrivance or premeditation – he rendered the event in a *haiku*. This endeavour demanded considerable skill and the end result was a supreme artistic achievement. Yet it was effortlessly natural, flowing in a pure, unmediated way from the immaculate depths of Bashō's newly awakened mind.

Many Japanese artists – and also those from elsewhere – have been guided by these principles of simplicity, freedom and naturalness to produce beautiful works of art. But these are also well-worn pathways to personal wellbeing. In Chapter 1, we saw that Buddhism teaches that liberation from *duḥkha* (suffering or dissatisfaction) can occur when people eliminate craving and attachment from their lives. Well, living according to principles such as *kanso* is a powerful means of advancing towards this extraordinary goal.

In the meantime, though, we all live imperfect lives in an imperfect world. Yet, there is still beauty to be found in that world ... sometimes in the imperfections themselves.

Wabi-sabi

Imperfect, weathered or aged beauty

Western art is often characterised by a preoccupation with *kairos* – order, symmetry and proportionality. By contrast, to the untrained eye, Zen paintings can seem wildly irregular, even chaotic, with seemingly crude brushstrokes. But this style is not indicative of a lack of technique. Rather, as per the naturalness of *datsuzoku*, it reflects great artistic skill combined with deep spiritual insight. Moreover, it displays elements of three further aesthetic ideals – *fukinsei*, *koko* and, above all, *wabi-sabi*.

Zen masters of *fukinsei* eschew regular, geometrical shapes in favour of compositions that are 'jagged, gnarled, irregular, twisting, dashing, sweeping'.[22] Similarly, *koko* signifies a sort of austere sublimity in which beauty and depth are discerned in objects that are furrowed and cracked, wind-dried and weathered. So, an artist imbued with the spirit of *fukinsei* and *koko* might paint a desolate, lightning-scarred tree in the depths of winter rather than a perfect cherry tree bedecked in the blossom of spring. But why would they *want* to do this?

Well, for a start, in terms of representational accuracy, such aesthetics are more faithful to the natural world. One rarely encounters perfect symmetry or straight lines in nature: life is usually skewed, imperfect, irregular. Moreover, the aim is to express the 'perfection of imperfection'.[23] In Taoism – a formative influence on Zen[24] – it is believed that everything is a 'perfect' expression of the *Tao* (the natural order of the universe), so nothing is incomplete or lacking. In this sense, *fukinsei* and *koko* both accord with a 'perceptual–emotional mood' that is much prized in Zen: *wabi-sabi*. Essentially, this phrase captures the strange, desolate beauty of aged or imperfect objects, and the depth and meaning they can evoke. Think of the eerie sensations that are aroused by seeing a withered tree or an abandoned ruin on a remote hillside. These may not be conventionally attractive images, but they have magnetic power that elicits thoughts of legends, ghosts and mysteries.

Ultimately, then, *wabi-sabi* involves a reappraisal of beauty. We do life a disservice if we only value that which is perfect and complete. As the fourteenth-century monk Kenkō asked, 'Are we to look at cherry blossoms only in full bloom, at the moon only when it is cloudless? ... Gardens strewn with faded flowers are worthier of our admiration.'[25] We should not disdain anything for its imperfection but rather respect its unique gifts. This is a dark – almost melancholic – form of appreciation. Yet it helps us make peace with a flawed world.

Moreover, it provides the perfect bridge to our next chapter, which focuses entirely on these kind of strange, ambivalent sensibilities. First, though, let's take a moment to glance back over the ground we've just covered.

Summary

This fifth leg of our adventure has seen us delighting in the graceful power of aesthetic appreciation and its almost limitless potential to alter our perception of the world. We began by revelling in the natural world's bounty, from the 'scenery poetry' of *fuubutsushi* to the sparkling light of *èit* and the quiet sanctuary of a *smultronställe*. Next, we savoured a leisurely *passeggiata*, the connoisseurship of the *gourmet*, the knowledgeable enthusiasm of the *aficionado* and the 'mind-captured' absorption of *hugfanginn*.

From there we dived into a wealth of perspectives on beauty itself. In classical Greece, we encountered the inspiring order and coherence of *harmonía* and the delicate proportionality of *kairos*. Then the Renaissance presented us with the graceful elegance of *leggiadria*, Enlightenment philosophers used *Gestalt* to explain that the whole can be more than the sum of its parts, and the twentieth century broke down conventions with the avant-garde art of *Dada*. Finally, the spiritual power of art and aesthetic appreciation was seen in a series of Zen principles, from the elegant simplicity of *kanso* to the weathered beauty of *wabi-sabi*.

This leads us gently into our exploration of the complex notion of ambivalence.

CHAPTER SIX

Ambivalence

Whenever we think about wellbeing, we tend to be dazzled by the brightness and warmth of positive feelings, as explored in Chapters 1 and 2. But is happiness only ever the province of unambiguously upbeat emotions? Intriguingly, the answer may be 'no'. For it may also involve rather more complex and ambivalent sentiments. These are complicated blends of light and dark, hot and cold, feeling simultaneously positive and negative. Mind you, ambivalence usually has a bad reputation. Any search through a thesaurus for its synonyms results in a host of unwelcome qualities – from 'dithering' and 'indecision' to 'conflict' and 'confusion'. Yet, many cultures acknowledge that some of our most precious feelings are dialectical blends of light and shade, rather than simple states of pure brightness.

My colleagues and I have taken a keen interest in this notion of wellbeing as a dialectical process.[1] In essence, a dialectic is a dynamic relationship between opposites. Accordingly, we have identified several dialectical principles at the heart of wellbeing. First, it can be difficult to define a phenomenon as wholly positive or negative, since such appraisals always depend on context. For instance, is crying necessarily negative? Weeping at the departure of a loved one is certainly an expression of sorrow, yet tears of joy upon being reunited signals a pinnacle of happiness. Therefore, the nature of crying is invariably context dependent.

Moreover, many emotional states can be both positive *and* negative simultaneously. Consider the longing you feel when your loved one is in a distant country. Of course, this is painful, but at the same time your heart is suffused with love, and your mind is full of precious memories of the times you've spent together as well as sweet hopes for the future. The Greeks call this strange intermingling of happiness and sadness *charmolypi*, a term that encapsulates Shakespeare's 'sweet sorrow' of pining for a loved one.

Finally, these light and dark elements are often deeply connected, or even co-dependent. For instance, it is the very fact that you love someone which makes parting from them distressing. Likewise, the sorrow you experience during their absence makes the reunion even more joyful. These are two sides of the same coin. As Sir Francis Bacon reportedly said, 'In order for the light to shine so brightly, the darkness must be present.'

Hence, wellbeing is not only a question of bright, positive emotions; it also involves feelings that may seem dark and dispiriting. Yet these can be just as valuable, and they may make a significant contribution to our overall happiness.

I broached these somewhat counter-intuitive notions in my previous book, *The Positive Power of Negative Emotions*.[2] However, in general, both academic psychology and the English-speaking world have tended to neglect them. By contrast, other cultures – particularly those of the East[3] – seem much more attuned to the idea of dialectics. As such, our appreciation of this vital area of human experience is sure to be enhanced through the study of untranslatable words.

We have already encountered a number of ambivalent states in the preceding chapters, such as the melancholic beauty of *wabi-sabi*. However, this chapter focuses squarely on rich, complex words that are imbued with this dialectical spirit. We begin with a familiar yet mysterious concept that serves as an archetypal symbol for the dialectical processes that are explored in the rest of the chapter.

Yīn yáng

The dynamic interaction of opposites

These days, almost everyone is well acquainted with the legendary *yīn yáng* motif: two curved halves of a circle, one black, one white, locked in a dynamic embrace, with a subtle dash of each appearing in the other half. It mesmerised me as a teenager, and even adorned a crude pendant I cobbled together for a high school assignment. But what does it *mean*? I had no idea back then, and I'm not sure I fully understand now, but the fog has cleared a little over the last twenty years.

The concept is central to Taoism, the venerable Chinese philosophical tradition introduced in Chapter 1. Taoism's roots stretch back into antiquity – to the shamanic practices of the Chou people around 3000 BCE. These included divinations based on yarrow stalks that were thrown on the ground, which were interpreted as constituting one of sixty-four 'hexagrams' (permutations of six broken or unbroken lines). A guide eventually emerged around the twelfth century BCE to assist in their interpretations – namely the *I Ching*, or *Book of Changes*. The key point is that the hexagrams represent states of *becoming*, rather than *being*. The focal points are the 'moving' lines: any of the six that are dynamic or 'unstable' and thus herald the shift to a different hexagram.

As its name suggests, the overarching principle of the *I Ching* is change, which, somewhat paradoxically, is the one constant in the universe. As Hellmut Wilhelm explained, 'He who has perceived the meaning of change fixes his attention no longer on transitory individual things but on the eternal, immutable law at work in all change.'[4] This is the very origin of Taoism, for that 'eternal, immutable law' is 'the *Tao*, the course of things, the principle of the one in the many'. Moreover, the *I Ching* taught that change occurs through the dialectical interaction between opposites, as is captured symbolically by *yīn yáng*.

In literal terms, *yīn* denotes 'darkness' or 'cloudiness', while *yáng* refers to 'sunlight'. Symbolically, it encapsulates various aspects of duality.[5] First, *holistic* duality holds that reality comprises innumerable co-dependent opposites. This is then augmented by *dynamic* duality: those opposites tend to transform into each other in a fluid process. Consider the arc of the sun: its meridian is the precise moment when the decline into night begins. Thus, *yīn yáng* does not refer simply to static opposites – light *versus* dark, say. Rather, it evokes the ceaseless process of becoming – light *gives way* to dark, which in turn *starts to return* towards light.

Eastern philosophies seem to have a particular gift for

appreciating dialectics. That said, other cultures have been graced with comparable insights. Classical Greece, for example, coined the notion of *agón* – a clash of oppositional forces that ultimately results in progress and growth. Similarly, Roman scholars such as Horace developed the principle of *concordia discors* – the possibility that conflict and opposition may create a sort of discordant harmony. More recently, the German philosopher Georg Hegel argued that the tension between a thesis (i.e., a viewpoint) and its antithesis (an opposing perspective) can lead to synthesis (that is, a product that harnesses the best of both sides).

All of these ideas resonate throughout this chapter, not least in the next entry, which returns to the dizzyingly dialectical phenomenon of love.

Duende

Heightened emotion, spirit, passion

A scene from my childhood reverberates through my memory. I was on holiday in France and my parents had invited a neighbour round for dinner. Late in the evening, as often happened, my dad got out his guitar. Among his favourites is the French classic 'Plaisir d'amour', with its mournful refrain: *'Plaisir d'amour ne dure qu'on moment / Chagrin d'amour dure toute la vie'* – 'The joys of love last but a moment / The pain of love endures all life long'. As the chorus rang out, I saw our neighbour weeping, but also singing along entranced. Hungarians call this *sirva vigad* – taking one's pleasures tearfully (or one's sorrows smilingly). At the age of twelve, I was mystified by what was happening, so the next morning I sheepishly asked my dad why his friend had been crying. He replied, in a tone that was both approving and profound, 'He's an emotional man.'

This was my first real encounter with *duende* – a heightened state of emotion that is usually inspired by a work of art. Think perhaps of the dramatic swirls of passion that surge through a Flamenco dancer *and* her captivated audience. The term derives from a mythical, elf-like creature in Spanish folklore, which gives an indication of the capricious, irrational, other-worldly experiential state it symbolises.[6] In its power to transport people to other realms, *duende* is a close cousin of the musically induced enchantment of *tarab* (see Chapter 2), but of greater relevance here is the insight it provides into the dialectical nature of love.

Consider the etymology of 'passion' – from the Latin *pati*, meaning 'to suffer or endure'. As noted above, the deeper one's love, the greater the pain of separation. As C.S. Lewis wrote: 'To love at all is to be vulnerable. Love anything and your heart will be wrung and possibly broken.'[7] But this means that the light and shade of love are inextricably intertwined: it's impossible to experience one without the other. In the words of Zygmunt Bauman, 'To love means opening up to that most sublime of all human conditions, one in which fear blends with joy into an alloy that no longer allows its ingredients to separate.'[8]

Duende epitomises this dialectic, encompassing the euphoric highs and terrible lows of love, passion and, indeed, life as a whole. Thus, according to Nick Cave, all love songs 'must contain *duende*' if they are to be genuine and touch people's hearts. 'The love must resonate with the susurration of sorrow, the tintinnabulation of grief. The writer who refuses to explore the darker regions of the heart will never be able to write convincingly about the wonder, the magic and the joy of love.'[9]

These are powerful words for a powerful emotion, one which most of us crave and cherish, and which goes to the heart of what it means to be human. As such, we not only accept that works of art must feature darker elements, if they are to convey truth; we actively seek them out, and then find ourselves – like our French neighbour – reverberating with their power.

Páthos

Empathetic suffering and sorrow

Close your eyes and call to mind your favourite pieces of music. Which songs comprise the soundtrack to your life? To which do you repeatedly return, especially when you're feeling down and long for comfort? Which words and melodies have become embedded in your heart? How many of them are melancholic? More than a few, I imagine.

For some reason I can't quite fathom, one of my personal favourites is 'In the Bleak Midwinter', and I'm not alone: in a survey of choirmasters and choral experts, it topped the list of favourite carols.[10] Yet its verses are full of sorrow, of struggling to express one's gratitude and devotion to Christ: 'What can I give Him, poor as I am?' Moreover, these words are set to a poignant lament whose melody alone can bring tears to my eyes. So why do I listen to it so frequently, and not just at Christmas?

This brings us to the quiet power of *páthos*. In its original Greek context, it denoted suffering, but also emotion in general and even, simply, experience.[11] However, since entering the English lexicon in the sixteenth century, it has come to signify the capacity of certain phenomena to *evoke* sorrow and sadness. One might wonder why this term merits an entry in a book about wellbeing. While the inclusion of *duende* – which blends the highs and lows of passion – makes sense, surely a word that is so closely associated with melancholia doesn't belong here? Indeed, there is a widespread tendency to regard sadness as entirely invidious, and even to pathologise it as a form of mild depression.[12]

However, emotions with overwhelmingly negative connotations, such as sadness, can perform a valuable function and might even be fundamental to a fulfilling life, as I explored in my previous book.[13] For a start, sadness can reflect refined *moral* sensitivity, particularly the admirable capacity to be moved by the suffering of others.[14] It has been argued, for instance, that exemplary individuals, such as Abraham Lincoln, are compelled to act by the distress they experience at the troubles of the world.[15]

Sadness may also reflect *aesthetic* sensitivity and sophistication.[16] Indeed, feeling moved by art is integral to wellbeing. That's why we listen to laments, watch tear-jerkers, read tragic novels, view harrowing art and visit sombre memorials. We recognise the importance of engaging with the full spectrum of our emotions. As much as we enjoy the sweetness and light of life, we understand the value of periodic solemnity and pensiveness, since these are equally vital aspects of being human. If nothing else, they make the good times seem all the more precious ... as do gentler moments of melancholic absorption.

Ambedo

Melancholic sensory absorption

Have you ever gazed out of the window and started to feel the enveloping touch of a gentle sadness? This isn't precipitated by anything in particular; you are not aware of any suffering or lamenting some sort of loss. It's just a strange form of mellow hypnosis. You might be entranced by sensory ephemera – raindrops gliding down the windowpane, say, or *komorebi* as the sun descends (see Chapter 5). Lost in thought, or rather *out of* thought, you suddenly feel porous, listless, even abandoned – not unhappy, per se, but certainly lost in reverie and shadows.

There's a word for this sensation: *ambedo*. This may be viewed as something of an interloper in our lexicon of untranslatable terms. For, while it has roots in the Latin *ambedere* (literally, 'to erode' or 'gnaw around the edge'), John Koenig coined it just a few years ago for his evocatively titled collection of neologisms, *The Dictionary of Obscure Sorrows*. *Ambedo*'s etymology reflects how we can disappear into the mists of self-absorption and fade away at the edges when lost in melancholic reverie. This delicate, dream-like state is so familiar that it certainly merits its own word, and Koenig came up with the perfect solution. On his lexicon's accompanying website, a video voice-over associates *ambedo* with 'Those moments when everything falls quiet. When words lose their meaning and it all mixes together, until you can't tell the difference between the ordinary and the epic, and you stop waiting around for some other meaning to arrive … Life is not just a quest, or an opportunity, or a story to tell. It's also just an experience that exists for its own sake.'[17] Meanwhile, the subtle ambivalence of this other-worldly state is readily apparent in the video's images.

Indeed, I would encourage you to peruse all of the entries in Koenig's collection. For, despite the title, his dictionary is not a litany of suffering but a compendium of intriguing, complex emotional states. For instance, another neologism with its origins in Latin is the alluring *chrysalism* – 'the amniotic tranquillity of being indoors during a thunderstorm, listening to waves of rain pattering against the roof'. Or consider *kenopsia*, which derives from the Greek *kenosis* ('emptiness') and *opsia* ('seeing'). This conveys the eeriness of empty or abandoned places and, more generally, that odd sense of perceiving absence, especially of people.

We have all experienced these kind of feelings, which is why Koenig's dictionary is so evocative. Moreover, his neologisms merit inclusion in this book because they are all rooted in concepts that evolved in other languages before Koenig playfully adapted them in ways that remain consonant with their original meanings. This process of bricolage has occurred throughout the history of language evolution, so Koenig is simply the latest in a long line of imaginative thinkers to 'fill a hole in the language' by creating new words. His project also aligns perfectly with the philosophy of this book: borrowing – or, in Koenig's case, coining – words to bridge semantic gaps. His creations mostly pertain to ambivalent states of mind, hence their inclusion in this chapter. However, there is nothing to stop us coining our own neologisms for any or all of the other themes in this book.

For the time being, though, we must turn our attention to another untranslatable term that is closely associated with emotional ambivalence.

Gedenkstätte

Places and acts of rememberance

Among the most thought-provoking entries in Koenig's lexicon is *klexos* – the art of dwelling on the past. This should not be confused with simple nostalgia or the unfiltered recollection of previous experiences. Rather, it concerns the ongoing project of *creating meaning* out of our shape-shifting memories. This is reflected in the neologism's etymology, as it derives from the German term *klecksography* – the art of perceiving images in inkblots, as with the famous Rorschach tests that are used in psychological analysis. Enriching the present by reflecting on the past is truly an art, and a crucial one at that.

Time is a recurrent theme in this chapter. Later, we shall encounter the yearning for better days ... either gone by or, hopefully, ahead. We shall also hear laments of lost time: the poignancy of life ebbing away; and the urge to seize the moment before it slips from our grasp. But all of these temporal reveries rest on reckoning with the past. In that respect, it is appropriate that Koenig chose a German term as the root for *klexos*, because Germany has developed a particularly nuanced lexicon in this area.

In part, this may simply reflect the conceptual and lexical innovation for which that nation is rightly renowned. But it is also surely a consequence of the fact that it has been compelled to reflect critically upon its past, and above all the Second World War. Hence, a nuanced vocabulary has emerged to describe how people today engage with this dark history. For instance, German has four words for the single

English term 'memorial', each of which casts the difficult but essential process of memorialising the past in a slightly different light.

First, *Gedenkstätte* means a place of remembrance or memory, but it implies rather more than a location where memories are instantiated, such as a wall with a list of names and dates. For people tend to visit a *Gedenkstätte* specifically to *reflect* upon the past. In that respect, Lance Neckar has written about Berlin's 'topography of contemplation' and the fact that the city's troubled history remains visible in its many *Gedenkstätten*.[18]

The three remaining terms delineate the varying emotional quality and moral weight of Germany's memorials. Most neutral are the country's *Denkmale* (literally, 'think signs'), whereas those that celebrate someone or something are known as *Ehrenmale* ('honour signs'). Finally, and most powerfully, there are the *Mahnmale* ('warning signs'). These have been described as 'monuments to national shame',[19] and they serve as insistent reminders of past tragedies. Moreover, they function as 'bearers of admonition' that we must guard against revisiting such tragedies.[20] Of course, such warnings are applicable to most nations, not just Germany, in the aftermath of the global conflicts of the twentieth century and beyond.

It should be remembered that ostensibly negative emotions such as shame and guilt – as painful as they may be – can have ameliorative power at the individual as well as the national level.[21] If we engage with them skilfully – that is, without sinking into a spiral of self-recrimination and with a compassionate determination to make amends – they can help us become better versions of ourselves. Guilt, especially, can serve as a moral compass by reminding us of times we've gone astray and pointing us in the direction of better behaviour and towards goals that may be more conducive to happiness. For instance, the guilt you experience after snubbing a friend will often steer you away from behaving in a similarly thoughtless fashion in the future.

Similar paradoxical benefits may result from reflections on the ephemeral nature of life itself.

Mono no aware

Páthos and appreciation of life's transience

Each spring, a dazzling sight suddenly materialises along the quiet stretch of riverbank near my home: a radiant explosion of cherry blossom, as if the earth itself were rejoicing. It's beautiful, of course. But recently it's come to take on a deeper significance for me. For I now know that it is the symbol of a vital emotional sensibility that Zen seeks to inculcate: *mono no aware*.

This phrase describes a melancholic aesthetic that was especially revered during Japan's Tokugawa period (1603–1868).[22] The eighteenth-century scholar Motoori Norinaga coined the term by combining *aware* ('*páthos*') and *mono* ('things'). Thus, it reflects a person's capacity to be 'touched or moved by the world', and particularly by its transiency.[23] However, the mood it encapsulates long predates this relatively recent neologism. It can be discerned, for instance, in the opening lines of an epic fourteenth-century Japanese folktale, *The Tale of the Heike*: 'The sound of the *Gion shōja* bells echoes the impermanence of all things ... The proud do not endure, they are like a dream on a spring night.'[24]

As these evocative lines suggest, *mono no aware* encompasses a refined *páthos* of the fleeting nature of all life; hence its importance within Zen. We have already seen that Buddhism teaches that existence is impermanent and that suffering arises from developing attachments to that which is inherently subject to change. By contrast, a deep understanding of ephemerality may lead to liberation from pain. Thus, Zen – and Japanese culture more broadly[25] – encourages not only acceptance but a strange kind of *appreciation* of life's transiency.[26]

It's not that impermanence is welcomed or celebrated; there is still sadness at someone's or something's passing. But *mono no aware* is a complex state in which grief mingles with gratitude for having the opportunity to experience the beauty of life, however fleetingly. Moreover, one recognises that ephemerality can be integral to this very beauty: cherry blossom is precious in part because of its brevity; childhood innocence is treasured when we understand that those years pass all too quickly. As Yoshida Kenkō wrote, 'If man were never to fade away like the dews of Adashino . . . how things would lose their power to move us.'[27]

In a sense, cherry blossom is a *memento mori* – the Latin injunction to remember one's own mortality. Yet, it is delicate and light when compared with laying a skull symbolically upon a table (a standard *memento mori* motif). In the midst of *mono no aware*, one is sighing rather than weeping or despairing; one is standing with upturned palms amid the falling blossom rather than trudging through the gloom. A similar mood resonates through the fragile hope of *magari*.

Magari

The wistful hope of 'if only'

In Frank Darabont's masterful film *The Shawshank Redemption*, one of the two central characters reads a letter from the other. It urges the ageing recipient to choose hope over a downhill spiral of despair: 'Hope is a good thing, maybe the best of things, and no good thing ever dies.' Indeed, earlier in the film, the same character essentially equates hope with the will to live, saying, 'Get busy living, or get busy dying.' Keep the flame of hope alight. Have faith that good things are possible and even likely or risk sinking into apathy and resignation.

Contemporary psychology aligns with these dictums. Hope is invariably seen as not only desirable but central to wellbeing.[28] Yet, curiously, on closer inspection, it is also decidedly ambivalent. It is a fragile blend of some confidence that a longed-for outcome will occur *and* anxiety that it might not (otherwise, one would have certainty).[29] This doesn't devalue hope: on the contrary, it remains an absolute good. It just reinforces this chapter's central message: many of our most precious experiences are fundamentally ambivalent.

The power of hope is reflected in countless terms from around the world. These can be usefully situated on what is effectively a spectrum from optimism to pessimism, reflecting shifting degrees of confidence that a desired outcome will eventuate. For instance, at the optimistic end of the scale, the Icelandic phrase *Þetta reddast* roughly translates as 'everything will work out OK'. Deployed especially as a rallying cry when a positive outcome seems in doubt, it has been described as the country's motto, evoking a determination to thrive in the face of adversity.[30]

A rather different perspective is adopted by terms that allude to fate and destiny. Some of these are theistic, placing the future entirely in divine hands, such as the Arabic invocation *in sha' Allah* – 'God willing'.[31] Similarly, albeit without reference to a deity, the Russian term *avos* expresses faith or hope in luck or fate.[32] Meanwhile, with a shrug of resigned acceptance, the well-known Spanish loanphrase *que será será* recognises that 'what will be will be'. Rather than exuding confidence in a particular outcome, all of these expressions contain an inherent acknowledgement that much of our future is out of our hands. As such, they allude to the tranquil acceptance of *ataraxia* or *Gelassenheit* (see Chapter 1).

Conversely, in other terms the balance of expectation is more pessimistic; yet, crucially, they are not bereft of hope. For instance, while the Italian word *magari* may imply equivocation (e.g., 'I might come round tonight'), it can also convey dreamy, hopeful longing, possibly tinged with forlorn regret: 'If only ... '[33] Finally, the melancholic Korean noun *han* describes a state of deep sorrow and regret, and so is usually characterised as almost entirely dark. Yet even it contains faint flickers of hope that redemption will eventually arrive.[34]

However, whatever our level of confidence in the future, or indeed satisfaction with the present, it is only human to long for better days ahead.

Sehnsucht

Life longings

In 1516, Sir Thomas More published an account of a fictional society on an Atlantic island which he named 'Utopia'. His neologism had a revealing etymology, deriving from the Greek for 'place' (*topos*) and the prefix 'not' (*ou*). Thus, 'no place': a non-existent land. Given the definition that 'utopia' has today – an idyllic, perfect world – one might assume that More had adapted the Greek prefix *eu* ('good' or 'beautiful') instead. But his Utopia was merely an alternative to the society in which he lived – not necessarily better or worse. Indeed, many aspects of his fictional world – such as slavery – would be abhorrent to people today. However, because More shortened the prefix to *u*, the word's meaning morphed over time into 'the land of our dreams'. It may not exist, but we can long for it, and maybe even try to fashion it ourselves.

Humans have a particular aptitude for longing. It may even be what sets us apart from other animals. We previously thought our uniqueness rested on such qualities as sentience and symbolic language. However, our self-elevated status has gradually diminished as ethnologists and zoologists have discerned these characteristics in numerous other creatures. We now believe that many animals even have the ability to think about objects that are absent, such as food. Yet we alone perhaps – though we can never know for certain – have the imaginative capacity to conceive of phenomena that do not and have never existed. It is perhaps this unattainability that ultimately characterises longing ... and renders it supremely ambivalent.

In fact, longing is almost synonymous with ambivalence, being defined as 'a blend of the primary emotions of happiness and sadness'.[35] More poetically, it has also been termed 'an emotional state suffused with a melancholic sweetness'.[36] We yearn for something we do not have, which brings sorrow. Yet there remains a possibility, however small, that our dream might come true. In this respect, longing differs from wishing, as the latter may be utterly unattainable. I might *long* to visit India, but I can only *wish* to be a child again. Moreover, there is that sweet element to longing: in yearning for my beloved, she is right there in my mind, calling to me, whenever I think of her.

The German term *Sehnsucht* relates to a particularly interesting form of longing. Translated as 'life longing', its etymology implies an 'addiction' or commitment to yearning itself, as opposed to pining for a particular person or thing. This is a sort of utopian dreaminess in which a person becomes preoccupied with how life could be.[37]

It is particularly noteworthy because, of all the terms included in this dictionary, it is one of the few to have been the subject of rigorous empirical investigation. Psychologist Susanne Scheibe and her colleagues designed a survey featuring all manner of questions relating to *Sehnsucht*.[38] By statistically analysing patterns in the respondents' answers, they ascertained that it comprises six key elements: a utopian notion of personal development; a sense of life's incompleteness and imperfection; a blended focus on the past, present and future; ambivalent or bittersweet emotions; a tendency towards deep reflection on life; and a mental world imbued with symbolic richness.

Such is the nature, it seems, of diffuse, general longing: a dreamy sense that life could be better than it is. But there are more specific forms of yearning, too.

Hiraeth

Nostalgic longing for one's homeland

Identity is a strange and powerful phenomenon. What makes us who we are? Our individual personalities, certainly: whether we are excitable, shy, conscientious, gregarious or any of the myriad ways in which people differ from one another. Our commitments and ideals are important, too – from political persuasion to religious affiliation. But one of the most potent factors is our connection to a certain place. For the land to which we feel we belong constitutes our roots.

This is no mere metaphor. Our physical being is literally produced by the combined natural forces of a particular place's air, sunlight, water and food. Then there are our biological roots – in the form of DNA – which stretch back through history. Finally, somewhat more abstractly, we are woven from threads of culture, history and tradition. Of course, many migrants move from place to place, either willingly or unwillingly, as did their ancestors. Hence, richly complex roots are common, with people having some form of attachment to more than one place. Yet, most of us still feel a strong sense of belonging to one particular land, one that we might call home.

In Chapter 3, we saw that *chōros* encapsulates one's love for such a land. However, this theme warrants further exploration, since a number of words – including *hiraeth* in Welsh, *saudade* in Portuguese and *toska* in Russian – evoke heartfelt *longing* for home. Moreover, these are not general terms for homesick yearning, but are all intimately linked to their respective cultures. So, *hiraeth* is 'a Welsh cultural longing for Wales',[39] *saudade* is a 'key Portuguese emotion'[40] or 'an emotional state that pervades Brazilian culture and thought',[41] and *toska* is 'one of the leitmotifs of Russian literature and Russian conversation' which help to define the unique Russian character and culture.[42]

These are much more than sensations of objective appreciation. In the course of many visits to Wales, I have been entranced by its natural beauty and much else besides. Yet, I will never fully understand the notion of *hiraeth* because I was not born and raised there. My own grounding is in England, and I'm liable to yearn for it if I'm away for any length of time. But this emotion is not *hiraeth*. Indeed, I'm not aware of an equivalent English term for a longing for England. Maybe we need one.

Obviously, emigrants are most likely to feel these strong emotions, but such terms can also imply a yearning for an earlier age or even for an idealised image of a country that never existed. Inevitably, such longings are rarely, if ever, satisfied, which is what makes them so bittersweet. For instance, Robert Macfarlane poignantly defines *hiraeth* as an 'acute longing for a home-place or time to which you cannot return and without which you are incomplete'.[43]

At other times, though, we might be more inclined to look ahead and crave pastures new.

Fernweh

Yearning for distant places

I well remember the powerful emotions I experienced when deciding, at the age of eighteen, to venture to China and teach English before starting university. Nervous anxiety mingled with the heady thrill of unprecedented adventure and freedom, a combination aptly referred to in Swedish as *resfeber* – 'travel fever'. My choice of China was actually prompted by my mum, who wanted an excuse to visit the country! But the urge to take flight had long been brewing within me. Moreover, as my departure date neared, China exerted an increasingly powerful pull. It seemed to be calling me.

Most people have surely dreamed of fleeing their daily burdens and responsibilities and taking wing to distant lands. Romantic visions of exotic territories, limitless possibilities and the chance to reimagine oneself merge with the enticing notion of escape. This potent yearning is captured in the word *Fernweh*, a typically ingenious German term that combines 'pain' (*Weh*) with 'distance' (*Fern*). While it can denote longing for one's homeland, equally, it can imply the 'call of faraway places'.[44] Therefore, it may describe somewhat paradoxical 'homesickness' for a place one has not yet visited. In this sense, it functions as a counterpart to *Heimweh* – 'regular' homesickness. Indeed, many people may experience the two emotions in swift succession or even simultaneously, as they yearn for global adventure yet miss the comforts of home almost as soon as they depart.[45]

The loanword 'wanderlust' is a close relation. It literally denotes a desire (*Lust*) to hike or roam (*Wander*), rather than wandering per se. However, it has come to mean a longing to wander the world, untethered to any specific place.[46] Although this is imbued with romanticism and excitement, there is also a melancholic undertone, reflecting general dissatisfaction with one's current situation. After all, if we were wholly content, would we yearn to be elsewhere?

Maybe we would. It could be argued that it is only human to dream of a brighter future, irrespective of our opinion of the present. Such utopian visions are found in a rich tapestry of imagined lands – from the ease and plenty of Cockaigne to the pastoral harmony of Arcadia. Moreover, even though these lands are – almost by definition – unattainable, there may be great value in yearning for them. Doing so might, for instance, generate concerted efforts to improve our existing world. Indeed, there may be no stronger spur to human progress than the question 'What if . . . ?'

But what happens if we manage to realise such ambitions?

Vorfreude

Anticipatory pre-pleasure

It's a beautiful summer afternoon in London as I type these words. After an unseasonably cold, grey week, the sun has finally graced us with its presence. However, at the moment, I'm sweltering in a stuffy train carriage. Mercifully, though, my stop is only a few minutes away and I can already imagine the cool breeze on my skin. Moreover, I'm picturing the shop just outside the station where I will obtain succour in the form of an ice-cream. I can almost taste the sweet vanilla on my tongue. There's no ambivalence here, no undertone of melancholy. Everything in my mind's eye – from the anticipation to the reward itself – is pure delight.

Earlier, when discussing *magari*, we saw that doubt and anxiety are intrinsic aspects of hope. However, if the possible becomes probable – and especially if it develops into certainty – hope makes way for *anticipation*. At this point, unfettered optimism overwhelms any lingering hint of pessimism and we experience *Vorfreude* – the German notion of 'pre-pleasure'.[47]

In light of this definition, you may be wondering whether this term merits an entry in this chapter. In what way is luxuriating in the anticipation of a pleasurable outcome in any way ambivalent? Surely it is total joy? Well, not necessarily.

What if the train does not pull into the station quite as quickly as I would like? What if other people have had the same idea as me and they are already at the shop's freezer cabinet, grabbing the last of the ice-creams? This sort of tantalising anticipation mixed with impatience and worry has echoes of the intriguing Inuit verb *iktsuarpok*, which specifically describes the act of repeatedly going outside to see if an expected visitor is arriving.[48] And finally, it can be hard to shake the suspicion that the reality will fail to measure up to the dream, that the ice-cream – or whatever it is we're so keenly anticipating – might not provide the joys we had hoped it would. Not for nothing do some people say that it is better to travel than to arrive.

On the other hand, sometimes an outcome may not only match but exceed our expectations.

Frisson

A spine-tingling thrill

If you have a computer to hand, go online and type 'Jayne's Blue Wish' into Google. You're looking for a recording of the Tom Waits song of that name, ideally the version on the album *Orphans: Brawlers, Bawlers & Bastards*. Now settle comfortably in your seat, close your eyes and let its subtle glory wash over you. That's all I'll say. In fact, read no further for the next three minutes. I'll be right here, awaiting your return.

How was it?

Every time I listen to that song, its opening half soothes my restless mind with its quietly powerful refrain: 'Life's a path / Lit only by / The light of those I love.' Amen to that. Then, even though I know exactly what's coming next, I always feel a quicksilver jolt of electricity down my spine. Having heard the song, I'm sure you'll understand what I mean: the trumpet solo that echoes through its own hallowed space. Is any sound more evocative than a trumpet – melancholic and majestic, a lament and a call to arms? I feel shivers all over my skin and deep inside even when I *think* of that solo, let alone hear it.

The word for this sensation is *frisson* – from the Latin *frigere* ('to be cold') – which captures that familiar spine-tingling blend of fear and excitement.[49] Neurobiologists explain it with reference to the release of endorphins in the nervous system and the galvanic skin response that can accompany anxiety.[50] Meanwhile, musicologists suggest that it can be prompted by specific auditory stimuli, such as 'enharmonic change' – when one note remains constant while others subtly shift, for instance by changing from a major to a minor chord.[51] Or perhaps a haunting trumpet solo will do it?

Of course, not every *frisson* has a musical accompaniment. Consider the last time you looked deep into another person's eyes. You might have gazed longingly at your lover, or perhaps you simply stared at a stranger for a fraction too long. The experience can be strangely unnerving. On a recent meditation retreat, one exercise involved maintaining eye contact with a partner and accepting whatever feelings arose. Over the course of just a few minutes, we were all assailed by a riot of emotions: mirth, awkwardness, solemnity, tenderness. After searching in vain for a word to describe the mysterious, almost painful pleasure of this close encounter, I was gratified to find *opia* among John Koenig's neologisms.[52] Derived from the Greek word for eye (ṓps), this has long served in English as a suffix for conditions relating to eyesight, such as myopia. However, as a standalone word, it perfectly evokes the *frisson* of prolonged eye contact.

Of course, we may experience shivers of thrill in far less intimate circumstances, not least when witnessing something truly staggering.

Vidunder

An awe-inspiring miracle or monstrosity

Have you ever hiked in a mountain range and found yourself gazing around the inhospitable, icy vastness? It can be rather unsettling. The sheer scale can leave you feeling like a speck of dust in an overwhelming void of time and space. Likewise, the forces that create such vistas – from the relentless tectonic shifts that form the peaks themselves, to the gravitational dynamics that define life at altitude – can inspire and terrify in equal measure.

Edmund Burke called this experience 'sublime', from the Latin *sublimis*, which – in addition to its literal definition of 'uplifted' – conveys the idea of approaching an important threshold (*limen*). For Burke believed that the natural world can carry us to the very edge of human experience and understanding as we become overwhelmed by its power and grandeur. As he wrote, 'The passion caused by the great and sublime in nature is ... astonishment; and astonishment is that state of the soul, in which all its motions are suspended, with some degree of horror. In this case, the mind is so entirely filled with its object, that it cannot entertain any other.'[53]

The Swedes have a word for a phenomenon that may provoke this reaction: *vidunder*. This pertains not only to natural objects, such as mountains, but to anything that is highly impressive or deeply threatening. It can, for instance, be used to describe a prodigy, a miracle or even a monster. For geniuses can seem rather monstrous – not in an ugly or an evil way, but simply because their talent appears to be inhuman ... or possibly superhuman. Think of those fortunate souls who witnessed the ten-year-old Mozart performing one of his own concertos with what seemed to be preternatural skill. They must have been in speechless awe of what they were seeing and hearing.

It's telling that two diametrically opposed adjectives stem from 'awe': the bright positivity of 'awesome' and the wholly negative 'awful'. (That said, a couple of centuries ago, their definitions were rather similar: a Keats poem celebrates 'an awful rainbow once in heaven'.[54]) For awe itself is situated phenomenologically at 'the upper reaches of pleasure and on the boundary of fear'.[55] In sublime contexts, the combination of admiration and terror can generate uneasiness but also respect, astonishment and even reverence, as we saw when exploring the worshipful love of *sébomai* (in Chapter 3).

This exemplifies the strange power of ambivalent emotions and experiences, which reaches its apotheosis in this chapter's final entry.

Yūgen

The unfathomable depths of existence

In 1680, the master poet Bashō composed another seemingly simple *haiku*:

> *On a withered branch*
> *A crow is perched*
> *In the autumn evening.*

This may sound unremarkable, even mundane, to Western ears. But it has been celebrated as perhaps the ultimate expression of *yūgen* in Japanese poetry.[56] In turn, *yūgen* is hailed as one of the three principal 'perceptual–emotional' moods that Zen aims to inculcate among its adherents.[57] We have already discussed the other two: *wabi-sabi* – appreciation of the desolate beauty of aged or imperfect phenomena (see Chapter 5); and *mono no aware* – making peace with life's ephemerality (see above). As delicate as these moods are, though, *yūgen* may be even more ineffable and elusive.[58]

Nevertheless, attempts have been made to encapsulate it, with one tentative definition being 'profound grace'.[59] D.T. Suzuki explains that both *yū* and *gen* signify depth and remoteness, so together they convey unknowability, impenetrability, obscurity and 'beyond intellectual calculability', but *not* 'utter darkness'.[60] As such, *yūgen* points obliquely towards the unfathomable depths of existence – the 'mysterious quiescence beneath all things'[61] – and the fundamental inability of the human mind to penetrate those depths. However, while these mysteries elude rational understanding, we may still sense them in some vague, inchoate way.[62] Suzuki continues: 'It is hidden behind the clouds, but not entirely out of sight, for we feel its presence, its secret message being transmitted through the darkness however impenetrable to the intellect.'[63]

Japan is not alone in viewing the profundity of existence as 'veiled', as intimated by St Paul's immortal phrase: 'For now we see through a glass darkly'.[64] Indeed, Christianity has a tradition of apophatic, mystical theology that draws on the Greek notion of *aphaíresis*, which describes a process of abstracting. Such teachings hold that the nature of God cannot be stated explicitly, and can only be alluded to in 'mystical languages of unsaying' and negative statements, such as 'God is not x, God is not y'.[65] More recently, John Keats formulated the concept of 'negative capability' to characterise 'being in uncertainties' and tolerating 'mysteries, doubts, without any irritable reaching after reason'.[66]

Negative capability echoes *yūgen*. Moreover, both terms imply that we may be moved to the core of our being by these mysteries, albeit without knowing why. In the thirteenth century, Kamo no Chōmei suggested that *yūgen* 'is like an autumn evening under a colorless expanse of silent sky. Somehow, as if for some reason that we should be able to recall, tears well uncontrollably.'[67] Similar sentiments are evident in Bashō's *haiku*. Deeply profound and moving, such moments go far beyond mere hedonic pleasure and may even promote far-reaching self-transcendence.

What is particularly striking about *yūgen*, however, is that apparently commonplace phenomena may evoke it, as in Bashō's *haiku*. It need not be occasioned by awe-inspiring vistas or rarefied moments of life-altering grandeur. Rather, the ordinary – which is always within reach – may be revealed as extraordinary.

This seems the perfect place to conclude our investigation of ambivalence. We now move from the unknowable to the knowable as we investigate understanding. First, though, it's time for a brief recap.

Summary

This latest leg of our journey has covered some unusual terrain. We encountered the counter-intuitive notion that wellbeing does not rest entirely on positive emotions, but may relate to states of mind that are rather more ambivalent. Although these may be dark or even distressing, they are integral to our flourishing, central to a life well lived. In that vein, we began with the potent Taoist notion of *yīn yáng* – symbol of the dynamic interaction of opposites – which served as an overarching motif for the chapter.

From there, we explored the spirited passion of *duende* and the empathic suffering of *páthos*, followed by the melancholic trance of *ambedo*. We took in the memorialising of the past with

Gedenkstätte and the pathos of life's transience with *mono no aware*. We then moved into the delicate nuances of longing – the wistful hope of *magari*, the life-longings of *Sehnsucht*, the place-specific nostalgia of *hiraeth* and *Fernweh*'s lure of distant places. Next, we embraced a clutch of more tantalising, spine-tingling terms – the anticipatory pre-pleasure of *Vorfreude*, the thrill of *frisson* and the awe of *vidunder*. Finally, *yūgen* captured the mysterious, unfathomable depths of existence.

However, while we may never comprehend everything, it is only human to try, as we shall see in the next chapter.

CHAPTER SEVEN

Understanding

Thus far, we have covered three great swathes of territory in the vast landscape of wellbeing. First, we looked at positive feelings, spanning contentment (Chapter 1) and pleasure (Chapter 2), from the mindful awareness of *sati* to the ecstatic delight of *jouissance*. Next, we took in the hallowed ground of relationships, exploring the contours of love (Chapter 3), such as the protective care of *storgē*, as well as social connections more broadly (Chapter 4), as exemplified by the common humanity of *ubuntu*. Then we investigated a range of valuable mental states characterised by appreciation (Chapter 5) and ambivalence (Chapter 6), from the graceful elegance of *leggiadria* to the spine-tingling thrill of *frisson*.

But there is yet more to wellbeing. And so, finally, we turn to the central issue of who we are as people. As such, the remainder of the book explores the profound possibilities of personal development: our often untapped potential to improve ourselves. For we are not static entities, like a stone carving. Rather, we are immeasurably dynamic, with a limit-less capacity to learn, change and evolve.

Indeed, academia is increasingly attuned to the possibility of personal growth throughout life, including into old age. Numerous psychological theories celebrate this potential, most famously Abraham Maslow's hierarchy of needs.[1] Imagine a pyramid. Its base comprises our fundamental physiological and biological needs for food, warmth and health – everything we require to survive. If and when these needs are met – at least to some extent – others begin to assume prominence, such as safety concerns, which constitute the next step of the pyramid. In turn, once these are catered to, our main priorities become love and belongingness, then self-esteem. Finally, at the top of the pyramid is 'self-actualisation' – fulfilling our potential. It's best not to conceive of this model too rigidly; after all, many people are concerned with, and indeed attain, the higher levels before meeting all of their lower-level needs.[2] However, the central notion of an upward spiral of personal growth has been corroborated by thousands of studies.[3]

And so, our remaining three chapters focus on this spiral, which is woven from three broad threads: first, understand-ing, including insight, knowledge and wisdom; secondly, spirituality, encompassing contemplation, self-transcendence and the search for the sacred; and, finally, character, spanning virtue, flourishing and fulfilment.

This chapter concentrates on the bracing promise of under-standing. This has been valorised throughout history, perhaps most famously by the ancient Greeks, who venerated the god-dess Sophia and the wisdom she represents. Indeed, her name is the root of the term 'philosophy' – the 'love of wisdom'.[4]

Moreover, Greek thinkers engaged in more than the dry, abstract theorising that all too often characterises academic philosophy today. They undertook an ambitious quest to understand the nature of existence and the good life, then put their insights into practice and inspired others to do the same.

Of course, the Greeks were not alone in appreciating the life-changing power of wisdom and understanding. Every culture in the world has surely coined words relating to this phenomenon. When considering some of these, it is useful to adopt a chronological approach – beginning in the mists of human history and wending our way gradually to the present era – as this will give us the best chance of appreciating the full depth of human thinking as it has unfolded over the millennia. At first glance, the ideas that are presented here may seem rather remote and esoteric, with little direct relevance to your life. Naturally, I shall endeavour to point out subtle resonances that you may find personally helpful, but in addition I hope you will find all of these words objectively fascinating. After all, they represent the very foundations of the human mind, the building blocks of our modern psyche.

With that, let's begin our journey by venturing back to before the dawn of recorded time.

Aljerre-nge

All-encompassing 'Dreamtime'

Our frenetic contemporary age has been called 'liquid modernity',[5] because everything is in a state of constant flux. In this context, a century ago seems like the 'olden days'. We look at black-and-white photos from the early 1900s and it seems like a distant era. Therefore, it's almost impossible to fathom what life must have been like for our ancestors hundreds or even thousands of times further back in time.

Stone tools, fashioned by early hominid species, have been dated to a bewildering 2.6 million years ago,[6] far predating the emergence of *Homo sapiens*, which occurred around 200,000 years ago (or possibly even 350,000, according to recent discoveries[7]). But it was 'only' around 60,000 years ago – for reasons that are subject to intense debate – that dramatic changes began to occur in the development of humanity. Essentially, around that time, our ancestors embarked on a stunning journey of exploration and discovery. Their horizons expanded both literally (they ventured out of Africa) and metaphorically (they developed language, art and abstract thought). For the first time, they began to earn the title *Homo sapiens*: 'wise human'.

Consider Australia. Although it is thousands of miles from Africa – across a perilous ocean – humans managed to make their way there some 50,000 years ago.[8] Thereafter, they gradually developed a rich and complex culture. For instance, some of their rock art has been definitively dated to 26,000 BCE, with other examples potentially far older.[9] As this long process of cultural development continued, forms of wisdom – modes of understanding life and the world – began to take shape.

One such is known as *aljerre-nge*, which denotes the complex cultural–religious belief system of the Aranda (or Arrente) people. Other Aboriginal peoples have comparable knowledge systems that are known by different names, such as the Kija's *Ngarrankarni*. You may have noticed the use of the present tense here. This is no accident, because these epistemologies are not confined to prehistory. Nor are they simply vestiges, acknowledged for some vague previous significance but no longer relevant today. Rather, they are living, breathing ways of understanding and engaging with the world that still have great resonance for many Aboriginal people today.

So, what does *aljerre-nge* actually mean? In English, it is sometimes rendered as 'Dreamtime' or 'the Dreaming' – a pair of evocative terms that were coined by the anthropologist William Stanner in the 1950s.[10] However, both have been criticised for implying an air of unreality, among other obfuscations.[11] Stanner's intention was probably to highlight the epistemological significance of dreams as a means of acquiring knowledge, including receiving instruction and guidance from ancestors. But *aljerre-nge* and related concepts are about much more than dreaming in the literal sense of the word (i.e., cognitive activity while asleep). They are holistic and all-encompassing ways of perceiving all forms of life as interconnected.

Stanner coined another term for this mode of understanding – 'everywhen' – to encompass past, present and future. Rather more than a synonym for 'timeless', this acknowledges the ongoing relevance of the great primordial ancestral beings and powers that supposedly shaped the world. This is not simply an 'origin myth': everywhen is a vibrant, complex, *living* reality. Aboriginal peoples consult and engage with their stories about these progenitors for guidance about how they should behave now, from their relationship with the land – including designations of sacredness and issues of stewardship and responsibility – to their personal interactions.

Terms like *aljerre-nge* are windows onto entire worlds.

Just glancing through them can expand all our horizons. Admittedly, it's surely impossible for non-Aboriginals to come close to appreciating such philosophies in all their nuanced detail and depth, but they still have valuable lessons to impart. For example, could we do more to honour the memory and traditions of our own ancestors? And what of our relationship to the land from which *we* spring, wherever that may be? Are we dutiful custodians who cherish and preserve it for future generations, with an everywhen perspective that is not exclusively preoccupied with our immediate desires and needs?

Reflections on concepts like *aljerre-nge* may prompt us to ask such questions. And we may be equally stimulated by the great narrative power of myth.

Enkidu

A mythological wild-man

In 1853, the archaeologist Hormuzd Rassam made a stunning discovery that would radically change how the modern world viewed its forebears. He was excavating the ruins of Nineveh, capital of the ancient empire of Assyria, a dominant force in Mesopotamia (literally, the 'land between rivers') that spanned most of present-day Iraq and Kuwait as well as parts of Syria, Turkey and Iran. Also home to the Babylonian and Akkadian empires, this region is widely regarded as one of the 'cradles of civilisation'. From as early as 4000 BCE, many of the first instances of cities, monumental architecture, agriculture and innovations in metallurgy and writing occurred there. In short, it could be said that modern human existence sprang into life in places like Mesopotamia.

Yet, in the nineteenth century, much of this history had been lost to the ravages of time. It was only thanks to the likes of Rassam that the world began to remember.[12] The first wonder he unearthed was the magnificent palace of King Sennacherib, who ruled Assyria from 705 to 681 BCE. Digging further, he stumbled upon a great library. Among its treasures were twelve clay tablets covered in indecipherable, wedged-shaped marks. Once these symbols had been decoded, it transpired that the tablets contained the oldest surviving work of literature in the world, dating from around 2100 BCE. (The marks themselves were termed 'cuneiform', one of the first writing systems, which the Sumerians had invented more than a millennium earlier.) This great epic provides an insight into the wisdom that started to evolve all those years ago. Indeed, it speaks to many existential issues that remain paramount concerns of humanity today. Above all, it is a tale of our attempts to come to terms with our own mortality.

The story centres on a semi-mythical king of Uruk and his companion, Enkidu. The latter is a primitive wild-man, created from water and clay by Aruru – the goddess of creation – in order to quell the arrogance of Gilgamesh, who had been oppressing his subjects. Raised by animals, Enkidu initially stands apart from society, representing the primordial power of the natural world. However, he eventually meets and befriends Gilgamesh, and they embark on a series of dramatic adventures that are full of notable encounters.

The key episode occurs halfway through the tale, when the gods sentence Enkidu to death after he slays a bull that has been sent from heaven. This judgment greatly distresses

Gilgamesh, who spends the rest of the story searching for the secret to immortality. Although he fails in this quest, in the remainder of the narrative he finds comfort in various endeavours that ultimately help him to become reconciled to his own mortality. Moreover, in doing so, he does attain an immortality of sorts, for he commits to creating a legacy of great works that will last for posterity.

The epic therefore constitutes one of the earliest known compendiums of wisdom, as well as an exposition on the nature of existence. For that reason, 'Enkidu' warrants inclusion here. Granted, this is a name rather than an untranslatable word, but he symbolises numerous important truths that were forged at the dawn of civilisation and remain pertinent to this day. Moreover, he is a great exemplar of the vast repository of wisdom that is housed in the world's mythologies. For all peoples and cultures have formulated similar creation and mortality myths.

Once again, as with *aljerre-nge*, you may find subtle resonances with your own life here. It's unlikely that you have an abiding interest in Enkidu himself, or in Mesopotamian myths generally. But some narratives among the world's great stock will surely animate you and give shape and meaning to your life. These may be religious, such as the morality tales of the Bible, or secular, encompassing everything from *The Lord of the Rings* to the Harry Potter series. For, despite their recent provenance, these latter adventures are suffused with timeless, archetypal themes, such as the 'Hero's journey' – as identified by the renowned scholar Joseph Campbell[13] – in which a fledgling hero or heroine embarks on a perilous but ultimately transformative quest.

It is illuminating and edifying to explore the extent to

which our current stories and concerns echo back in time to the very first myths, as personified here by Enkidu. Indeed, this primordial mythologising and philosophising constitutes the fundamental basis for modern human consciousness. For we still think along the tracks laid down by the founders of civilisation, not least the illustrious sages of the Axial age.

Ahura Mazdā

All-wise, supreme being

In the long, winding history of humanity, the development of thought stretches back many millennia into the mists of unrecorded time, as intimated above. But there was a dramatic collective shift between the eighth and third centuries BCE – a qualitative jump in consciousness. This wasn't precipitated by the emergence of an individual genius; nor is it associated with a single geographical area. In multiple locations – from China to India to Greece – profound and unprecedented cognitive and philosophical revolutions occurred almost simultaneously. The psychologist and philosopher Karl Jaspers called this the *Achsenzeit* – the 'Axial age' – to signify that it marked a pivotal moment in the earth's history.

The earth is still spinning from the creative energy that was unleashed at that time. For, as intimated above, the mind of contemporary humankind is still structured according to the concepts and theories that were forged more than two millennia ago. Hence, over the next few pages, we shall explore a few of the systems of thought that developed during that world-shaping era.

We begin in Persia with the epochal figure of Zarathustra – otherwise known as Zoroaster – who lived in the sixth or seventh century BCE, or perhaps even earlier.[14] As that equivocation attests, the details of this distant age remain shrouded in mystery, but we do know that this prophet was one of the most influential thinkers of his (and in fact any) time. Indeed, his teachings coalesced into a powerful belief system known as Zoroastrianism that continues to attract adherents, making it one of the oldest extant religions. Of course, attempting to summarise a religion as rich and complex as Zoroastrianism in a few paragraphs would be a fool's errand, but a brief discussion of some of its key ideas may be illuminating.

In contrast to the bountiful polytheism of many cultures at the time, Zarathustra was one of the first theologians to develop the notion of a single, supreme divinity. And at the core of this vision was an unstinting respect for wisdom. For he named this almighty power Ahura Mazdā – 'Lord of Wisdom' – and acclaimed him as the originator of truth, order and justice.

But this was not straightforward monotheism. In fact, possibly uniquely among the world's great religions, Zoroastrianism combines belief in a supreme deity with a form of cosmic dualism.[15] That is, it begins with a dualistic account of the origin of existence, with Ahura Mazdā engaged in a primordial struggle with his antithesis, Angra Mainyu, an equally powerful god of destruction who represents darkness and chaos. This will eventually resolve into a monotheistic eschatology (i.e., a theology of ultimate destiny) when Ahura Mazdā is finally triumphant. However, this outcome is far from guaranteed, at least not within our human timeframe. Forces of strife and chaos remain ever present and must be held at bay until they are finally overcome. And we are active participants in this struggle: we have a responsibility to join Ahura Mazdā and contribute to his war against the darkness by cultivating wisdom and undertaking good deeds.

Of course, it is not only Zoroastrians who believe that existence is an eternal struggle between the benevolent powers of light, goodness, truth and beauty and the destructive forces of darkness, evil, falsehood and ugliness. Irrespective of whether we choose to personify the former as a deity and give it a name, we can all align ourselves with benevolence and help secure its ultimate victory over evil.

Indeed, these ideas have been pervasive throughout recorded history, influencing and inspiring not only Zarathustra's followers, but also adherents of other traditions that developed around the same time, such as Judaism.[16]

Mitzvah

Commanded ethical observance

The second book of the Jewish Torah, Exodus, recounts the liberation of the Israelites from captivity in Egypt. Led by the prophet Moses and, subsequently, his brother Aaron, they travelled to Canaan, the land they believed God had promised to Abraham, their founding patriarch. This journey predates the Axial age by roughly half a millennium: it is thought that Abraham lived around 2000 BCE, or even earlier, while Moses appeared some seven centuries later[17] (although this chronology is still much debated). Whatever the exact historical details, however, these epochal figures became central to the narratives of the Jewish people when their legends were transcribed in the great books of the Torah during the Axial age.

Exodus tells us that the Jews eventually reached Mount Sinai, where their encampment was visited by violent thunder and lightning. They interpreted this as signalling the presence of YHVH – or Yahweh – their God. Moses climbed to the summit of the mountain, where God presented him with the *Aseret ha-Dibrot* – also known as the Ten Commandments or the Decalogue – on two stone tablets. Each commandment constituted a *mitzvah* (literally, 'law' or 'precept') that his people, as 'children of God', were obliged to follow. These laws became the foundation of Jewish ethics: a divinely inspired guide to good and evil.[18]

The injunctions themselves are legendary: exhortations to worship one God, honour one's parents and respect the Sabbath, along with proscriptions against idolatry, blasphemy, killing, adultery, theft, dishonesty and covetousness. These were then augmented by many further *mitzvot* (plural) throughout the Torah – as many as 613, according to popular reckoning.[19] Taken together, these laws constitute a codification of wisdom, a practical rubric for how people should live. And people of Jewish faith and heritage still find solace, guidance and inspiration in them.

Meanwhile, other traditions have comparable ethical precepts and codified tenets of wisdom (some of which we shall explore below, such as those within Buddhism). Even people who categorise themselves as agnostic or atheistic abide by certain principles and secular laws. So, irrespective of whether we use the term *mitzvah*, most of us are the grateful heirs of some sort of tradition of ethical living. Many such frameworks have been formulated over the centuries. Indeed, the

Babylonians developed a legal code as early as 1700 BCE,[20] which commentators have even suggested may have informed the instantiation of the Decalogue.[21] Nevertheless, the latter is arguably the most influential code of ethics in the world, whose moral perspective continues to shape mindsets in the twenty-first century. As such, it remains a foundational legacy of the Axial age.

Meanwhile, far to the east, similarly epochal ideas were starting to percolate.

Shù

Forgiveness, mercy, reciprocity

As we continue to explore ancient modes of wisdom and understanding that still shape the modern world, our focus inevitably turns to China. Another cradle of civilisation, this may constitute the oldest uninterrupted society on earth. Its first dynasty, the Xia, was founded around 2100 BCE, but a multitude of kingdoms and emperors had previously ruled the territory we now know as China, and there is evidence of settled Chinese communities from as early as 8000 BCE.[22]

Systems of knowledge gradually evolved throughout those epochs. However, as in the Middle East, there was a sea change in Chinese thinking during the Axial age. Particularly note-worthy is a remarkable era known as the Spring and Autumn period (722–476 BCE), which occurred in the middle of the Zhou Dynasty (1046–256 BCE). Although this was a time of great political conflict and chaos, it was also a golden era of intellectual development as numerous philosophies competed with one another for precedence.[23] Out of this creative ferment emerged two luminaries in particular – Confucius and Lao Tzu – whose philosophical systems are still influential today.

Born into the middle stratum of Chinese society in 551 BCE, Confucius's vision and impact became so singular that the system of thought he devised now bears his name. He occupied various governmental positions before travelling to nearby provinces, where he visited courts and engaged in political and philosophical debate, with his final years devoted to setting his wisdom down in writing.

It is hard to overstate his impact on Chinese culture. His teachings brought new degrees of public order through a clear system of well-defined roles and social stratification. Moreover, he encouraged harmony among the people through such virtues as *lǐ*, *rén* and *shù*. The first of these relates to adherence to and appreciation of decorum, etiquette and ceremony, all of which should be practised as expressions of *rén* – humanity and humaneness – rather than in a cold, emotionless way.

In turn, *rén* is exemplified by *shù*, which was Confucius's answer when he was asked for a 'single word that can serve as a guide to conduct throughout one's life'. He defined this ideal as: 'Do not do to others what you would not want others to do to you'[24] – often referred to as the 'golden rule'. Although analogous precepts are found in many other traditions, Confucius was among the first to articulate this ethic of reciprocity, which remains the bedrock of almost every code of ethics and legal systems around the world.

Meanwhile, elsewhere in China at around the same time, a similarly influential philosophy was germinating.

Tao

All-pervasive, generative power and path

While Confucius's life is well documented, Lao Tzu remains a semi-mythical figure who may (or may not) have lived at some point between the sixth and fourth centuries BCE. According to tradition, he was a keeper of the archives at the Chinese imperial court, before becoming disillusioned with the scheming ways of men and setting off into the mountains. At the Xiangu Pass, a border guard, presumably aware of Lao Tzu's wisdom, begged him to transcribe his philosophy. The result was a collection of just five thousand ideograms, yet this short book proved to be revolutionary, and went on to become one of the most widely disseminated texts in history: the *Tao Te Ching.* Having created this legacy, Lao Tzu disappeared into the mist, never to be seen again.

Unfortunately, as is the way with myths, there is no concrete evidence for this tale. Moreover, given the generic nature of Lao Tzu's name – it means simply 'old' or 'venerable master' – 'his' book may actually be a compendium of earlier texts, rather than the work of a sole author. Nevertheless, the *Tao Te Ching* did come into being around that time – written (or compiled) on bamboo tablets – and it is regarded as the foundational text of Taoism (even if the roots of Taoism stretch back many centuries before that).

But what, exactly, is the *Tao*? There is no easy answer to that question. As alluded to in relation to *wú wéi* (in Chapter 1), by its very nature it is utterly ineffable and ungraspable. As the book's first line states, 'The *Tao* that can be spoken is not the eternal *Tao*.' Essentially, though, we might say that the *Tao* is both the origin and the fabric of existence itself – a 'nameless, formless, all pervasive power which brings all things into being and reverts them back into non-being in an eternal cycle'.[25] This definition hints that it may relate to living in a certain way and following a path towards ultimate freedom. Indeed, *Tao* itself is sometimes rendered simply as 'way'. Meanwhile, *te* means 'power' or 'virtue' and *ching* denotes a scripture or classic text. Hence, the title may be translated as 'The Book of the Way and Its Power'.

Fundamentally, this 'way' entails first understanding and then aligning oneself with the *Tao*, as we saw with *wú wéi*. A wealth of concepts then flesh out this singular vision of wisdom. For example, Taoism emphasises the importance of *lǐ*. This is not to be confused with the Confucian *lǐ* above, pertaining to decorum. Although the Taoist *lǐ* is also concerned with order, it is a different concept, being more about the organic laws of nature, such as the intricate organisation of living systems. Understanding this is the key to wisdom, effective action and ultimate liberation.

For instance, a Taoist carpenter would always try to work with the wood's grain, rather than hack artlessly against it. This serves as a metaphor for a whole way of living. It's about being attuned to the unfolding patterns of life and learning how to harness their energy rather than fight against them. As the saying goes, you can't stop the waves, but you can learn how to surf. Like the skilful carpenter, this might mean knowing how to work adeptly with materials to achieve a desired end. Or, in a social context, it might mean knowing exactly when and how to raise an issue in the workplace to get one's point across.

These ideas have been hugely influential over the centuries, shaping not only Taoism but other systems of thought. For instance, as noted in Chapter 1, when Buddhism was exported to China, it mingled with Taoism to produce a unique interpretation of the Buddha's teachings that eventually became known as Zen.[26] As such, Zen has a decidedly Taoist flavour. Consider this early Zen aphorism from around 600 CE, attributed to Seng-ts'an: 'Follow your nature and accord with the Tao ... Don't be antagonistic to the world of the senses. For when you are not antagonistic to it, it turns out to be the same as complete awakening.'[27]

Of course, such directives are not only Taoist but unequivocally Buddhist, too.

Dhárma

Teachings and laws for living

Around the time Confucius and Lao Tzu were formulating their philosophies – possibly in or near 550 BCE – Gautama Siddhārtha was born into a royal family in what is now Nepal.[28] Legend has it that he witnessed four sights on venturing out of the palace for the first time as a young man: a frail, elderly person; someone racked with sickness; a dead body; and a wandering ascetic. His protective father had previously shielded Siddhārtha from the terrors of life, and so these images precipitated a profound crisis.

He spent the next few years wrestling with the problem of existence, seeking the solution to suffering. He consulted various teachers and tried a variety of methods, including extreme asceticism, but none seemed to work. Eventually, at the age of thirty-five, he resolved to sit in meditation and persist until he arrived at the answer. After forty-nine days, he attained *nirvāṇa*.

Of course, as we saw in Chapter 1, Siddhārtha is now known the world over as the Buddha, the awakened or enlightened one. And he spent the next forty-five years propagating his insights and explaining to others how they could reach the same luminous goal. He referred to these teachings as the *dhárma*. This term has broader meanings that are not connected specifically to Buddhism, so it lends the teachings power by implying that they are grounded in the nature of reality. It connotes laws and truths, denoting 'how things are' and the 'correct' way of living. In Hinduism, for instance, it designates actions that are attuned to *rta* – the universe's inherent order. So, those who accord with the *dhárma* align themselves with the currents of life and navigate them skilfully.

Wisdom is at the core of the *dhárma*. The Buddha proclaimed this as one of two paramount qualities that people must possess to attain enlightenment. (The other is compassion, as we saw in Chapter 4 in relation to the *bramha-vihārās*.) Specifically, he taught the importance of cultivating *prajña*. Although translatable simply as 'wisdom', this can also be rendered as 'insight' or 'discernment'. Moreover, it implies *experiential* understanding, rather than rote memorising of teachings, or dry, abstract knowledge with no bearing on how one lives one's life. It is about gaining deep understanding as a consequence of intimately experiencing the truths in question. To achieve full comprehension of the power and importance of *mettā*, for example, one must have felt and practised this quality intensely, rather than merely read about it.

Furthermore, Buddhism does not merely proclaim the value

of *prajña*. The *dhárma* is replete with guidance about its nature. Indeed, vast libraries have been written in which these teachings are expounded in great detail. We can only scratch the surface here, but the merest sample of this deep repository of insight may prove beneficial.

For instance, a central component of *prajña* is an understanding of *pratītya-samutpāda*. Translated as the 'law of conditionality' or 'dependent origination', it articulates the Buddha's pivotal insight into the causal nature of the universe.[29] In short, life is not dictated by chance or whim: laws of cause and effect operate everywhere at all times. This is as true in the psychological domain as it is in the physical world. Just as dropping an object causes it to fall to the ground, there are reasons for *duḥkha* (suffering or dissatisfaction; see Chapter 1). *Duḥkha* may occur due to the confluence of multiple and often complex factors. Nevertheless, we can develop insights into them and thereby improve our lives.

Every culture has its own versions of *dharma* and *prajña*, such as the Judaic *mitzvot* (see above). So, whatever your tradition, personal philosophy or religion, you are likely to have access to a path that will guide you towards the light. For, mercifully, an in-depth understanding of the causes of suffering may lead to some kind of salvation.

Ashtangika

The Noble Eightfold Path

Given that we live in a causal universe, the value of wisdom is self-evident. If we understand why we experience *duḥkha*, then we can work towards alleviating it. Of course, discontent may be due to myriad factors that lie outside our control. Equally, though, it may also be partly attributable to our own negative thoughts and actions, as encapsulated by the concept of *karma* (see Chapter 9). Hence, it would be useful to have access to a guide that might help us forge a better path. Fortunately, many of these are available – not least, Buddhism.

The Buddha began his teaching by propounding the *catvāri āryasatyāni* – 'four noble truths'.[30] These amount to a medical diagnosis of *duḥkha*, outlining both its causes and its cure. The first truth is *duḥkha* itself, meaning that life is pervaded by this dolorous quality. The second is *samudaya* (literally, 'origin' or 'cause'). Here, the Buddha identified attachment and craving as the main causes of *duḥkha*. Of course, there may be others: if I break my arm, that certainly is painful. But we often exacerbate such pain by feverishly resisting it and/or craving good health. The Buddha likened this situation to coming under attack from two arrows. The first arrow is the misfortune of becoming hurt or ill, while the second is the mental distress we generate in response, which can potentially be even more insidious and damaging.[31] As this teaching is sometimes paraphrased: pain is inevitable, whereas suffering is optional.

The third truth is *nirodha* (literally, 'cessation'), which refers to ending *duḥkha* by liberating oneself from craving and attachment. No easy task, you might think. However, the Buddha offered a solution, namely the fourth truth, *mārga* – meaning path – which in this case denotes the Buddha's path of salvation, which he termed the *ashtangika*, or 'eightfold path'.[32] Unsurprisingly, this contains eight strands, all of which are prefixed by *samyak* in Sanskrit (meaning 'right', 'correct' or 'best').[33] The first two relate to wisdom: *dṛṣṭi* ('view') and *saṃkalpa* ('resolve'). The next three concern morality and ethics (*śīla*): *vāc* ('speech'), *karmānta* ('action') and *ājīva* ('livelihood'). The final three pertain to meditation: *vyāyāma* ('effort'), *smṛti* (*sati* in Pāli; 'mindfulness') and *samādhi* ('concentration').

Each of these elements is a multifaceted jewel in itself, full of nuance and fine detail. Indeed, we explored both *sati* and *samādhi* as such in Chapter 1. However, ideally, one should not pick and choose individual elements, or even work through them sequentially. They are best embraced as a total package, a single path. A prominent symbol of this path is the *dhármacakrá* – a wheel in which the eight elements comprise the spokes. Following the *dhárma* means keeping this wheel turning, with all of the spokes in play all of the time.

In another sense, though, the two 'wisdom' elements are foundational, since we are unlikely to embark on this journey unless we have some understanding that it is necessary ('right view') and have the motivation to start walking ('right resolve'). Wisdom, then, is the ignition that sparks the *ashtangika* motor into life. It does *not* mean we know everything from the outset. Indeed, the pursuit of wisdom is never-ending. However, in the early stages of walking down the path, we need to have at least some understanding that continuing will be worthwhile.

Hopefully, you are already on your own path of wisdom, be it the *ashtangika*, the teachings of another religion, a school of philosophy, or even something you have devised largely on your own. Although I am concentrating on Buddhism, I do not wish to imply that this is the only valid path. The ways to liberation are manifold, and each of us follows whichever speaks to us personally.

Indeed, that is precisely why I have focused more on Buddhism than on other traditions: it happens to be the one that speaks most clearly to me, and which I have endeavoured to follow (however haphazardly) for the last twenty years. As such, it is the path that I feel most able to discuss with confidence, even though my knowledge of it is assuredly imperfect and incomplete. Hence, I shall return to it in the final two chapters. For the time being, though, we must turn westward.

Phrónēsis

Practical wisdom and knowledge

Of all the intellectual furnaces of the Axial age, few burned with as much intensity as classical Greece. Over a few short centuries, its scholars developed an astonishing body of thought that spanned everything from physics and medicine to politics and morality. Indeed, as we've seen many times over the course of the preceding chapters, their ideas are foundational building blocks of the modern human mind. Inevitably, Greek philosophers held a wide variety of views about wisdom, but these generally all sought to resolve one key question: if we wish to fulfil our potential and develop as people, how do we determine the best course of action?

For Aristotle, the answer was *phrónēsis*.[34] In contrast to *sophia*, which is rather abstract and theoretical, *phrónēsis* is a practical form of wisdom.[35] It means being able to judge which goals to pursue *and* the best means of achieving them. In particular, *phrónēsis* is crucial for a calculation that Aristotle regarded as essential to virtue and ethics: determining the *mésos* – literally the 'mean' or 'middle' – often better known as the 'golden mean'. The adjective 'golden' – implying a fundamental law that one is best advised to heed – may ring a bell. After all, we have already encountered the 'golden ratio' in the proportionality of *kairos* (Chapter 5) and the 'golden rule' in the reciprocity of *shù* (above). In this case, Aristotle argued that virtue resides in the middle ground between the opposing vices of excess and deficiency[36]: courage is the fine line between rashness and cowardice; generosity is the optimal point between profligacy and miserliness; and so on. This isn't a simplistic appeal to split the difference between two opposites. For instance, Aristotle didn't recommend navigating the tension between honesty and lying by being partially truthful. Rather, it means using *phrónēsis* to calibrate one's actions carefully on the basis of context.[37]

Hence, the best action may fall anywhere along the continuum between two poles. For example, the optimal degree of warmth to display towards a friend who has hurt you – and thus warrants gentle admonishment – differs from that which should be shown to a pal who is feeling down and needs cheering up. Similarly, with respect to courage, sometimes it is right to be bold and take risks, while on other occasions it is advisable to be cautious and refrain from taking action.

Many other philosophies offer analogous advice. For instance, the Buddha referred to his path as the 'middle way' – *madhyama mārga* – which involved, among other things, avoiding either punitive asceticism or indulgent sensuality.[38] There are secular varieties too, such as the Swedish *lagom*, which relates to doing something to just the 'right amount'.[39] In terms of fashionable Nordic philosophies, this may be fast superseding *hygge*.[40] Whichever name we give it, though, there are obviously great benefits to skilful and wise moderation.

Next, we remain in classical Greece and explore another

of its many gifts relating to wisdom – namely an esoteric approach to knowledge.

Gnôsis

Secret, esoteric wisdom

Fourteen miles north-west of Athens lies the ancient town of Eleusis. Although somewhat overlooked by tourists today, it was once one of the most important, and most mysterious, places in all of Greece. For here, nestled in the hills, an annual ritual took place – possibly from as far back as 1600 BCE – to which only select initiates were invited. This ceremony became known as the Eleusinian *mustérion*, with the latter term meaning a secret doctrine or truth (and the root of 'mystery'). It was shrouded in secrecy at the time, and to this day no one is certain what transpired. All we know is that it centred on the myth of Dēmētēr, the Greek goddess of the harvest, and her beautiful daughter Persephónē.

The legend tells of Persephónē's abduction by Háidēs, King of the Underworld, who had coveted her from afar. Dēmētēr was distraught and wandered the earth in search of her lost daughter, but her abandonment of her duties had dire consequences: the harvest failed and humanity was imperilled. Eventually, the crisis came to the attention of Zeus – not only King of the Gods but husband to Dēmētēr and father to Persephónē – who vowed to secure his daughter's release. Finally, Háidēs freed Persephónē and humanity's crops flourished once again. However, while in captivity, he had tricked Persephónē into eating six pomegranate seeds, an act that bound her to the underworld for ever. Consequently, she was obliged to return there for six months each year. During that time, Dēmētēr would sink back into sorrow, and no crops would bloom.

This extraordinary tale is a vivid origin myth for the cycle of the seasons. With customary imagination and insight, the Greeks created a compelling explanation for the earth's slumber each winter and miraculous rejuvenation each spring. Moreover, it was central to the Eleusinian mysteries, underpinning a transformative process that was granted to the initiates. For, it is believed that these select individuals experienced a form of death and resurrection in the course of their rituals. They would 'die' – not literally, of course, but symbolically and experientially – before returning to life, transformed. As such, they were initiated into *gnôsis*.

In conventional usage, *gnôsis* can simply mean 'knowledge'. But it also has connotations of *initiate* knowledge – levels of understanding to which only select people are granted access, usually because they are deemed worthy of receiving it. Such was the wisdom imparted to the Eleusinian initiates and other 'mystery cults' that flourished across the Hellenistic world and beyond. Indeed, most religions have their own gnostic traditions, veiled from the rank and file believers, reserved for the select few. More generally, secret knowledge has long been a feature of innumerable walks and domains of life. Perhaps you have been an initiate yourself ... or, alternatively, know that you have been kept out of the loop. If so, you'll surely appreciate the power of *gnôsis* as well as its potential pitfalls, such as the discomfort felt by those who are excluded.

With that, we must leave the world-shaping insights of the Axial age. But our story of the progress of wisdom and understanding is far from over. Indeed, the revelations and revolutions have continued throughout the centuries, although few can rival the one that occurred just over two millennia ago.

Et

The alpha and the omega (beginning and end)

The Hebrew word *et* (את) is used grammatically to identify a definite object (and, as a result, occurs more frequently than any other word in the language). For instance, it appears twice in the first line of the Torah: *'B'rasheet bara Elohim et HaShamayim v'et HaEretz.'* *Et* has no equivalent in English, so this sentence is literally translated as: 'In the beginning, God created את the heavens and את the earth.' However, while *et* may simply be serving its standard grammatical function here, some people believe it could also have much more powerful symbolic connotations. For its two letters – *aleph* (א) and *tav* (ת) – are the first and last of the Hebrew alphabet. As such, the term can imply both the beginning and the end of something – its creation and conclusion – in the same way that *alpha* and *omega* do (the first and last letters of the Greek alphabet).

This brings us to Christianity, for Jesus referred to himself as 'the *aleph* and the *tav*' (or 'the *alpha* and *omega*' in the Greek New Testament). To explain this nomenclature, many Christian writers drew on the Greek notion of *logos*, which literally means 'discourse', 'speech', 'reason', 'account' or, famously, 'word'. However, following the Greek philosopher Heraclitus

(535–475 BCE), this term also came to denote a divine plan that animates and pervades the *kosmos* (the universe as a complex, rational, orderly system). Hence the immortal opening lines of the Gospel of St John: 'In the beginning was the Word [*logos*], and the Word was with God, and the Word was God.'

By invoking *logos* and drawing on the philosophical lineage of the Axial age in this way, Christian writers such as John upheld a vision of the universe as sacred and full of wisdom. This is why Jesus' use of the appellation *et* is so significant. It encapsulates the whole alphabet, and so it symbolises the full realisation and expression of *logos*. Christ, therefore, is the earthly embodiment of *logos*. As John continued, 'The Word became flesh and made his dwelling among us.'[41] This constitutes a powerful salvational message. By engaging with *logos* – the 'word of God' and the Bible's 'good news' – believers could partake in this divine language.[42]

Perhaps you are religious yourself, or are even just open to the possibility that the universe may be animated by a wise, rational, purposeful spirit. If so, you probably have some appreciation of the power of concepts such as *et* and *logos*. The same could be said too of mathematicians.

Şifr

Absence, void, zero

The Arabic world has played a profoundly important role in shaping civilisation as we know it today. Understandably, histories of this region tend to highlight the epochal revelations of the Prophet Mohammed and the religion he founded. This makes sense, given his immense influence: Muslims now account for almost a quarter of the earth's population, some 1.6 billion people.[43] Perhaps less universally appreciated is that, at around the same time, other similarly revolutionary ideas were emerging that would likewise transform our understanding of the world. A prime example is *ṣifr*.

This is nothing less than the notion of zero, upon which all modern mathematics, science and technology is founded. As such, few concepts have been more pivotal in shaping the world we see around us today.[44] A number of Islamic scholars contributed to the formulation of *ṣifr* around the beginning of the ninth century CE, most notably the Persian mathematician Muhammad al-Khwarizmi, director of the House of Wisdom in Baghdad.[45] He also created algebra – a name adapted from *al-jabr*, a technique he developed to solve quadratic equations – and his work is the foundation of modern mathematics.

Al-Khwarizmi's theories marked the culmination of insights dating back more than two millennia. As early as 1700 BCE, an Egyptian hieroglyph, *nfr*, was used to denote occasions when items received and disbursed by the royal court cancelled each other out. Later, the Babylonians (around 300 BCE) and the Mayans (around 350 CE) employed similar symbols. However, these were mere placeholders rather than numbers – they simply denoted an absence, and could not be used in calculations. The first revolutionary shift occurred in fifth-century India, where the idea of zero as a *concept* was conceived (denoted by the term *sūnya*, literally meaning 'void' or 'space'). Then, in 628, the astronomer and mathematician Brahmagupta made a second crucial cognitive leap: he conceived of zero as a *number* and depicted it with a dot. By 773, his work had arrived in

Baghdad, where the likes of al-Khwarizmi and other scholars set about fine-tuning it. It was there that it became *ṣifr* (possibly an adaptation of *sūnya*).

Thereafter, its revolutionary power began to be harnessed, paving the way for modern mathematics. Given that this is among the most potent systems of knowledge we possess – the 'alphabet with whose aid God wrote the universe', as Galileo put it – the creation of *ṣifr* was a seminal moment. Thus, although the concept itself may seem rather abstract – with little direct relevance to our personal lives – it is one of the foundation stones of contemporary civilisation.

Moreover, aside from its mathematical importance, *ṣifr* is a potent symbol of intellectual endeavour, with far broader significance. Among other things, it reminds us that crucial dimensions of existence – the concept of zero in this instance – may remain unseen and unconceptualised until some pioneer, a Brahmagupta or al-Khwarizmi, has the foresight to notice and harness them. And that idea *is* directly relevant to us. What 'zero' are you overlooking in your life? What phenomena are you failing to notice but might capitalise upon to your benefit? In one sense, this whole book is devoted to helping you discover such phenomena by furnishing you with novel formulas and symbols that, like *ṣifr*, may enrich your understanding and experience of life.

With that, our brief, selective tour of the development of wisdom, from prehistory to the modern age, is almost complete. We just have time to explore two more cognitive revolutions that altered our conception of life, starting with the disconcerting insights of psychoanalysis.

Ego

The self, I-hood

In 1882, a young Austrian doctor began his medical career at Vienna General Hospital. His name was Sigmund Freud, and he would revolutionise our understanding of the human mind. In a nutshell, he radically challenged the prevailing view of our species as rational, clear-headed creatures who are fully in control of our actions and thoughts. In fact, he took a figurative sledgehammer to this confident, uncritical conception of humanity.

In its place, he revealed a shocking truth: we are riven by multifarious drives and biases of which we are scarcely aware. The mind is not a pristine engine of level-headed deliberation. Rather, it is a maelstrom of competing desires, many of which are motivated by the evolutionary necessity of fulfilling basic physiological needs. Sensationally, and almost immediately, humanity began to teeter precariously on the pedestal upon which it had placed itself.

Freud surely ranks as one of the most original and influential thinkers of all time. Not only did he invent an entirely new lexicon to communicate his ideas to other psychologists, but the terms he coined are now familiar to the general population around the world. That's not to say he owed no debt to previous and indeed contemporary thinkers. For instance, he drew extensively on Greek philosophy and mythology to explain his patients' psychological issues.[46] And considerable credit must go to James Strachey, Freud's English translator, whose renderings of the latter's terminology are the phrases that most of us know today. Caveats aside, however, ultimately it was Freud who gave us this new language for understanding ourselves.

His insights first emerged through his work with patients who were suffering from various psychological ailments, including the ubiquitous – if ill-defined – 'hysteria'. An early interest in hypnosis helped him appreciate the value of *freier Einfall* – 'free association' – a spontaneous, free-form sequence of thoughts. This technique revealed that his patients' utterances were driven by forces that lay somewhere below their conscious mind, inhabiting a realm that Freud called the *Unbewusste* – the 'unconscious'.

Armed with this insight, he began to explore the structure of the psyche and eventually identified a tripartite configuration. First, there is the energetic *id* – primeval, instinctive drives that originate in and surge from the unconscious. This battles against the strict, authoritarian voice of the *superego*, which forbids certain actions and encourages others on the basis of internalised cultural norms and rules. Finally, caught in the middle and constantly trying to negotiate a truce between the *id* and the *superego* is the bewildered *ego* – Freud's label for who we feel and experience ourselves to be.

Freud's meanings are a little clearer in the original German: the *id* is simply *Es* ('it'); the *ego* is *Ich* ('I'); and the *superego* is *Über-Ich* ('over-I'). Thus, for example, an instinctual *id*-driven desire that wells up inside is termed 'it' because it seems inexplicable and alien, a marauding interloper who is not part of the self (or *ego*) we understand ourself to be. A central task of psychoanalysis is therefore to help the patient make sense of such impulses and integrate them into their 'I'.

Some of the clarity of these vivid ideas was lost in Strachey's translation, which featured the Latin equivalents of these terms, possibly because he thought they conveyed more scientific authority than simple English translations. Nevertheless, terms like *ego* and 'unconscious' have entered the public consciousness in an astonishing way. The vast majority of us have surely employed these terms when trying to articulate the strange dynamics of our own selfhood and those of others. Thus, even if Freud's theories are no longer widely endorsed by current psychologists, his influence endures. All of us still see ourselves, to some extent at least, through his eyes.

While Freud focused on the mysterious workings of the human mind, another group of thinkers focused on an equally daunting task: to understand the nature of existence itself.

Geworfenheit

The existential condition of thrownness

Born in 1813, Søren Kierkegaard had a gloomy upbringing under the stern religious discipline of his father. But worse was to come. By the age of twenty-five, he had lost both parents and all but one of his seven siblings. Given this background, it is perhaps unsurprising that he developed a dark, foreboding perspective on life. Yet he also understood the vital power of resilience, faith and even hope in the face of the daunting forces of darkness. For Søren Kierkegaard was the father of a bracing new philosophy that came to be known as existentialism.

He viewed life as being pervaded by *Angst* (a German term meaning 'fear' or 'dread'), by which he did not mean fear of a specific terror, but general unease. He argued that this arises, in part, from the 'dizziness of freedom'[47] – the vertiginous notion that we are responsible for our own existence, the choices we make, the paths we choose. For each moment is suffused with potentially life-defining possibilities, and we cannot but act. Indeed, most existentialist discourse is concerned with this realisation that we are 'condemned to be free', as Jean-Paul Sartre put it,[48] and how best to cope with that burden (or, seen more positively, to maximise freedom's opportunities).

Martin Heidegger offered some intriguing suggestions. Such was his conceptual innovation that, like Freud, he fashioned an entirely new lexicon – including repurposing existing words in unconventional ways – in order to express his ideas. For a start, his preferred term for human beings was *Dasein* (literally, 'being there'), to imply that we always exist in a particular context.[49] Crucially, though, we rarely have much choice over those contexts; they are often thrust upon us. As such, the human condition is characterised by *Geworfenheit* – 'thrown-ness'. We perennially find ourselves thrown into situations that are not of our choosing – from the haphazard events that make up everyday life to more fundamental constraining factors, such as the place and time of our birth.[50] Yet, still, we must try to make the most of these circumstances.

And in doing so, rather than slavishly following the crowd – or *das Man* (literally, 'the they') – we should strive for *Eigentlichkeit* ('authenticity'). The existentialists' philosophical forebears, the Romantics, had framed this in terms of a quest to 'find' oneself, a notion that Jean-Jacques Rousseau first articulated in his autobiographical *Confessions* (published post-humously in 1782).[51] But it was only when Heidegger, Sartre and others refined the concept in the twentieth century that it became pivotal in creating the modern sense of self.[52] As with Freud – and indeed all of the thinkers and philosophies discussed in this chapter – we understand ourselves through the prism of their thought. Thus, surely all of us can appreciate the noble ideal of authenticity and striving to attain the truest version of ourselves.

Clearly, much more could be said about existentialism and indeed all the schools of thought we've encountered over the last few pages. However, I hope this brief discussion has managed to convey some of the sheer breadth of ideas relating to understanding that have been forged throughout the long evolution of humanity.

Next, we turn our attention to a similarly vast topic: the elevated peaks of spirituality. First, though, a short summary is in order.

Summary

This chapter has attempted to chart some of the key milestones in the development of human wisdom and understanding. These ideas not only helped form the modern mind but continue to have direct relevance for us today. We began with the Aboriginal concept of *aljerre-nge*, which spoke to the importance of honouring ancestral traditions and responsibilities. The mythological figure of *Enkidu* then symbolised the power of narrative, while the Zoroastrian god *Ahura Mazdā* highlighted life's dualism – the eternal conflict between light and dark – and the importance of aligning ourselves with the good.

Next, *mitzvah* represented the importance of ethical observance, while *shù* epitomised the golden rule of reciprocity. Our consideration of the *Tao* emphasised the importance of flowing harmoniously with life, while *dhárma* indicated the value of following a personal path and *ashtangika* served as a useful example of one such path. We then encountered the practical wisdom of *phrónēsis* and the secret knowledge of *gnôsis*. *Et* symbolised a cosmos that is imbued with reason and spirituality, while the conceptualisation of *ṣifr* showed the human mind's capacity to conceive of new dimensions of existence. Finally, we touched on the Freudian notion of *ego* and the existentialist concept of *Geworfenheit*, both of which have helped to shape contemporary ideas of selfhood.

With that, our selective whirlwind tour of the history of understanding is complete. Now we move into the rarefied air of spirituality.

CHAPTER EIGHT

Spirituality

Our path starts to wind upwards into more elevated territory as we broach the opaque notion of the sacred. At first glance, this mist-shrouded terrain seems daunting, even inaccessible. However, attempting the ascent should prove worthwhile. For most cultures acknowledge that one must cultivate some kind of spirituality in order to experience life's highest peaks. Hence, many of their most evocative words relate to this mysterious area.

These terms might seem challenging to some ears, given the long migration towards secularism and, indeed, atheism in many societies. Yet, they may help us redefine the term 'spirituality' itself and consequently increase its relevance to the modern world. For instance, atheists often resist the notion of spirituality because they feel it is inextricably linked to religion, but many cultures have conceptions of the sacred that are far removed from traditional theistic forms of religious observance.

That said, spirituality *has* been closely associated with religion throughout much of human history, to such an extent that they are still frequently regarded as synonymous.[1] Etymologically, 'spirituality' derives from the Latin *spiritualis* – itself an adaptation of the Greek *pneumatikós* – which implied being 'with' or 'of the spirit' of God.[2] This meant that the spirit dwelt *within* a spiritual person, or the person was at least receptive to that spirit. Often, only particularly devout sections of a religious community, such as the priesthood, were described as spiritual.

Correspondingly, the term 'religion' was coined to describe the social institutions that coalesced around these revered spiritual teachers.[3] It entered the English language in the twelfth century, via French, from the Latin *religio*, which possibly derived from *religare* – 'to bind' – and conveyed obligation and reverence.[4] Thus, religious people were 'bound together' by a common form and focus of reverence. Initially, this usually meant the members of monastic orders, but it eventually came to signify the community of the faithful more generally.[5]

Many people still view religion and spirituality as being intertwined, as noted above, perhaps with the former pertaining to their spiritual community and the latter to their personal experience of God. For others, though, the two terms are not necessarily enmeshed. Such people may have parted ways from a traditional religion, yet still feel themselves drawn to spirituality.[6] This is reflected in a modern definition of the latter term as 'something individuals define for themselves that is largely free of the rules, regulations and responsibilities associated with religion'.[7]

Whatever 'spirituality' means to you, the entries in this

chapter may help you increase your understanding of it. And your wellbeing might benefit too, since a burgeoning corpus of empirical research shows the importance of spirituality to personal development and fulfilment.[8]

However, before we proceed, we need to address an important question: if the concept of spirituality is so malleable, what makes it cohere as a theme? The answer may lie in the notion of the sacred. In one way or another, most of the terms discussed below revolve around this concept. They fall into four distinct categories: first, notions of the sacred as an *overarching power* that exists outside human beings, possibly embodied in a divine being or beings; second, words that describe a sacred dimension *within people themselves*, as conveyed by English terms such as 'soul' and 'spirit'; third, *spiritual practices* that are designed to bring people into contact with the sacred; and, finally, consequent *self-transcendence*, when people overcome their usual self-imposed restrictions and experience a connection with the sacred.

We'll discuss each of these four themes in turn. First, though, let's consider what we mean by the 'sacred' itself.

Sacer

Sacred, hallowed, set apart

Among everything you own, which items are most precious to you? An heirloom, passed down through the generations; an old photo of your parents; the comfort blanket that you or your child clutched in infancy? Such objects are intriguing. Their value not only exceeds their ostensible material worth but is, in effect, incalculable. If they were lost, you couldn't simply buy a replacement. Nor would you casually repurpose them. For instance, you would never dream of using the comfort blanket to clean the kitchen because, to you, it is so much more than a piece of cloth. Such objects are suffused with memories, imbued with meaning and significance. They are vessels of love, connections to those we hold most dear. As such, it would not be inaccurate to call them 'sacred'.

This term derives from the Latin word *sacer* and arrived in the English lexicon via French in the twelfth century. *Sacer* had a variety of meanings, but all related to being 'set apart' in some way – outside the normal human realm. Hence, in ancient Rome, it was not always a positive term: it could be used to signal that something was horrible or detestable. Increasingly, however, it came to imply a close connection to God: a holy, hallowed or consecrated place, object or person. Indeed, this was the standard definition when it entered English along with a host of other Latinate words with the same stem, such as *sacrifus* ('sacrifice'), which combined *sacer* with the verb *faciō* ('to make' or 'to do') to denote a holy offering to God.[9]

Above all though, *sacer* meant 'set apart'. But from what? This brings us to a significant antonym – 'profane' – from the Latin *profanus*, which originally meant 'outside the temple'. If the temple is isolated, hallowed ground where God's spirit dwells, the profane must be the rest of the world – everything from the noise of the market place to the mess of the kitchen. Such ideas occur in most religious traditions. Moreover, the distinction is not only spatial. It can be configured temporally, with certain times reserved for worship. We see this in the Hebrew concept of *Shabbat* – anglicised as 'Sabbath' – which sets aside one day each week for rest, contemplation and religious observance.

Although many people continue to link the term 'sacred' to divine beings, and to religious ideas and practices, more generally it has come to signify any phenomenon, object or experience that is qualitatively out of the ordinary and cherished. Hence, it is now almost synonymous with 'mystical' and 'numinous', and (relatedly) is frequently used to evoke feelings of awe or to convey the profundity of existence, as we saw with *yūgen* (see Chapter 6). But also, it can simply refer to something that one holds dear, such as an old comfort blanket. Whatever meaning it has for you, I hope that some of the entries in this chapter will resonate.

Our first broad theme is the notion of an external spiritual power, realm and/or being(s) that exist outside or around human experience. This encompasses various conceptions of the sacred, such as animism, polytheism, panentheism and pantheism, each of which we'll explore in turn. We begin, appropriately enough, by once again peering back to the dawn of humanity.

Vættir

Nature spirits

The earliest conceptions of the sacred are usually grouped under an overarching label coined by nineteenth-century anthropologists: 'animism', from the Latin *anima* (literally, 'soul', 'breath' or 'life'). This word was chosen because animists generally believe that spirits breathe life into every bird and animal, every plant and tree, even every stretch of water and rock. Literally *everything* is alive, invigorated by a unique soul, just as humans are.

Animist beliefs defined countless cultures around the world far into prehistory.[10] Indeed, animism was probably the dominant mode of cognition among the social groups that started to coalesce some sixty thousand years ago or even earlier. It's understandable that these early societies reached the conclusion that every natural phenomenon must possess some sort of consciousness and soul, given that humans themselves were just starting to acquire cognisance of their own thoughts, feelings, agency and volition. After all, a rushing river, full of energy and caprice, must have seemed no less alive than the person who bathed in it.[11]

Hence, their world was truly 'enchanted', as Max Weber put it.[12] It was brimming with spirits, agency and significance. Moreover, humans felt compelled to engage with these spirits, whether in gratitude for their apparent benevolence, to placate them after causing some sort of offence, or in the hope of future good grace and fortune. In short, our ancestors viewed the earth as a deeply spiritual place.

But this is not an exclusively ancient perspective, consigned to the prehistory of humanity. Even today, people continue to incorporate elements of animism in their personal credos. Consider the mythology of the Norse. While these Scandinavian legends were millennia in the making, they were not transcribed until the eleventh century CE. Ever since, they have comprised a living, breathing, animistic belief system for the people of the region.

Norse mythology is populated by a multitude of *vættir* – wights or 'nature spirits' – including *landvættir* ('land spirits'), *vatnavættir* ('water spirits') and *sjövættir* ('sea spirits'). Each such spirit is connected to a specific location, like a particular river or forest, which they guard and infuse with their presence. In addition, other mystical beings, such as *ljósálfar* ('light elves') and *dǫkkálfar* ('dark elves'), roam the earth on the edge of human perception. And, to reiterate the point above, this is a mythology that continues to have meaning and resonance. Iceland still celebrates four *landvættir* – *Dreki* the dragon in the east; *Gammur* the griffin to the north; *Griðungur* the bull in the west; and *Bergrisi* the giant of the south – on its coat of arms. Perhaps more surprisingly, the country's officials have also been known to assess the potential impact on *vættir* habitats when debating urban planning proposals.[13] Like many of their fellow Icelanders, they continue to find the world enchanting.

We can all glean inspiration from this perspective. There's no need to be Icelandic or a committed animist to do so. And you certainly do not have to regard natural phenomena as *literally* vitalised by spirits. Instead, you might prefer to think of them as alive in a more poetic, figurative sense of the word, and consequently precious and worthy of respect. Personally, I don't perceive rivers or trees as possessing a divine soul per se, but I still regard them as sacrosanct, and endeavour to treat them with care.

Thus, even in the twenty-first century, animism can still speak to us and broaden our perspective on life. The same may be said of another aspect of Norse mythology. For the Scandinavians' sophisticated lore is not *wholly* animistic. It also boasts a pantheon of legendary gods: Odin, Thor, Loki and many others. This brings us neatly to our next conception of the sacred: polytheism.

Gaia

Primordial Mother Earth

In the late 1960s, James Lovelock was looking for a name for his new scientific theory of 'atmospheric homeostasis by and for the biosphere'[14] – that is, the earth's dynamic ability to perpetuate the conditions it needs to maintain viability as a living planet. This involved a radical reconceptualisation of what might constitute a living organism, for Lovelock argued that the earth, in its entirety, is one such organism. Of course, it is home to trillions of other organisms – from bacteria to giant redwoods – but it is also a living being unto itself.

Although this was a revolutionary concept in the context of modern science, it is an ancient notion. Throughout history, most cultures have regarded the earth as animate or sacred in one way or another. Indeed, Lovelock found the name for his theory in one of those cultures: 'Gaia', the primordial goddess of the earth and 'mother' of all living things in Greek mythology.

As awe-inspiring as the notion of Gaia may be though, the Greeks never felt that all the wonders of the world and the universe could be attributed to just one deity. Indeed, they envisaged three separate generations of divinities, spanning aeons, as detailed in epics such as Hesiod's *Theogony* (written around 700 BCE), which outlined their genealogy.[15] First came the Prōtógonos ('first-born'), a primeval triad of creative forces that fashioned all existence. In the beginning was Kháos – the void that preceded the cosmos. The cosmos then came into being through the union of Gaia and Ouranus, the deities of earth and heaven. Moreover, together they created the second generation of twelve Titânes, including such primordial powers as Mnemosyne – the personification of memory and mother of the Muses. However, the Titânes were subsequently overthrown in a mighty battle by the twelve Olympian gods, so-called because they convened on Mount Olympus. The latter deities were contemporaneous with the Greek people and exerted a powerful influence on their daily lives. Their names are still legendary – Zeus (god of the sky and the supreme deity), Poseidôn (god of the sea), Háidēs (god of the under-world), Dēmētēr (goddess of the harvest) and so on.

Perhaps the most important aspect of Greek polytheis-tic mythology is the way in which it casts these deities in intricate narratives to explain the mysteries of existence. For instance, in Chapter 7 we saw how a tale involving Dēmētēr and Persephónē was used to account for the changing sea-sons. Similarly, human characteristics such as memory and desire were personified as deities, who were then deployed in an extraordinarily rich anthology of stories that served to enhance the ancient Greeks' understanding of the human condition.

Moreover, *we* have all been influenced by these narratives, as countless familiar words and concepts have their origins in the fertile Greek imagination. We've already seen how 'memory' and 'music' derive from the mythical figures of Mnemosyne and the Muses, respectively (see Chapter 5). Or consider the tale of Tantalus, for instance, who was condemned to stand for ever beneath a bough of delicious fruit that always just eluded his reach, from which we get the word 'tantalising'. Hence, I'd encourage you to delve into these timeless stories, as they still provide valuable insights into why we think and behave as we do.

By now, though, you may be wondering how polytheism differs from animism. Well, the principal distinction relates to the level of abstraction. As we have seen, in animism, all life is pervaded by spirits. By contrast, in polytheism, the deities are somewhat removed from the phenomena they represent, existing in another realm. Although they exert a powerful influence over the earth – for instance, an angry Poseidôn might shake his trident and generate a tidal wave – they are fundamentally transcendent. Which brings us to panentheism.

Brahman

Transcendent and immanent supreme spirit

Our spiritual journey now leads us to the Indian subcontinent and the mystical notion of *Brahman*. This is a central feature of the sacred vision that is expressed in the *Upaniṣads* – Sanskrit texts that are among the foundational works of what is now called Hinduism – composed between 1500 and 500 BCE.[16] Hundreds of millions of people still adhere to this great body of wisdom, also known as *Vedānta*.[17] But *Brahman* is fascinating not merely because of its venerable age and enduring, extensive influence.

Of greater relevance here is that *Brahman* is one of the earliest examples of a doctrine known as panentheism, which revolves around the notion of one all-encompassing divinity (in contrast to the multiple deities of animism and polytheism). However, panentheism is not synonymous with monotheism, in which a unitary God is separate from 'His' creation, as in Christianity. With panentheism, the divinity is immanent.

Hence, *Brahman* is immersed within the cosmos. Indeed, it *is* the cosmos.

In addition to being immanent, though, *Brahman* is also transcendent. So, it is both *of* the cosmos and simultaneously *outside* it. The etymology of 'panentheism' helps to clarify this complex concept. It combines the Greek terms *pān*, *en* and *theó*, and thus means 'all in god', and was coined by Karl Krause in 1828 to differentiate it from 'pantheism', which simply means 'all god'. With the latter concept – as we shall explore in the next entry – the cosmos and the divine are one, so the divine is immanent but not transcendent (that is, it doesn't exist other than as the cosmos).

By contrast, as an exemplar of panentheism, *Brahman* suffuses and interpenetrates all existence, but *also* transcends it by standing apart. That said, at the risk of complicating an already labyrinthine picture, *Vedānta* could also be construed as *polytheistic* – depicting the cosmos as the playground of a pantheon of deities.[18] It's hardly surprising that such a vast body of teachings, which was supplemented repeatedly over many centuries, encompasses a range of theologies. Nevertheless, *Vedānta* does attempt to identify a unifying force beneath the multiplicity and flux of life – which it called *Brahman* – so it is reasonable to view it as one of the first instances of panentheism.

Today, many people might see these ideas as rather arcane, with little or no relevance to their lives. However, as with animism and polytheism, panentheistic perspectives have the power to inspire and subtly transform our view of existence. It's all too easy to hold rigid, clichéd ideas about the sacred, such as picturing God as an old, bearded man who lives somewhere beyond the stars. Such notions almost invite scepticism and consequent rejection of *all* religion and spirituality. By contrast, reflecting upon a concept like *Brahman* – a divine creative power that suffuses the cosmos but resides outside it – has the potential to open us up to new ways of contemplating sacredness.

Our final perspective on the divine – pantheism – has similar mind-expanding potential.

Natura naturans

Nature as a divine, creative process

Rabbi Herbert S. Goldstein once asked Albert Einstein whether he believed in God. His subtle response has passed into legend: 'I believe in Spinoza's God, who reveals himself in the orderly harmony of what exists, not in a God who concerns himself with the fates and actions of human beings.'[19] But who is Spinoza's God?

Baruch Spinoza was born in Amsterdam in 1632 to a Jewish family that had recently fled persecution in Portugal. As an adult, he made his living as a lens-grinder before dying at the age of forty-four. Yet, in the course of his short life, he became one of the pioneers of rationalism and helped lay the foundations for the Enlightenment. Indeed, by the age of twenty-three, he had already published critiques of the Bible and the nature of God that were so incendiary that the Portuguese Synagogue in Amsterdam felt compelled to issue a *herem* against him – equivalent to Christian excommunication. Later, his works were also placed on the Catholic Church's List of Prohibited Books.

So, what did he write that so enraged the religious

authorities of the day? His critics often accused him, simply, of atheism. But his perspective was much more nuanced than a straightforward rejection of the divine. In fact, he is now regarded as one of the first proponents of pantheism: the view that God and the cosmos are indivisible. This conclusion rested on the concept of *substantia* – namely, something that is capable of self-subsistence. For Spinoza, there was only one substance in the universe: God. Consequently, there was nothing outside God. Here, he employed the Latin phrase *natura naturans* – 'nature naturing'. God is nothing more or less than the dynamic process of creation – nature unfurling in all its glory.

In Spinoza's day, it would have been nearly unthinkable – regardless of one's personal perspective – not to invoke God when discussing the universe. Since then, however, numerous thinkers have endorsed his theory of pantheism without reference to a theistic being. In this modern sense of the term, the cosmos itself is regarded as divine – a sacred process. Hence Einstein's reference to 'the orderly harmony of what exists'. Many contemporary scientists and philosophers share this view. They may not believe in God, per se, but the awe they feel for the universe may come close to religious devotion. For instance, Richard Dawkins – a prominent atheist – has spoken approvingly of 'Einstein's God', which he defines as 'the laws of nature which are so deeply mysterious that they inspire a feeling of reverence'.[20] Moreover, we humans are not only part of *natura naturans*, but are conscious of the fact. Thus, through our minds, nature is becoming aware of itself.

This intriguing notion leads us to the next stage of our spiritual journey, as we start to explore the sacred within ourselves.

Qì

The breath of spirit

In Genesis 2:7, we are told: 'The Lord God formed man of the dust of the ground, and breathed into his nostrils the breath of life.' Thus, spirit and breath are inextricably linked in Judaism and Christianity, as they are in countless other traditions around the world. Indeed, the word 'spirit' derives from the Latin *spiritus* – 'breath'. This is entirely appropriate, given the centrality of breath to life itself. In a very real sense, to be animated by breath is to live.

These ideas echo across languages, from *qì* in Chinese to *prāṇā* in Sanskrit, terms that are sometimes rendered in English as a vitilising 'life force'.[21] Modern science tends to leap on the supernatural or mystical implications of that phrase before dismissing the notion itself. But one need not interpret *qì* and *prāṇā* in this way. Even when one understands the physiological mechanics of respiration, the idea of a 'life force' seems rather more than a mere metaphor. Of all our physiological processes, breathing is probably the one that is most associated with life itself.

The spiritual significance of terms like *qì* is not limited to their centrality to life. Over the centuries, various traditions have developed techniques to help people work with their breath. We've already touched on this in relation to *sati* and the mindfulness of breathing (see Chapter 1). But *qì* is not only about the breath. In Chinese medicine and philosophy, it is regarded as a suprapersonal 'force' or 'energy'. It flows through us, and we can even use it to our advantage, but it is not contained within or defined by us. (By contrast, the breath is a product of our body and cannot exist apart from it.) For instance, *qì chang* denotes an energy 'field' that operates between or around people.

Numerous methods have been devised to harness *qì*. For instance, *qì gōng* (literally, '*qì* work') includes a focus on the body's *dān tián* ('energy centres'), which are believed to be significant routing points in currents of *qì*. Similarly, martial arts such as *aikido* (literally, the 'way of *qì*', as *ki* is the Japanese cognate of *qì*) are based on a mastery of *qì*. In a more therapeutic vein, *reiki* practitioners endeavour to heal their patients by 'laying hands'– usually without touching the skin – to 'direct' the flow of *qì*.

You may have possibly felt these mysterious currents of energy flowing within you, without necessarily knowing how to harness them. This is why spiritual practices that can help us tap into them are so valuable. We shall explore more of these later, as numerous cultures have developed techniques that increase our access and connection to the sacred. First, though, we need to look deep into the human soul.

Akh

The composite, enduring soul

Returning to Genesis 2:7, once 'man' received the spirit (or 'breath of life') from God, he 'became a living soul'. This curious phrasing suggests that humans possess not only a spirit but also a soul, and that these are two distinct, separate entities. Moreover, it implies that the latter can in some way exist outside the living human body.

These strange meanings are reflected in the term's roots. It is thought to derive from the Proto-Germanic word *saiwala*, meaning 'of the sea'. This etymology seemingly relates to the idea that, according to ancient northern European mythologies, some essence of personhood dwelt in the sea both prior to birth and after death.[22] We are moving into esoteric, metaphysical terrain here. But is it not possible that some vital aspect of what makes us 'us' might exist beyond the horizons of mortal life?

To say that modern science has a problem with these notions and possibilities is something of an understatement. But should we take that scepticism as cast-iron proof that the soul does not exist? Many people, including some eminent scientists, think not. Indeed, a fascinating field of research known as parapsychology (or noetic science)[23] has emerged to investigate phenomena that lie outside the paradigms of conventional science. These include the possibility that consciousness – which is, perhaps, a modern way of thinking of the soul – is not dependent on the body, as tentatively seems to be suggested by 'out-of-body' experiences. Such notions are, to some extent, supported by a degree of empirical evidence that cannot simply be dismissed as flawed methodology, fraud or chance.[24]

Hence, we should not dismiss the possibility of the soul just yet, not least because it has occupied a central role in so many cultures and traditions. Unsurprisingly, some languages have developed a particularly rich lexicon in this regard. For instance, the ancient Egyptians had a complex theory of the soul which comprised three main elements – the *ka*, *ba* and *akh*. The first of these was akin to the spirit, the animating principle that distinguished a living body from a dead one. In an allusive echo of Genesis, it was thought that a deity – in this case the goddess Meskhenet – breathed *ka* into a recipient in order to turn them into a sentient being. *Ba* then represented that being's personality or character – the attributes that made them unique. Finally, *akh* was the enduring soul, which would be reanimated in the afterlife when *ka* and *ba* reunited.

This tripartite soul was further augmented by various aspects of personhood, including *ib*, *ren* and *sheut*. *Ib* was the physical and metaphysical heart – the person's emotional centre, their locus of passion and motivation. *Ren* was their unique name, which was believed to have magical properties they needed to live. Indeed, the ancient Egyptians thought that a person did not truly exist until they had received their *ren*, and moreover that they would continue to exist as long as it was invoked after death – hence the importance they placed on recalling the names of the deceased. Less is known about *sheut* – 'shadow' – although it seems to have been considered a companion of the soul that could in some form be detached from it.

Clearly, then, although people have conceptualised the sacred spark within themselves in a variety of ways, most of these notions relate to either the 'spirit' or the 'soul'. Some ideas are not so easily categorised, however.

Anātman

The insubstantiality and ephemerality of the self

A curious phrase recurs in *Vedānta* teachings in relation to the all-encompassing power of *Brahman*: *tat tvam asi*. This is often translated, opaquely, as 'thou art that'.[25] In other words, the inner essence of the person – the soul, perhaps, or *ātman* in Sanskrit – is of the same order as *Brahman*. Remember, the concept of *Brahman* is an example of panentheism: as well as transcending the cosmos, this divine power also interpenetrates every aspect of it … including human beings. Thus, in some ineffable way, we ourselves are divine.

This philosophy is known as *ádvaita* ('non-dual'), since *ātman* and *Brahman* are not separate entities but are ultimately one.[26] If *Brahman* were an infinite ocean and I were a drop of water within it, I might be minuscule in comparison, but I am nevertheless part of the totality. Or, if *Brahman* were a great fire, I might be a spark, flickering briefly to life. In *Vedānta*, liberation comes from realising this oneness through personal experience.

This was the spiritual and metaphorical context into which the Buddha was born some 2,500 years ago. Like the Brahmanic preachers around him, he held out the promise of liberation – *nirvāṇa*. Yet, his teaching was revolutionary and different, not least because, whereas *Vedānta* spoke of the *ātman*, the Buddha spoke of *anātman*. The prefix *an* equates to 'non-' in English. So, if *ātman* describes the soul, or inner self, *anātman* evokes the elusive notion of *non*-soul or *non*-self!

According to the Buddha, *anātman* is the first of three *lakṣaṇa*s – inherent characteristics of existence – and it applies to *everything*. No phenomenon – be it a person, a mountain or an idea – can exist in a self-determined and self-supporting way. Rather, everything is continually brought into existence through other phenomena. Consider a whirlpool in a river. It is created by the temporary interactions of water flow, river bed and rock formation. It does not and cannot exist in isolation from these. I couldn't venture down to the river with a bucket, collect the whirlpool and take it home. Similarly, people are formed by the shifting play of circumstance, with no fixed essence. This is not some nihilistic denial of our very existence, it's vital to add. It's just that our personhood is not permanently engraved somewhere inside us. It is a dynamic, kaleidoscopic product of all our encounters with other people, situations, events, the whole world around us, and it does not exist outside these interactions.

The second *lakṣaṇa* is *anitya*, often rendered as 'imperma-nence' – a theme we explored in relation to *mono no aware* (see Chapter 6). This conveys the notion that all phenomena are ephemeral, subject to change and, eventually, dissolution.[27] Alter any element in the river – the direction of the current, the depth, the configuration of the rocks – and the whirlpool will disappear. Similarly, every human being is in a state of continual flux. With a few exceptions, most of our cells are replaced repeatedly throughout life, some as frequently as every couple of days. We are like Plutarch's Ship of Theseus, of which a substitute had to be made for every single component in the course of a long voyage. So, by the time it reached its destination, was it the same ship? Likewise, in ten years' time, will I be the same person?

Such questions can be unnerving, but the Buddha provided some solace to his followers by approaching them from a dif-ferent angle. In his teachings, the third *lakṣaṇa* is suffering or dissatisfaction: *duḥkha*. Therefore, he believed that it is just as prevalent as the first two *lakṣaṇa*. However, he taught that *duḥkha* is generated by our habitual denial of *anātman* and *anitya*, so it can be attenuated if we are able to change our ways. This means ceasing to covet and rigidly attach to people, objects and ideas in the hope that they will never change, because, invariably, they do. This isn't an ethic of cold detachment, I hasten to add. It doesn't mean that we cannot or should not love and be loved. Indeed, as we saw in Chapter 4, the loving-kindness of *mettā* is at the very heart of Buddhism. At the same time though, it teaches that liberation from *duḥkha* does also involve the cultivation of a deep understanding – and ultimately acceptance – of *anitya* and *anātman*.

This can be a very long and arduous road, though. So the Buddha – and other teachers – developed techniques to make the going a little easier.

Vipassanā

Awareness, clear seeing, insight

Throughout history, and across cultures, people have engaged in a multitude of contemplative practices in the hope of establishing or improving contact with the sacred – from prayers to chanting, rituals to reflection. Such is the dizzying variety of these practices that Roberto Cardoso and his colleagues came up with a helpful classification system in which they can be assessed on the basis of four parameters.[28] First, 'behaviours of the mind': in cognitive terms, the nature of the contemplation. Second, 'object': its focus. Third, 'attitude': the emotional tone of the experience. Finally, 'form': how the body engages in the practice. We shall encounter each of these parameters over these next four entries, starting here with behaviours of the mind.

Firstly then, contemplative practices differ in terms of their deployment of the practitioner's psychological resources, or how the mind 'behaves'. Buddhism, for instance, distinguishes between *śamatha* and *vipassanā* forms of meditation. The former involves focused attention: concentration at length on a stimulus.[29] You may have tried this in the form of 'mindfulness of breathing' exercises. If so, you'll know that you sit quietly, attending to the rise and fall of your breath, perhaps counting as this occurs, or fixing your attention on a specific part of the body, such as the deep, rhythmic movement of the diaphragm.

There are many ways to experience *śamatha*. Indeed, to an extent, almost everyone practises it from time to time, even if unwittingly. For it could be defined as any prolonged period of highly focused attention – from a parent gazing adoringly at their newborn baby to an angler watching his line for a nibble. Some attentive people may be naturally able to do this effortlessly for hours on end. But most of us know that the human mind has a tendency to wander off like a capricious child and chase bright lights or seductive trains of thought. That is why so many people find it helpful to attend an organised class and practise the mindfulness of breathing: it teaches us how to concentrate by quietening the mind and ignoring distractions.

And, once this point is reached and the meditator's attention has 'stabilised', they may then choose to move into a state of *vipassanā*. At this point, they cease to fix upon a stimulus (such as the breath) and 'open' their mind. Therefore, in marked contrast to focused attention, *vipassanā* involves an expansive awareness, excluding nothing. The practitioner is alive to everything they perceive – thoughts, feelings, sensations, sounds – but in an unusual way. They are curious, but not fixated; inquisitive, but not invested. Think of the mind as a bright blue sky through which thoughts and emotions pass like clouds. They are not the same as the sky, nor can they sully it. So, if a self-critical thought hoves into view, rather than automatically accepting it as fact, the meditator ideally stands back and watches it pass through and then out of their mind, like a dark cloud disappearing over the horizon.

The ultimate aim of *vipassanā* is increased understanding of the nature of the mind and existence more generally. Indeed, its literal meaning is 'clear seeing',[30] especially in relation to the *lakṣaṇas* – *anātman*, *anitya* and *duḥkha*. If this is achieved, the end result may be self-transcendence and liberation, as we shall see below. First, though, let's consider the second aspect of contemplative practice: the object of attention.

Druptap

Advanced meditation practices

The Tibetan plateau is home to an esoteric branch of Buddhism that took root in the eighth century CE. Known as *Vajrayāna* in Sanskrit – the 'way of the diamond or thunderbolt' – or *Tantra*, this tradition has developed a wealth of advanced meditation exercises. In Tibetan, these are collectively known as *druptap*, and are reserved for select initiates. In that sense, they could be seen as a form of *gnôsis* (see Chapter 7). Key among them are *lha'i rnal 'byor* – 'deity meditation practices'.

Their details are well guarded, for they are deeply personal, tailored to specific worthy practitioners. But they all involve a skilled act of introspection, in which the practitioner imagines interacting with – or even being – a divinity or divinities of the

Tibetan Buddhist pantheon. These include Ö-pa-me, a deity of infinite light and the creator of Dewachen, a celestial pure land akin to heaven.

Some readers might be surprised to hear of such practices, since Buddhism is frequently portrayed as non-theistic. But several of its branches do feature divinities, even if their onto-logical status is a matter of debate. One could, for example, construe them as inner psychological potentials – perfect versions of ourselves – rather than external beings. Whatever their precise nature, though, they are among the most power-ful objects of contemplation.

And these are joined by a wide variety of powerful contem-plative foci across the spiritual traditions. Turning inwards, one might attend to one's subjective experience, such as phys-iological sensations, as in the mindfulness of breathing. Or one might contemplate an idea. For instance, Zen masters have devised a number of strange, unanswerable riddles known as *kōan*, including the famous 'What is the sound of one hand clapping?' These defy logical analysis, so they help the med-itator 'cut through' rational thought. After months or even years of focusing on them, the practitioner may finally break through to psychospiritual liberation.

Alternatively, the gaze can be directed outwards, perhaps towards a religious icon. These powerful objects of veneration can be full of meaning. For instance, Hindu and Buddhist iconography feature elaborate, symbolic postures and hand gestures known as *mudra*s. A prime example is the *abhay-amudrâ* – in which the fingers point upwards with the palm facing outwards – which signifies fearlessness and protection. A meditator might also fixate on a *mandala* – an intricate geometric symbol that represents the cosmos from a spiritual perspective. Or they could concentrate on a sound, perhaps that they generate vocally themselves. In that respect you may be familiar with *aum* – the sacred Sanskrit syllable that various traditions regard as the primordial cosmic sound, the *alpha* and *omega* of everything.

Whatever is contemplated during meditation, though, one's emotional state in the practice also matters. This leads us to the third of our four parameters of contemplation: 'attitude'.

Hallelujah

God be praised

I have long been spellbound by the way the Christian Church has managed to harness the power of music and song. Take 'Amazing Grace'. There are many different versions of this hymn, from the stirringly euphoric to the softly devastating, but each one can transport me to a higher realm while a frisson of electricity surges through my body. At those special moments, I am perhaps granted a glimpse of what pure faith must feel like.

It seems that no word captures the emotional force of this sensation better than the Hebrew term *hallelujah*. It was originally used as a declaration of devotion and gratitude towards God, with *hallelu* meaning 'give praise' and Yah one rendering of the Judaic deity (alongside YHVH and Yahweh).[31] Later, Christians adopted it to express their own heartfelt thanks for God's grace. To this day, it remains a central motif of worship across both traditions, with the capacity to transport the faithful into elevated emotional states, as exemplified by gospel singing.

Moreover, its resonance extends far beyond the walls of synagogues and churches. Consider Leonard Cohen's great secular hymn. Such is the emotive force of his 'Hallelujah' that entire books have been devoted to the original recording and the countless cover versions, above all the epochal iteration by Jeff Buckley.[32] It is a paean to the terrifying power of love, which can raise us to the heavens, yet also crush us in despair (as we saw with *duende* in Chapter 6). Thus, it can be heard without a religious dimension, but it can also still open a door to the sacred. The audience at a packed concert may not be praising the Lord as they sing along to Cohen's lyrics, but they are surely expressing sincere devotion to *something* – love, human connection, maybe even life itself?

Many other traditions have similarly evocative words for the emotions that accompany spiritual contemplation. For instance, Tibetan Buddhism features an exercise called *tonglen*, which has echoes of the *mettā bhāvana* – the cultivation of loving-kindness (see Chapter 4). *Tonglen*, though, involves both sending *and* receiving. Practitioners visualise breathing in the sufferings of others – in effect, inhaling a noxious cloud of distress – to relieve those people of their burdens. This may seem daunting, but it is not viewed as an act of self-flagellation or martyrdom. Driven by great love, the meditator incinerates the suffering in the furnace of their own heart. It is then transmuted into compassion and happiness, which the practitioner breathes out and transmits back to those in need.

They may often perform this act of spiritual alchemy while sitting cross-legged on a meditation mat. However, acts of contemplation can take many physical forms.

Tai chi

A graceful, balletic martial art

I vividly remember the first time I visited a public park in China. On a balmy spring evening, my colleagues and I left the bustling streets and entered an expanse of lush, spacious greenery. Our students had told us that such parks were hives of activity and community, and how right they were! In one courtyard, dozens of couples of all ages were waltzing. Nearby, there was a bank of open-air pool tables, and a huge crowd had gathered around a karaoke machine. Most intriguing of all, a large group of older adults were moving slowly and silently in graceful unison, as if collectively guided by unseen hands. It was my first encounter with *tai chi*.

Contemplative practice is usually associated with serene motionlessness: the meditator adopts the lotus position then ideally remains basically static for the next half hour or more (allowing for some restless fidgeting!). However, the spirit doesn't reside solely in the mind, and our bodies are more than mobile supports for our heads. We are *whole* beings, so our bodies have a vital role to play whenever we try to connect with the sacred. Hence, the fourth parameter that allows us to differentiate between the world's numerous contemplative practices is 'form': the physical nature of the technique. For the body can be harnessed in a variety of ways to access the higher dimensions of human experience.

One of those ways, *tai chi*, translates as 'supreme force or energy', and is one of a corpus of practices that aim to tap into the aforementioned *qì*. Practitioners learn extended sequences of slow, graceful movements that allow them to work with the body's energy currents. Particular attention is paid to the subtle dynamics of balance and the transference of weight during movement, which is one reason why it is so beneficial for older people.[33] The movements may also be incorporated into a martial art called *tai chi ch'uan* (the latter term means 'fist'). Collectively, such arts are known as *gōng fu* (anglicised as kung fu), many of which are well known in the West, from *jūdō* to *aikidō*.

Indeed, Western cultures seem to be increasingly enamoured of dynamic forms of contemplative practice. Consider the widespread enthusiasm for *yoga*, which rivals mindfulness in ubiquity. Actually, most Westerners practise just one branch of *yoga* – *hatha* – which is often erroneously portrayed in their cultures as the *only* branch.[34] This centres on adopting a sequence of *āsana* (physical poses that often entail deep muscular stretching), linked by *vinyāsa* (the dynamic transitions between those poses). *Hatha's* ultimate goal reflects the etymology of the term *yoga* itself – 'to yoke' or 'bind together' – as the idea is to unite body, mind and spirit. The other branches include *karma* (selfless service), *jñāna* (pursuit of knowledge) and *bhakti yoga* (devotion and care), but *hatha* is perhaps the supreme example of paying detailed attention to physical form during contemplation.

With that, we conclude our brief tour of contemplative practice and its wide range of techniques and methods. And yet, amid all the variety, there is arguably always one overarching aim: self-transcendence.

Aufheben

To transcend, to sublimate, to negate and also preserve

'Self-transcendence' is a mysterious term that attracts diverse interpretations. Indeed, each of its two components – 'self' and 'transcendence' – is itself an arena of confusion and contest.

Let's consider the self first. There appears to be as many perspectives on this topic as there are theorists who have attempted to explain it. However, I find Ken Wilber's approach particularly illuminating. He starts by differentiating between the self (with a small 's') and the Self (with a capital 'S'). He then essentially defines the self as the *ideas* we have about ourselves. In other words, it is our constructed identity, the collection of biographical facts that we accrue throughout life, our accumulated memories. Ask me who I am and I might say, 'I'm Tim, an Englishman from London, thirty-eight years old, a husband, son, brother, psychology lecturer, erstwhile musician, clumsy cook ...' and so on. All of these pieces of information are true and they constitute my self. Yet this self is limiting and narrow. It segregates me from my own potential, from other people ... and from the sacred.

In short, it is not my Self. Often called the 'witness', this Self comprises my conscious awareness and the strange feeling that accompanies it: of *being* someone and experiencing life. It is vast, pure, limitless; the expansive sky through which the 'contents' of my awareness – my thoughts, emotions, sensations, sights, sounds – effortlessly pass, as described above in relation to *vipassanā*. From a certain perspective, it is itself divine, as captured in the phrase *tat tvam asi.*

Therefore, from a certain perspective, the aim of almost all contemplative practice is to transcend one's constricting sense of self and enter the infinitely greater domain of the Self.

Now, though, we must ask what 'transcend' means in this context. Does it imply that the person must erase all traces of the self? Are they obliged to forget their name, identity and memories in a cataclysmic blitz of self-negation? Mercifully, Wilber suggests that the answer to both of those questions is 'no'. People who achieve the great feat of self-transcendence still answer to their names and they are unlikely to deny any of the facts in their biographies. They have simply gone beyond them, to some extent.

The key to understanding this process lies in the complex German verb *aufheben*, as deployed by Georg Hegel.[35] For he used it to define 'transcendence', suggesting that it means 'at once to negate and preserve'.[36] With self-transcendence, our exclusive identification with the self is negated. That is, we no longer define ourselves by our biography or our identity. But these 'facts' are not lost. Rather, they are preserved and set within the vastly more expansive experiential framework of the Self, which provides a far deeper context for them. So we don't forget the self, but we are no longer bound by it.

All of this might seem rather abstract, so it makes sense to conclude this chapter with an exploration of one way in which this mysterious process may unfold in practice.

Śūnyatā

Emptiness, boundlessness, boundarylessness

To conclude our spiritual journey here, let's return to the Buddhist notion of *anātman*, or 'non-self' – the idea that we lack a fixed, enduring self. Each of us is a whirlpool in the river of life: we don't exist apart from the temporary and dynamic configuration of the conditions that create us.

Yet, we tend to believe that we *do* have a self. We cling to it, protect it, cherish it. You might have no problem with that, or even argue it's admirable. And indeed, the self-preservation of our being is fundamental to life. And yet, from a Buddhist perspective, rigidly attaching to the constructions of the small 's' self lies at the heart of *duḥkha*. We suffer because we crave anything we think will benefit this self, direct anger towards anything that threatens it, and grieve over the prospect of losing it. As such, the solution is to transcend this narrow pre-occupation with the self and become our true, limitless Self (see *aufheben*, above).

Of course, this is easier said than done, so Buddhism – and other traditions – has developed a powerful repertoire of practices to facilitate it. A note of caution before we proceed, though: these techniques should be attempted only by those who are psychologically ready and sufficiently proficient at the difficult art of meditation, as assessed by and under the guidance of a skilled teacher. With that in mind, one such practice involves meditating on the so-called five *skandhas* – the elements that comprise the (illusion of) self. By reflecting on each of these in turn, practitioners are ideally able to see how their sense of self is generated in real time. They may then safely transcend that self and achieve some degree of liberation.

The first *skandha* is *rūpa* – 'matter' or 'form' – the material body. This comprises four *mahābhūta* ('great elements' or 'forces')[37]: *pṛthvī* ('earth'), *āp* ('water'), *tejas* ('fire') and *vāyu* ('air'). In relation to the body, these refer respectively to elements that are: hard (e.g., bones), fluid (e.g., blood), of varying temperature (e.g., sensations of heat) and insubstantial and in motion (e.g., the breath).

The second *skandha* is *vedanā* – 'feeling and sensation'.[38] At any moment, our experience is coloured by one of three basic *vedanās* – *sukha* ('pleasant'), *duḥkha* ('unpleasant') or *upeksha* ('neutral') – which arise in conjunction with perception. So, whenever we sense something, it is immediately coloured by one of those appraisals. This generates the push and pull of aversion (to phenomena that evoke *duḥkha vedanā*) and craving (to that which evokes *sukha vedanā*).

Next comes *saṃjñā* – the cognitive mechanisms by which these initial sensations of stimuli are processed. In turn, this generates the fourth *skandha*, *saṃskāra* – the psychological effects that are set in motion. These include runaway trains of thought, instinctive behavioural urges and physical actions (such as reaching out for something we find desirable). All of this takes place in a fraction of a second, whereupon we arrive at the final *skandha*, *vijñāna* – 'consciousness' or 'discernment'. In other words, unnervingly, we become truly conscious of a stimulus only once we have sensed, processed *and responded* to it.

Crucially, this sequence is not an abstract theory. People can be trained to see it happening, in real time, during meditation. As a result, they are better able to see the self for what it truly is – a construction, a useful fiction – and achieve liberation (to varying degrees). Specifically, they undergo an experiential realisation of *śūnyatā*.

In English, this term is often rendered as 'emptiness', but such a translation can be rather misleading, since it implies a nihilistic void in which nothing exists.[39] In fact, *śūnyatā* brings together the key ideas of *anātman* (non-self) and *anitya* (impermanence), in that all phenomena, including the self, are regarded as 'empty' of a fixed nature. This doesn't mean they aren't real; rather, they simply can't be pinned down. Hence, *śūnyatā* is not nihilism but liberation. Consequently, a better translation might be 'openness',[40] 'boundlessness'[41] or even 'boundarylessness'.[42] We are not the narrow self we usually assume ourselves to be. Instead, we are the infinite Self – uncontainable and free. Once we realise this, in a deep experiential way, we may approach the ultimate goal of *nirvāṇa*.

With that, we must conclude our lightning tour of spirituality. But before moving on to the final chapter, let's take a moment to see how far we've come.

Summary

We started with the foundational notion of *sacer* – the root of the term 'sacred' – which is central to our understanding of spirituality. Next, we explored the divine realm from four key perspectives: animism, represented by *vættir*, or 'nature spirits'; polytheism, symbolised by *Gaia*, the primordial Mother Earth; panentheism, with its concept of a transcendent and immanent supreme spirit, such as *Brahman*; and pantheism, where *natura naturans* presents nature as a divine, creative process. We then looked inwards – to the notion of a sacred dimension within people themselves. This part of our journey encompassed the spirit, captured by *qì*, and the soul, as per *akh*, as well as the strange and challenging idea of *anātman*, which relates to the ephemerality of the self.

From there, we examined the great range of contemplative practices that have been devised to help people connect with the sacred. These were classified according to four parameters: the mode of attention, such as the clear insight of *vipassanā*; its focus, such as the 'deity meditations' of *druptap*; its emotional tone, as epitomised by the reverential joy of *hallelujah*; and its physical form, exemplified by the balletic grace of *tai chi*. Finally, we saw that the ultimate goal of such practices is self-transcendence. This complex concept was illuminated by *aufheben*, while the Buddhist notion of *śūnyatā* clarified the resulting liberation.

With that, it only remains to tie everything together with the overarching notion of human character.

CHAPTER NINE

Character

What an adventure! We have traversed a vast realm of feelings, experiences and qualities, all of which relate to happiness in some important way. Together, these chapters have illuminated what it means to live a full and flourishing life. But there is one piece of the jigsaw remaining.

At the start of Chapter 7, I suggested that in addition to positive emotions, cherished relationships and valued mental states, our wellbeing intimately depends on personal development. I further proposed that such development could be viewed as involving three key strands. The first two, understanding and spirituality, were covered in chapters 7 and 8. And so, finally, we come to the third strand, the all-important issue of character: who we are as people and, more importantly, who we are in the process of becoming.

Great strides have been made in psychology over recent years towards understanding character and its vital role in flourishing. This work was long overdue. For much of the twentieth century, the field mainly studied people through the prism of disorder and dysfunction, for instance classifying them according to psychiatric categories (such as anxiety or depression). While this approach is valuable, it is not only dispiriting, but also highly incomplete. Does it even come close to portraying humanity's full potential? What about all that is *right* with us – the ways in which we excel and shine? Fortunately, emergent disciplines such as positive psychology have begun to redress this oversight by focusing on the good in people – the traits and talents that help them flourish.[1]

A prominent approach in this respect is the influential Values-in-Action (VIA) paradigm of character strengths[2] – defined as 'positive traits that a person owns, celebrates, and frequently uses'.[3] Its premise is that people are more likely to flourish if they use and develop their strengths.[4] Twenty-four key strengths have been identified – check out www.viacharacter.org for the full list – grouped into six broad virtues: wisdom and knowledge; courage; humanity; justice; temperance; and transcendence. While this taxonomy is interesting in itself, even more intriguing in the context of this book is the cross-cultural methodology through which it was developed. For the researchers created their framework by consulting foundational religious and philosophical texts – from the *Upaniṣads* to the *Tao Te Ching* – and recording those qualities that have been most valued throughout history and across cultures.[5]

We shall undertake a similar exploration in this chapter, but with two key differences. First, while VIA focuses on concepts that are shared across many cultures, here we concentrate on notions that appear to be unique to specific cultures, as signalled by an untranslatable word. This may allow us to unearth previously hidden gems. Second, while VIA aims to explore specific strengths, we are more concerned here with the principles and mechanisms that underpin flourishing more generally: that is, with the broad dynamics of character that work across a variety of attributes.

With that in mind, there is only one place to start: with the idea of character development itself.

Bildungsroman

A coming-of-age story

One of my favourite novels is Hermann Hesse's *Siddhartha*, which tells the meandering story of a spiritual seeker living around the same time as the Buddha. Significantly, *Siddhartha* is not only the name of the protagonist, but was also the Buddha's too (before his honorific was bestowed upon him). This shared appellation is imbued with meaning, since it denotes someone who has attained a worthy aim. For both Siddharthas, this is liberation from suffering. Indeed, the two meet in the narrative and discuss their respective paths towards this eternal goal. However, while our protagonist cedes to the Buddha's wisdom, he ultimately decides he must discover his own truths, having realised that salvation will not be handed to him on a plate. He must be the author of his own deliverance.

Siddhartha is what the Germans call a *Bildungsroman* – a novel that explores the possibility of *Bildung* ('self-cultivation'). Sometimes known as 'coming-of-age' stories, many of these chart a journey from the turbulence of youth to the goal of 'finding oneself' in adulthood. But some, including *Siddhartha*, emphasise that character development continues long after one reaches one's twenties. Although most people have acquired a stable sense of themselves by that age, we are not set in stone, and our story is not complete until we leave this life. Hence, Hesse insists that we can – indeed should – aim to continue learning, evolving and developing.

Contemporary psychologists are increasingly attuned to the possibility of lifelong personal development – in the realms of understanding, spirituality and, above all, character. Whatever our unique arsenal of talents and strengths, the message is that we can nurture them and realise our full potential. In this respect, it can help to think of one's *own* life as a *Bildungsroman*. Such novels are not intended to be mere entertaining diversions. Their ultimate aim is to awaken readers to the possibility of self-cultivation. Indeed, Hesse wrote *Siddhartha* in the hope of finding a cure for his own *Lebenskrankheit* – world-weariness or, literally, 'life disease' – by immersing himself in the *Upaniṣads* and studying Buddhist teachings. Your journey may well be different of course. As noted above, Hesse's protagonist learns the importance of discovering *his own* path, writing *his own* story. The rest of us must learn that lesson, too. Then the question becomes: what kind of story will we tell about our life?

As in fiction, much of life lies outside our control; we are often 'thrown' into circumstances that are not of our own making (as we saw with *Geworfenheit* in Chapter 7). But these situations need not rigidly dictate our life story. For ultimately, we are the authors of our own narrative. Even when life throws plot-points and dramatic scenes at us, we have some say in the tale we tell about these. Moreover, we have agency in how we *respond* to the challenges we face and the person we become along the way.

This, then, is the overarching theme of this final chapter: fulfilling our potential and becoming the hero or heroine of our own *Bildungsroman*. And this quest begins by us first acknowledging the very *possibility* of self-development.

Areté

Excellence, quality, virtue

When I was a teenager, I longed to 'make it' as a musician. I'd watch videos of Jimi Hendrix and Slash and dream of making my guitar sing like theirs. I pursued this vision as best I could. I started my first band in my early teens, then found the perfect outlet for my passions in an eccentric ska-rock band that provided the soundtrack for many a great night during my university years and beyond. We definitely had our flaws – as a singer, I was certainly no Freddie Mercury – but I loved getting up on stage and performing. We played hundreds of gigs throughout our twenties and enjoyed many thrilling adventures and beautiful experiences (as well as some moments I would rather forget). And, looking back, through all of that I was haphazardly exploring the promise and the potential of *areté*.

In classical Greece, in addition to connotations of excellence, quality and goodness, this term spoke to the fulfilment of one's potential and purpose. It could be applied to almost anything: for instance, a strong, athletic horse might be described as possessing *areté*, as might a well-made cooking pot that never leaked, since both had met or even exceeded people's expectations of them. With the band, I felt my passion and talent for music were harnessed in a similarly purposeful way. I had no illusions of 'achieving excellence', whatever that means, but I was drawn towards quality in ways that reflected who I was and who I still am.

We all have our unique interests, values and skills. Quality and excellence are not uniform; each of us excels in our own ways. But we must *try* to excel. For, when we do, we flourish. In VIA terminology, the band enabled me to put values and strengths that are close to my heart *into action*. Writing songs allowed me to exercise my creativity. Practice sessions and performances satisfied my thirst for learning. Visiting new places on tour stimulated my curiosity. Connecting with people through the music resulted in reciprocal love and kindness. Pushing towards our goals required perseverance and zest. Getting along with my bandmates demanded humility and prudence. And the whole endeavour imbued me with gratitude and hope.

Perhaps you have already harnessed your strengths – whatever these may be – in the pursuit of your own dreams. If so, you will know the fulfilment this can bring. If not, I hope you soon find an outlet for your unique but currently untapped talents. Mind you, it's not that your whole life has to be a continual expression of your deepest values and greatest gifts. All of us sometimes have to perform mundane tasks that don't really engage us. Even then, though, we can exercise some of our best qualities – from honesty and humour to fairness and forgiveness. And it bears repeating that *areté* does not necessarily mean *attaining* excellence. It just means doing your best in ways that remain true to who you are ... ideally in a spirit of consideration.

Apramāda

Earnest, diligent, moral watchfulness

Earlier, we discussed ideas pertaining to morality and ethics, from the Buddhist *brahma-vihārā*s (Chapter 4) to the Judaic *mitzvot* (Chapter 7). But this topic warrants revisiting here. For goodness is universally acknowledged as indispensable in the cultivation of character and consequent flourishing. The question is: beneath all the moral precepts, what *is* 'goodness'?

A large part of the answer, it seems, is 'consideration', for this comprises two essential qualities that are central to morality and goodness: awareness and care. That is, considerate people are acutely aware of the impact of their actions – on others and themselves – and, moreover, care deeply about that impact.

These qualities are embodied in another intriguing Sanskrit term, *apramāda*. Like *sati* (see Chapter 1), this is sometimes rendered simply as 'mindfulness' or 'awareness'. However, *apramāda* has an explicit ethical dimension, whereas this dimension is only implicit and understated in *sati*.[6] Indeed, in the latter's extraction from its original Buddhist context – where it was embedded within the ethical framework of the *dhárma* – and its repackaging as mindfulness, this ethical dimension may even be missing entirely. That's not to say that contemporary Western approaches to mindfulness are unethical. It's more that, in attending to the present moment in a non-judgemental way – a common modern definition of 'mindfulness'[7] – ethics are not really part of the equation.

By contrast, *apramāda* is suffused with appreciation of the ethics of one's actions. As such, it has been translated using phrases such as 'earnestness',[8] 'vigilant care'[9] or 'moral watchfulness'.[10] I have personal experience of the power – and the challenge – of trying to cultivate this kind of awareness. As someone who tries – not always successfully – to live a Buddhist life, I've come to appreciate the *pañcasīlāni*: the 'five precepts' to which lay followers are exhorted to adhere. These encourage people to refrain from five main forms of noxious behaviour: *pāṇātipātā* (harming or killing living beings); *adinnādānā* (stealing); *kāmesu micchācāra* (sexual or sensual misconduct); *musāvādā* (lying); and *surāmerayamajja pamādaṭṭhānā* (intoxication).

At first glance, these proscriptions seem pretty straightforward. However, on closer inspection, they are very nuanced. Take the second precept, *adinnādānā*. I might say, 'No problem – I would never dream of stealing anything,' and feel fairly self-satisfied. But a more accurate translation might be: 'taking the not given'. Suddenly there's an element of doubt. If I gossip about someone, am I taking their privacy and dignity? And what about when I turn on my heating or use my laptop? Fossil fuels are providing the energy, so I'm contributing to global warming and possibly robbing future generations of a clean planet. Seen in this light, the five precepts encourage us to reflect carefully on almost every action. Moreover, they caution against complacency because, even if I manage to do some good, I can always aim to do better.

Why should I, though? How do we benefit from being a considerate person?

Karma

A theory of ethical causality

Of all the ideas found in Buddhism, *karma* is probably the most fleet footed and well travelled. Indeed, it has featured as a loanword in many languages, including English, for decades. Thus, it is roundly invoked, including by people with no particular adherence to or familiarity with Buddhism. In that respect, it often gets used as a quasi-mystical explanation for someone's suffering by linking their current misfortune to previous wrongdoings in this or another life. Less frequently, positive outcomes are seen as rewards for earlier virtuousness or good deeds.

This is certainly a beguiling idea, and comparable notions have been developed in other cultures. For instance, the ancient Greeks identified the twin dynamics of *hubris* and *nemesis*. The former denoted overweening arrogance or pride, especially in the form of behaviour that challenged or defied the gods. Thereafter, *nemesis* was the process of divine justice and retribution, personified as a goddess who restored balance in the universe – through vengeance, if necessary. The Christian concepts of sin and the Last Judgment are not dissimilar. These Western ideas have helped frame English-speakers' interpretion of *karma*, but does this correspond in any way to the original Buddhist concept?

Well, to some extent. The key to understanding *karma* is the principle of *pratītya-samutpāda*, the law of conditionality we encountered in Chapter 7. The essential point is that the Buddha did not view *everything* we experience as our fault or responsibility. Our existence is woven together from many different threads of cause and effect. While we are directly accountable for some of these, we are merely swept up in others. Specifically, Buddhist teachings identify five distinct levels of conditionality. Known collectively as the *niyāmas*,[11] these are defined as 'laws, conditions or constraints that govern processes or phenomena'.[12] Crucially, *karma* is just one of these levels; many other forces and processes also influence what happens to us. It is important to remember this; otherwise, we risk falling into unhelpful patterns of blame or credit for outcomes that are not our responsibility.

The first level is *utu-niyāma* – the 'law of the seasons'. This relates to non-organic physical laws and the regularity of environmental phenomena. If I get wet in a rainstorm, that's due to precipitation and gravity, rather than my *karma* (although the latter might account for why I find myself in the rain in the first place).

Second is *bīja-niyāma* – the 'law of seeds', which concerns patterns in the realm of organic phenomena, such as biochemistry, including genetic inheritance. I'm tall and slim because these traits run in my family, not because I caused them. However, I can *contribute* to these outcomes through my actions, such as taking regular exercise, which *is* an aspect of *karma*.

Third is *citta-niyāma* – the 'law of the mind' – which refers to causality with respect to mental processes, such as the psychological associations we form throughout life. I'm wary of dogs because I was bitten by one as a child – an event over which I basically had no control.

Karma-niyāma is the fourth level. Here, we *are* personally involved and responsible for our outcomes. Indeed, *karma* means 'action'. When people talk about the consequences of their actions – which is how many people deploy the term *karma* – this is *karma vīpāka*, with the latter word meaning 'ripening' (i.e., of the fruit of past actions).[13] In essence, Buddhism argues that ethical actions help to generate future positive mental states, whereas unethical behaviour contributes towards negative mental states. Thus, there is a powerful incentive to behave morally, because such actions benefit ourselves as well as others, while conversely we suffer as a consequence of our own misdeeds.

The final level is *dhárma-niyāma*, the 'law of nature'. This builds on the inherent promise of *karma-niyāma* in suggesting that ethical behaviour can result in even more than a positive mindset. Indeed, if we align ourselves with the *dhárma*, we can make far-reaching spiritual progress towards the ultimate goal of *nirvāṇa*. And aside from this awe-inspiring possibility, *dhárma-niyāma* reflects the overarching theme of these final three chapters, namely our potential for psychological growth ... including honing our life skills.

Savoir faire

Confidently knowing how to behave

In the 1980s, TV-viewers were introduced to an effervescent new character – a secret agent called MacGyver. His name quickly became synonymous with a certain type of skill: quick-thinking repurposing of everyday objects to save the world from peril, usually at the very last minute. MacGyver's appeal has not diminished, as is evidenced by the success of a recent reboot. Indeed, his kind of daring, creative, practical intelligence is celebrated in a number of terms.

Perhaps the most well known is the breezily confident *savoir faire*. French uses *savoir* – 'know' in the sense of practical know-how, rather than abstract knowledge – in several related phrases, such as *savoir vivre*, which means 'knowing how to live' (which we encountered in relation to *joie de vivre* in Chapter 2). In this case, the verb *faire* is appended to convey the notion of 'knowing how to make or do'. Hence, *savoir faire* is usefully vague, covering a multitude of desirable qualities, including MacGyver-like practical problem-solving skills.

Such capacities are similarly celebrated in other languages, such as Italian, with its concept of *arrangiarsi*. This translates as 'to make do or get by' – often prefixed by *l'arte d'* ('the art of') – and is especially invoked when such skills are deployed in a tight spot.[14] That said, it can have negative connotations, implying that underhand machinations may potentially be involved. Similarly, the Portuguese word *desenrascanço*, which roughly translates as 'disentanglement', describes a useful ability to extricate oneself from a difficult situation, often through a combination of nerve and verve.

But *savoir faire* has implications beyond the cunning inventiveness of MacGyver, as it can also refer to an intuitive understanding of how to behave in any given situation.[15] In this sense, synonyms include 'diplomacy', 'finesse' and 'poise'. People who are blessed with these qualities have an uncanny ability to say and do the right thing, and to put people at ease. They may even be able to kindle *eunoia*.

Eunoia

Beautiful thinking

Some people just seem to exude social grace. Think of Barack Obama and his alchemical blend of vital qualities – from kindness and emotional intelligence to *panache*, courage and principled determination. In short, he embodies what the French call *savoir être* – 'knowing how to be' – the ability to act skilfully and carry oneself elegantly. In this sense, the term overlaps with *savoir faire*, being almost synonymous with 'diplomacy' and 'tact'. However, the emphasis is on interpersonal skills – often known as 'soft' skills, for some reason – in contrast to the more hard-boiled practicality of *savoir faire*.[16] Those who possess *savoir être* might not be able to dismantle and reassemble a car engine, but they will certainly have an appealing character.

The classical Greeks had a wonderful term for this quality: *eunoia*. This captures the idea of a good or beautiful (*eu*) mind (*noia*). This does not merely convey intelligence and clear thinking, but also qualities such as goodwill and elegance. Thus, people who possess *eunoia* are able to communicate benevolence and humanity, and elicit these attributes from others. For instance, a rhetorician might cultivate a warm reception from their audience through the moral substance of their speech and the sympathetic tone of their delivery.

When viewed from this perspective, *eunoia* is not simply an enviable character trait but also a communicable phenomenon that is 'aroused by virtue and goodness'.[17] Hence, someone who strikes us as noble, beautiful and brave inspires *eunoia* within us, too. Moreover, our newfound *eunoia* will be directed not only towards this moral exemplar but to life in general. Obama's soaring oratory could inspire this sort of reaction among his supporters. They felt ennobled and capable of making great progress in their own lives, invigorated by the audacity of hope.

Once the way forward is clear in our minds, and we have the necessary skills to realise our potential, we then need the will to proceed.

Orka

Sufficient energy and resilience

So far, our exploration of character has dwelt on various key components: the pursuit of excellence and self-expression; morality and ethics; knowing how to act and behave skilfully. All of these are certainly vital aspects of personal development and flourishing more broadly. However, in themselves, they are insufficient. In addition, we must be *able* to follow these pathways to a better character.

This brings us to the mysterious concept of human willpower. This encompasses our drive, our motivation and, indeed, our ability not only to identify a worthy goal but to march steadfastly towards it. It's one thing to think that a daily run would be good for your health. It's quite another to lace up your trainers and head outside on a bitter winter's evening. This point applies to just about every aspect of character, and it can be really hard. Two millennia ago, St Paul lamented, 'The good that I would, I do not; but the evil which I would not, that I do.'[18] Even when we know the best course of action, it can be strangely difficult to follow it.

This and the next two entries all address willpower, teasing apart its internal dynamics. For it appears to have three inter-related elements: energy, grit and autonomy. We begin here with energy – the initial spark of vitality, the primal urge to *do* something. An influential notion in this respect is the Greek concept of *thymós*. Sometimes rendered as 'spiritedness', in various contexts it can mean 'soul', 'spirit', 'will', 'courage' or even 'the principle of life'.[19] For instance, it drives *epithymía* – the urgings of 'uncontrollable desire' – which we encountered in Chapter 3.[20]

Ideally, of course, we are able to skilfully harness this energy – through qualities such as *savoir faire* – in much the same way as we competently steer a car towards our destination. However, we won't be going far without that initial combustion or the requisite fuel in the tank to reach our goal. An evening run doesn't amount to much if the first drop of rain forces us back inside after twenty metres. In that respect, we need what the Swedes call *orka*: sufficient energy to achieve a particular aim.[21]

Sometimes, though, unexpected challenges arise and the going gets tough. In such circumstances, we need *sisu*.

Sisu

*Extraordinary courage and determination
in the face of adversity*

At the start of this book, we met a remarkable woman named Emilia Lahti. I owe her a debt of gratitude, since it was her work that sparked this entire project. If I hadn't attended her inspiring presentation, I may never have stumbled upon the idea of exploring untranslatable words. Moreover, her topic itself has great relevance here. For her work involves introducing the world to the vital Finnish concept of *sisu*, a form of inner determination in the face of adversity.[22]

Indeed, Emilia herself personifies this quality, to the great benefit of others. She has founded an initiative called 'Sisu not silence', which aims to address the evil of interpersonal violence, particularly domestic abuse. Awfully, Emilia herself was a victim of mistreatment, and this ordeal led her into a long, challenging journey of recovery and rebuilding. While this path was often painful, Emilia suggests that it was also empowering, as she came to appreciate her own deep reserves of *sisu* – the strength and courage that enabled her to survive the trauma of the relationship. Moreover, she grew determined to help others who have suffered similar harm, which led to the formation of her initiative.

At the time of writing, she has just embarked upon an astonishing feat of physical endurance: a 1,500-mile run down the length of New Zealand that she aims to complete in just fifty days. Such extraordinary physical determination epitomises *sisu*, but this has a moral dimension, too. On her website, Emilia writes that *sisu* incorporates having 'the courage to take action against very slim odds, to stand up for what is right, and to have integrity and take responsibility for one's actions'.[23] Thus, her intention is to champion a good cause, pursue it with courage and stamina, and help others in its name. As such, throughout her run, she is convening events during which people will be encouraged to speak out, tell their stories, and become advocates for positive change within their communities.

Emilia's message is that *sisu* does not belong only to the Finns, even though they had the foresight to coin the term. It's a quality we all possess; we just need to learn how to tap into it. Whatever path you take, *sisu* can help you through. Indeed, it may prove invaluable, especially if you prefer, at times, to travel alone.

Solivagant

A lone wanderer

In astronomy, a 'free-floating' planetary object that drifts alone in the infinite silence of space is known as a *solivagant* – 'lone wanderer'.[24] This emotive Latin term can be used to describe people, too. In general, most of us prefer to orbit around those we love. Sometimes, though, we may feel called or compelled to keep ourselves to ourselves, and navigate a solitary path of independence for a time. We may even yearn for what the Japanese call *datsuzoku* – escape from mundanity and entry to the pristine realm of spontaneous freedom (see Chapter 5).

We've seen that willpower involves a combination of *orka* and *sisu*. However, in themselves, these qualities are insufficient to enhance character. Equally important is the nature of our goals, and how we arrive at them. Specifically, they must ideally be freely chosen and have intrinsic – rather than extrinsic – value to us. This relates to *areté* – possessing our own unique interests and talents – since an intrinsic goal is one which reflects those interests and talents. For me, becoming a musician was one such goal: a heartfelt desire, an unforced choice. In German, having the freedom to pursue one's dreams in this way is known as *eigenwillig* (literally, 'self-willed'). By contrast, passing my driving test was extrinsic: something I *ought* to do for various reasons. Of course, I still wanted to succeed, but it mattered less.

However, when it comes to choosing our goals, sometimes our ideals and ambitions conflict with what other people have in mind for us, and those people may raise their voices against our plans. Of course, sometimes these voices are right and we should at least consider heeding their advice and going in a different direction. At other times, though, no one else can fully understand the intrinsic goal we have decided to pursue. In such circumstances, there may be no option but to take a *solivagant* path and go it alone.

A note of caution is in order here though. Many cultures have words that tread a fine line between admiration for independent audacity and wariness about the dangers of excessive autonomy. Consider the Yiddish term *chutzpah*. Although it contains a hint of admiration – an implication of enviable boldness – it also has ambivalent connotations of effrontery and nerve.[25] Likewise, the German word *Willkür* evokes capriciousness and wanton disregard for norms and conventions rather than the free-spirited pursuit of one's personal goals.[26]

In general, though, a degree of autonomy enhances well-being, not least because it can help each of us become a more complete person.

Mensch

An all-round good person

So far in this chapter we've outlined the mechanics of personal development by identifying its individual components: deciding to seek excellence in the first place; maintaining consideration for others; behaving adeptly; possessing the willpower to pursue a chosen path; and having the freedom to follow intrinsic goals.

If you tick all those boxes – or at least are on your way to doing so – you may perhaps be sufficiently admired as to be deemed a *mensch*. Another Yiddish term – derived from the generic German term for a human being, *menschliches Wesen* – this denotes a 'good human being in its fullest sense'[27]: that is, a virtuous, upright person with fundamental decency and high moral standards. However, a *mensch* is not an inaccessible, remote exemplar. By definition, they also possess warmth, humour, humanity and compassion. One would have no qualms about turning to them for solace in times of trouble, for example, confident in the knowledge that their help would be forthcoming.

In other cultures, similar terms signal even more elusive qualities, such as the attainment of some sort of spiritual zenith. For instance, in the *Dhammapada* – the collected sayings of the Buddha – an *arhat* is said to be 'as firm as a high pillar and as pure as a deep pool free from mud ... wholly freed, perfectly tranquil and wise'.[28] Clearly, this is rarefied territory. Most of us will likely not quite attain these heights of personal development. But we can still cultivate good, noble characters. After all, it's not only exemplary people who are capable of flourishing. In our own fashion, we should all strive to be the best versions of ourselves, even with all our faults and weaknesses. Indeed, somewhat paradoxically, these flaws may even become positive attributes.

Kintsugi

Rendering fault-lines beautiful and strong

In his song 'Anthem', Leonard Cohen, that great poet of the human condition, sang of the cracked nature of the human condition; but, rather than lamenting this imperfection, he suggested that this is 'how the light gets in'.[29] Emmanual Kant once wrote that we are all fashioned from the 'crooked timber of humanity'.[30] Certainly, we can be strong, beautiful, noble, but we still have our vulnerabilities and flaws, wounded or damaged parts that we hide from the world. But Cohen's message is that we may yet find hidden value in these fault-lines.

It may be no coincidence that Cohen had a close affinity with Zen, and was even ordained as a monk. For his lyric strongly resonates with an artistic technique which has long been associated with Zen, namely a process of ceramic repair known as *kintsugi* – literally, 'golden joinery'. Rather than throwing out their broken pots and bowls, practitioners of this art apply seams of gold lacquer to the pieces and reassemble them with love and care.

In one sense, this is a vivid, practical manifestation of the *wabi-sabi* aesthetic (see Chapter 5) – cultivating an appreciation for beauty in phenomena that are worn, weathered or aged, and learning to perceive their inherent dignity and depth. However, in that spirit, one might equally see beauty in an object that has been repaired with invisible glue. Mending it with gold has added significance, because the aim is clearly to *highlight* the fault-lines. The cracks are not only rendered strong and beautiful battle-scars; they become the piece's defining features, its essence. They express its depth and history in a poignant, resonant and, above all, beautiful way. There is a powerful lesson for us in this metaphor: we are all broken in some way, but our flaws may become sources of strength, dignity and meaning – the places where the 'light gets in'.

Psychologists working with people who have suffered adversity sometimes invoke the image of a broken vase.[31] Our lives can be left broken by trauma and hardship, much like a dropped vase. Recovery is then a question of rebuilding ourselves, which is often a slow, painful process. The vase might not be rebuilt exactly as it was, because too much may have happened for us to resume our former life. And the pain may never be eradicated completely. However, people do have the capacity to fashion the broken pieces of their lives into something meaningful and even transformative. For instance, a brush with mortality may engender greater appreciation of life and a shift in priorities from material possessions to loved ones. As Friedrich Nietzsche put it, 'That which does not kill us makes us stronger.'

So, whatever our fault-lines, we may be able to discern their opaque beauty and come to appreciate that they are important aspects of who we are. They may even help us to find meaning in life.

Ikigai

Meaning and purpose in life

Another Nietzschean aphorism is pertinent here: 'If we have our own why in life, we shall get along with almost any how.'[32] This philosophy proved particularly providential for one of the great psychologists of the last century, Viktor Frankl, who suffered one of the worst traumas imaginable when he was interned in a series of Nazi concentration camps. He survived, but by the end of the war he had lost almost his entire family, including his beloved wife. However, amid the tragedy and barbarity, he arrived at a redemptive existential insight that has since provided great solace to millions of people. For he realised that those prisoners who continued to feel that they had something to live for seemed better equipped to withstand the traumas they faced. His own principal salvation was love. Afterwards, he wrote, 'I understood how a man who has nothing left in this world still may know bliss, be it only for a brief moment, in the contemplation of his beloved.'[33]

In the years that followed, as Frankl rebuilt himself and his life, this insight led him to formulate 'logotherapy'. We've already seen that *logos* forms the basis of a wealth of potent ideas, including the power of discourse and reason. Hence, Frankl incorporated it in the name of his new therapeutic process of 'healing through meaning', which helped his patients make sense of their problems and life in general.[34]

Indeed, the field of psychology is increasingly appreciative of the importance of meaning more broadly, not only in therapeutic contexts.[35] Here, we're not talking about 'the meaning of life' in grand, metaphysical terms, but rather the purpose and significance of individual people's lives – as beautifully encapsulated by the Japanese term *ikigai*. This has been translated as 'reason for being', capturing the sense that life is 'good and meaningful' and that it's 'worthwhile to continue living'.[36] It means having a reason to get up in the morning, and a positive answer to Albert Camus's fundamental existential question of why we ought to live at all. This has great significance for wellbeing, and even for physical health. Indeed, the ongoing cultivation of *ikigai* throughout life has been identified as one reason why Japan has such low mortality and morbidity rates (alongside more obvious factors, such as a diet that is rich in seafood and low in saturated fat).[37]

It's possible to find purpose in relation to just about anything: caring for one's family; a worthwhile career; good works; acts of kindness towards strangers; the creation of art. All of these activities and many more besides help bring meaning into people's lives and allow them to make the most of their days on earth. And in doing so, they are likely to experience the fulfilment of *eudaimonia*.

Eudaimonia

Flourishing and living life to the full

Our journey here is almost at an end. We've explored the length and breadth of wellbeing in great detail. We began with the peace and tranquillity of contentment, bathing in the cool waters of *ataraxia* and *xìng fú*. Then we moved into the intensely charged arena of pleasure, where we took in such delights as *joie de vivre* and the elevated peaks of *nirvāṇa*. Next, we encountered love in all its diversity, from the caring affection of *storgē* to the passion of *epithymía*. From there we delved into other forms of connection, from the humanity of *ubuntu* to the community spirit of *folkelig*.

Our gaze then lingered over the aesthetics of appreciation, from the savouring of the *gourmet* to the elegance of *leggiadria*. Next, we explored complex states of ambivalence, as symbolised by *yīn yáng* and the bittersweetness of *Sehnsucht*. Finally, our path led us into the mountainous terrain of personal development. First we viewed concepts relating to understanding, such as the Judaic *mitzvah*, and aspects of the self, including the *ego*. Further on, we arrived at the contemplative practices and self-transcendence of the spiritual realm, from *tai chi* to *śūnyatā*. And lastly, in this chapter, we have surveyed the notion of character, from *areté*'s pursuit of excellence to the grit and courage of *sisu*.

Most of us will have had experiences that relate to these themes individually – distinct moments of pleasure, aesthetic appreciation, connection and so on. But is it possible to encapsulate *all* (or at least the majority) of the themes in this book? Is there a word that ties them together in a neat, complete package? Psychology has some strong candidates for just such an all-encompassing term, from the generic 'wellbeing'[38] to the evocative 'flourishing',[39] both of which have featured repeatedly throughout this book. However, an untranslatable word from ancient Greece might be even more apt: *eudaimonia.*

For centuries, with science and medicine in their infancy, the classical Greeks by and large attributed prosperity and suffering to fate (or more specifically, to the preferences and whims of the gods). In light of this, *eudaimonia* originally described the happiness that was associated with the presence or guidance of a benevolent *daimon* ('spirit').[40] However, Plato, Aristotle and their fellow philosophers started to challenge this assumption, arguing that mortals had the power to influence their own wellbeing through self-cultivation. In that regard, Aristotle redefined *eudaimonia* as the 'activity of the soul in accordance with virtue'.[41]

Modern psychology no longer associates *eudaimonia* with Olympian gods and fate, but in other respects the term is still imbued with the meanings it evoked more than two millennia ago.[42] For it encompasses all the themes we have explored throughout this book, including learning to be content with our lot; accepting situations calmly; revelling in pleasure; loving and being loved; connecting and living in communion with others; savouring the beauty that graces our lives; welcoming the full spectrum of human emotions, including those that are bittersweet; understanding the world and our place within it; gaining some conception of the sacred; and being a good person while always striving to be a better one.

For these are the qualities we must strive for in whatever time we are given.

Tempus fugit

Time flies

Time is a strange thing. Indeed, our earliest ancestors may have had little or no concept of it. They probably sensed a general unfolding of events as some experiences receded into the past, but it must have been much harder to pin down the passage of time than it is today. If you've ever spent a few days in the wilderness, far from bleeping electronic devices and ticking clocks, you may have some inkling of what they experienced. In such circumstances, time becomes an expansive present rather than a rigid past, present and future. Moreover, there is surely less of the melancholy sense that time is slipping through our fingers, lost for ever.

Time, as we understand it today, entered human consciousness only with the invention of the first clocks. This may have occurred around the fourth millennium BCE, although the earliest extant timepiece is a sundial from Egypt's Valley of the Kings, dated to around 1500 BCE. Fashioned from limestone, it divides the working day into twelve segments, with elapsing time marked by the progression of the shadow cast by the *gnōmōn* (literally, 'one who knows') across the sectors. From that point onwards, our days were literally numbered. Quantifying time – and making it visible – means we all know our lot is limited and irretrievably ebbing away. A 75-year life comprises a mere 672,000 hours.

Given the sundial's pivotal role in fomenting our cognisance of time, and particularly its fleeting nature, it is apt that such timepieces often memorialise this insight with an inscription, usually in Latin. *Tempus fugit*, which laments the fact that time flees (or 'flies') from our grasp, is perhaps the most common. Or you may see the warning *Omnes vulnerant, ultima necat* – 'All hours wound; the last one kills'. In other words, each passing hour brings us closer to our end, with the last dealing a mortal blow. As melancholic as these messages may be thought, the intention was not to provoke despair. Rather, the idea was to remind us that time is precious. Hence, other sundials feature the more positive *Memento vivere* ('Remember to live') or *Carpe diem* ('Seize the day').

We must ideally approach our lives in this spirit. This doesn't mean succumbing to what the Germans call *torschlusspanik* (literally, 'gate-closing panic') – the urgent sense that time is running out and the gnawing fear of diminishing opportunities as one gate after another swings shut. Instead, we must strive to appreciate the time we have and make the most of it. Then, by the end, we may be fortunate enough to say that we have lived, and lived well.

Summary

Our final leg of this great adventure has taken us deep into the domain of character, and into the quest to become the very best version of ourselves. We began by viewing life as a *Bildungsroman*, a coming-of-age story. We then saw that this tale centres on the cultivation of *areté* – quality and excellence – which encompasses several key components. Firstly, it involves considerateness, as encapsulated by *apramāda*, as well as an understanding of why that matters, which relates to the ethical causality of *karma*. It further entails becoming skilled at the art of living, as per *savoir faire*, and cultivating a beautiful mind, or *eunoia*. Finally, it requires the energy and willpower of *orka*, the extraordinary grit and determination of *sisu*, and the autonomy and independence of the *solivagant*.

If we manage to put these components together, we may be sufficiently well-regarded to be considered a *mensch* – a generally good person. However, character development is not about embarking on an unrealistic quest for perfection. After all, we all have our flaws. Crucially, though, as we saw with the art of *kintsugi*, we may even find value and beauty in these very fault-lines. Overall though, whatever our circumstances and character, we may hope for *ikigai* – a redemptive sense of purpose in life – and the all-encompassing fulfilment of *eudaimonia*. Finally, we may be emboldened and motivated by the existential understanding of *tempus fugit*, and the knowledge that we must make the most of our precious days on earth.

On that note, in closing, let's take a brief look back over our entire journey.

Conclusion

I hope this whirlwind tour of the varied realms of wellbeing has helped you to articulate and understand valued experiences that you've previously lacked the words to express. Moreover, it may also have introduced you to new sensations and other phenomena that have the potential to enrich your life. We've certainly covered a great deal of ground, exploring no fewer than 124 key words in depth, together with numerous related terms. Therefore, let's conclude our travels by taking a moment to appreciate how far we've come and revel in some of the sights we've seen along the way.

We began with two chapters that focused on positive emotions. Chapter 1 embraced the more tranquil and peaceful arena of contentment, where we encountered the stoic acceptance of *ataraxia*, the mindful awareness of *sati* and the focused absorption of *dhyāna*. Serenity and stillness were conveyed by the natural spontaneity of *wú wéi*, the relaxed, alert *zanshin*, the self-surrender of *Gelassenheit* and the quiet reflection of *selah*. Well-rested satisfaction was found in *morgenfrisk*, cosiness and homeliness in *hygge* and *Gemütlichkeit*, and justified pride in *fiero*. Finally, gradations of happiness were evident in the ease of *sukha*, the blessing of *xìng fú* and the grace of *béatitude*.

In Chapter 2 we moved on to the more energised allure of pleasure. There were delights to be found in the revelry of the *craic*, the mischievous laughter of *pretoogjes*, the postprandial socialising of *sobremesa* and the cool refreshment of an *utepils*. Liveliness and passion featured in the boisterous *ramé* and the spirited *kefi*, *tarab* graced us with enchantment, and joyful appreciation was conveyed by *joie de vivre* and *njuta*. Finally, we encountered more intense, climactic experiences in the euphoric transportation of *ékstasis* and the orgasmic delight of *jouissance*, before arriving at the zenith of *nirvāṇa* and its promise of lasting liberation from suffering.

The next two chapters delved into human relationships and their immense influence over wellbeing. Chapter 3 explored fourteen 'flavours' of love, several of which may feature in a single relationship to create a unique 'taste'. First, we acknowledged three impersonal forms of love – for experiences (*meraki*), objects (*érōs*) and places (*chōros*). Next came bonds of friendship (*philia*), benevolent self-regard (*philautia*) and familial protection (*storgē*) – all of which are aspects of caring. In the realm of romance, we looked at desire (*epithymía*), playfulness (*paixnidi*), troubled intimacy (*mania*), relationship-building (*prâgma*) and star-crossed destiny (*anánkē*). Finally, we explored transcendent love in relation to compassionate benevolence (*agápē*), ephemeral connection (*koinōnía*) and devotional awe (*sébomai*).

Moving outside intimate relationships, Chapter 4 looked at connecting with people more generally. We revelled in the common humanity of *ubuntu*, the loving-kindness of *mettā*, the altruistic sensitivity denoted by *omoiyari*, the vicarious happiness of *mud$\bar{a}$*, the hospitality of *melmastia* and the sociability provided by a good *fika*. The importance of communication was noted with the civilised conversation of *enraonar*, the deep, contemplative listening of *dadirri* and the peaceful salutation *shalom*. We then touched upon the voluntary collective action of a *talkoot* and the will of the people as captured by *folkelig*. *Janteloven* served as a warning against restricting individual freedom before we celebrated the nurturing community of the *saṅgha* and the social harmony of *simpatía*.

The fifth and sixth chapters explored various mental states that are beneficial to wellbeing. Chapter 5 focused on the power of aesthetic appreciation to transform our perspective on life. The beauty of nature was highlighted in the scenery poetry of *fuubutsushi*, the sparkling of *èit* and the peaceful tranquillity of a *smultronställe*. Next, we were encouraged to savour a leisurely *passeggiata*, cultivate the connoisseurship of a *gourmet* and the informed enthusiasm of the *aficionado*, and experience the absorption of *hugfanginn*. Then came various perspectives on beauty itself, from the order of *harmonía* and the proportionality of *kairos* to the elegance of *leggiadria*, the coherence of *Gestalt* and the avant-garde inventiveness of *Dada*. Finally, Zen gave us the graceful simplicity of *kanso* and the weathered depth of *wabi-sabi*.

Chapter 6 considered the somewhat counter-intuitive notion that ambivalent states of mind can have an important role to play in wellbeing, as epitomised by *yīn yáng*, which symbolises the dynamic interaction of opposites. From there, we looked at the passion of *duende*, the empathy of *páthos* and the melancholic trance of *ambedo*. Next came the memorialising of the past with *Gedenkstätten* and the awareness of life's transience in *mono no aware*. We explored four forms of longing, from *magari*'s wistful hope to the utopianism of *Sehnsucht*, the nostalgia of *hiraeth* and the irresistible call of the unknown, as encapsulated in *Fernweh*. Then there were spine-tingling thrills, with the anticipation of *Vorfreude*, the shiver of *frisson* and the awe of *vidunder*. Finally, with *yūgen*, we acknowledged the mysterious, unfathomable depths of existence.

The final three chapters addressed the possibility of personal development. We began in Chapter 7 with understanding and wisdom. Adopting a historical perspective, we examined various ideas that not only helped to shape the modern mind but continue to be relevant to this day. Thus, *aljerre-nge* speaks to the value of honouring ancestral traditions, *Enkidu* symbolises the power of narrative and *Ahura Mazdā* highlights the necessity of aligning with goodness. *Mitzvah* reminds us of ethical observance, and *shù* the golden rule. *Tao* alludes to the flow of life, *dharma* highlights the importance of forging a personal path, and *ashtangika* is an example of one such path. We have practical wisdom in the form of *phrónēsis* and secret knowledge in *gnôsis*, while we see the cosmos imbued with reason and spirituality in *et*, and the discovery of new dimensions of existence with *ṣifr*. Finally, we have a new model of selfhood in *ego* and an insight into the 'thrownness' of existence courtesy of *Geworfenheit*.

Chapter 8 turned to the elevated territory of spirituality, which many cultures view as integral to flourishing. We began by defining this in terms of *sacer* – 'the sacred' – before exploring four perspectives on the divine: animism, polytheism, panentheism and pantheism. Respectively, these were symbolised by *vættir* (nature spirits), *Gaia* (Mother Earth), *Brahman* (a transcendent, immanent spirit) and *natura naturans* (divine nature). Next, we looked for the sacred within ourselves in the spirit of *qì*, the soul of *akh* and the ephemerality of *anātman*. We then turned to contemplative practices, which were arranged according to four parameters: mode of attention, as highlighted by the crystal-clear insight of *vipassanā*; focus, as in the deity meditations of *druptap*; emotional tone, exemplified by *hallelujah*; and physical form, as seen in the balletic grace of *tai chi*. Finally, we saw that the ultimate goal of such practices is self-transcendence via *aufheben* and consequent liberation through the attainment of experiences like *śūnyatā*.

Finally, Chapter 9 took us through the dynamics of character development. We began by viewing life as a *Bildungsroman* in which we nurture the quality and excellence of *areté*. Next, we saw that *areté* rests on consideration and an understanding of ethics, as per *apramāda* and *karma*, respectively. Also important is the cultivation of *savoir faire* (knowing how to live) and *eunoia* (a beautiful mind), along with the utilisation of *orka* (willpower) and *sisu* (determination), especially if one is called or compelled to become a *solivagant* (lone wanderer). When all of these qualities are combined, we may become a *mensch* (a generally good person), although we should always try to emulate *kintsugi* artists by valuing and finding beauty in our own and others' flaws. And then, overall, we must hope that our life has the meaning and purpose of *ikigai* and the fulfilment of *eudaimonia*, all in the knowledge that *tempus fugit* (time flees), and so we need to make every day count.

With that, we have reached our destination. I hope that this book has been and will continue to be a useful companion for you on your journey, wherever you have come from and wherever you are going. We've explored many important ideas in these pages, and it is my sincere wish that at least some of them have resonated with you. If so, I urge you to explore them further. Maybe you are already familiar with some of the emotions, qualities and experiences discussed here but didn't previously have words for them. If so, now you do. On the other hand, perhaps you have also been introduced to some novel notions that you are keen to encounter personally for the first time. If so, this book may help to smooth your path.

Whatever use you make of it, though, I hope that it has shed some light on the nature of happiness and how you might find more of it in your own life.

Glossary

This glossary includes all of the items in the lexicography that are discussed here in the book. Its main purpose is to encourage you to engage with these words in your own lives. For a complete, up-to-date version of the lexicography, please visit www.drtimlomas.com/lexicography.

A brief working definition is provided for each word to convey at least some of its meaning. However, given that most of the words have multiple meanings, the definitions are inevitably partial. More complete explanations are provided in the main text, but even there, though, the discussion may be limited. Therefore, if you are especially interested in a particular term, please consult additional sources, such as the references that are cited in the Notes.

Each word is also rendered phonetically, first as per the International Phonetic Alphabet (IPA) and then transliterated into 'regular' English. Words for which I was unable to source IPA renderings from established dictionaries I have sought to configure into an approximate IPA format myself, based on audio recordings and/or pronunciation guides. As such, this glossary should just be treated as a rough guide, rather than a final and definitive determination of pronunciation. Indeed, given regional dialects and so on, there is rarely a canonical way of articulating a given word. Nevertheless, my intention is to provide sufficient information for you to attempt a basic vocalisation.

A

Abbiocco. Italian / n. / abˈbjɔk.ko / ah-*byokk*-oh. The soporific drowsiness that can follow a meal, especially a large one.

Abhayamudrâ (अभयमुद्रा). Sanskrit / n. / ʌb.haɪ.ə.mʊ.dɹɑː / uhb-hy-uh-moo-drah. A gesture (e.g., in Hindu and Buddhist iconography) of fearlessness, protection, and/or peace; the palm faces outwards and the fingers extend upwards.

Achsenzeit. German / n. / ˈak.sən.tsait / *ak*-sen-tsiyt. Axis or Axial age; coined by Karl Jaspers to denote a key period in human history between the eighth and third centuries BCE, characterised by the emergence of new philosophies.

Adinnādānā (अदन्निदाना). Sanskrit / v., n. / ˈʌ.dɪ.nɑː.dɑːnɑː / *uh*-dih-nah-dah-nah. Taking the not-given (the second of Buddhism's Five Precepts).

Ádvaita (अद्वैत). Sanskrit / n. / ʌd.vaɪ.tʌ / *ud*-vy-tuh. Non-dualism; the notion that there is only one reality, such that the person and the sacred are not separate.

Aficionado. Spanish / n. / ə.fɪs.jəˈnɑː.dəʊ / a-fis-yun-*ah*-doh. Someone who is knowledgeable and/or enthusiastic about something; can have connotations of being an amateur in a benign sense. Lit. to inspire affection.

Agápē (ἀγάπη). Greek / n. / ˌɑˈɡɑːpiː / ag-*ah*-pee. Selfless, unconditional, devotional love.

Agón (ἀγών). Greek / n. / aɣón / ah-gon. Contest, competition, gathering, struggle; used to imply a clash of opposing forces that ultimately results in growth and progress.

Ahura Mazdā (اهورا مزدا). Persian / name / əˌhʊ.rəˌmæz.də / uh-hoo-rah-maz-duh. Lord of Wisdom; wise, intelligent spirit; the creator and supreme being of Zoroastrianism. Lit. Mighty Wisdom.

Aiki (合気). Japanese / n. / ɑ.iːkiː / ah-ee-kee. Blending or harmonising opposing forces within oneself; a dialectical relationship between matched equals; the ability to manipulate another person skilfully. *Aikido* (n.): the way of *aiki*.

Ājīva (आजीव). Sanskrit / n. / ɑːdʒiːwʌ / ah-jee-vwuh. Livelihood, work, mode of life; as per *samyak-ājīva* (i.e., right livelihood), of the Buddhist Noble Eightfold Path.

Akh (ꜣḫ). Egyptian / n. / ækʰ / akh. Thought, intellect; enduring soul; one of the three main constituents of the soul in Egyptian theology; reanimated after death by the union of *ba* and *ka*.

Aljerre-nge. Arrernte (aka Aranda) / n. / ˌaltʃəˈrɪŋgə / al-chuh-*ring*-guh / aka Alcheringa, Ülchurringa. A complex cultural–religious belief system, spanning all elements of life; sometimes referred to as Dreamtime or the Dreaming (occurring 'everywhen', embracing past, present and future).

Aloha. Hawaiian / int. / æˈləʊ.hæ / ah-*loh*-ha. Hello and goodbye, with love and compassion; cognate with Māori *aroha*. Lit. the breath of presence.

Alpha (ἄλφα). Greek / n. / ˈal.fa / *al*-fah. First letter of the Greek alphabet (A, α); can denote the first in a series, or the beginning of something.

Amateur. French / n. / a.ma.tœʀ / ah-mah-toer. Non-professional, hobbyist. Lit. lover or one who loves.

Ambedo. English (new) / n. / æmˈbiːdəʊ / am-*bee*-doh. A melancholic, trance-like state involving absorption in vivid sensory details; coined by John Koenig.

Amour de soi. French / n. / amuʀ də swʌ / a-moor-de-swuh. Self-regard that is not contingent on others' judgement. Lit. love of oneself.

Amour fou. French / n. / amuʀ fu / a-moor-foo. Mad, crazy, foolish love.

Amour propre. French / n. / amuʀ ˈpʀɔ.pʀ / a-moor *prrop*-ruh. Self-regard that is contingent on others' judgement. Lit. self-love.

Anánkē (ἀνάγκη). Greek / n. / aˈnæŋ.kiː / ah-*nang*-kee. Necessity, compulsion, inevitability, fate.

Anātman (अनात्मन्). Sanskrit / n. / anˈaːt.mən / an-*at*-mn. Insubstantiality; lack of permanent self or soul.

Angst. Danish (also German, Dutch) / n. / aŋ(k)st / angkst. Combination of anxiety, alarm, fear, dread and gloom; a prominent emotional state in existentialist philosophy.

Anima. Latin / n. / ˈa.ni.ma / *ah*-nih-mah. Soul; spirit; breath; mind.

Anitya (अनित्य). Sanskrit / n. / æˈniːt.jə / a-*neet*-yuh. Impermanence; the notion that existence is transient and evanescent.

Ansias. Spanish / n. / ˈæn.siːə / an-see-uh. Longing, yearning; worry, anguish; desparate or anxious love (e.g., worrying about a loved one).

Apéritif. French / n. / ap.ɛʀ.it.if / ah-per-ree-teef. A drink taken before dinner (and the associated social occasion).

Apheíresis (ἀφαίρεσις). Greek / n. / afəˈriːsɪs / aff-uh-ree-sis. Abstractive negation; to withdraw or take away and thereby reveal the truth (e.g., in mystical theology).

Aphrodíte (Αφροδίτη). Greek / name / a.fro.di.tiː / ah-froh-dee-tee. In Greek mythology, the goddess of love, beauty, sexuality and procreation; known as Venus in Roman mythology.

Apollo (Απόλλων). Greek / name / aˈpól.lɔ / a*poll*-oh. Greek and Roman deity; god of light, the sun, truth, prophecy and healing.

Apramāda (अप्रमाद). Sanskrit / n. / ʌ.prʌˈmaːdʌ / uh-pruh-*mah*-duh. Earnestness, alertness, diligence, moral watchfulness.

S'apprivoiser. French / v. / s͵apʀiˈvwa.ze / s-a-prre-*vwa*-zay. In the context of a relationship, a mutual process of learning to trust and accept the other person. Lit. to tame.

Arbejdsglæde. Danish / n. / ˈaːbaɪd̥ˢs͵glɪl / ar-bides-glil. Pleasure or satisfaction derived from work. Lit. work gladness.

Arcigola. Italian / n. / ͵art.ʃiˈgola / art-chee-*goo*-lah. The original name for the 'Slow Food' movement. Lit. society of gluttons (ARCI is an Italian social institution, while 'arch' can also imply authority; *gola* means gluttony or appetite).

Areté (ἀρετή). Greek / n. / aˈre.tḗ / ah-*reh*-tay. Excellence, quality; virtue.

Arhat (अर्हत्). Sanskrit / n. / ˈaːhʌt / *aar*-hut. A worthy or perfect individual; one who has attained enlightenment.

Arkadíā (Αρκαδία). Greek / n. / aɾ.ka.ðía / ar-kay-dthee-ah. A pastoral utopia; an idyllic realm; living in harmony with nature. Lit. a region of Greece.

Arrangiarsi. Italian / v. / a.ranˈdʒaːsiː / a-rran-*jar*-see. To make do, get by, get along.

Āsana (आसन). Sanskrit / n. / ʌːsə.nə / uh-suh-nuh. Yoga postures. Lit. seat or sitting position.

Aseret ha-Dibrot (תורבידה תרשע). Hebrew / n. / æˈseət hæ.diːˈbrɒt / ah-*sairt* hah-dee-*broht* / aka Aseret ha-d'varîm. The Ten

Commandments, aka the Decalogue. Lit. ten words, statements, sayings.

Ashtangika (अष्टांगिक). Sanskrit / n. / ʌʃ.tʌŋ.gɪ.kʌ / ush-tung-gee-kuh. Eightfold, as per the Buddhist Noble Eightfold Path.

Ataraxia (ἀταραξία). Greek / n. / ɑ.tə'ɹæk.siə / at-tuh-*rak*-sia. Robust and lucid tranquillity; peace of mind; calmness.

Ātman (आत्मन्). Sanskrit / n. / 'ɑːt.mən / *uht*-mn. Soul, spirit; breath.

Ātomos (ἄτομος). Greek / n. / æ.tɒ.mɒs / ah-toh-mos. The idea of the universe being composed of fundamental units. Lit. indivisible or uncuttable.

Aufheben. German / v. / 'aʊf.heːbən / *orf*-hee-bn. To sublimate; to raise up; to remove, suspend, repeal, set aside; to negate and also preserve.

Auṃ or Oṃ (ॐ). Sanskrit / particle / əʊmː / aohmm. A sacred syllable/ mantra associated with various traditions; the 'cosmic sound' encapsulating all teachings; the beginning (*alpha*) and end (*omega*) of all things.

Avant-garde. French / n. / a.vɑ̃.gaʀd / ah-von-gaard. People, artworks, ideas, etc. that are unorthodox, experimental, radical. Lit. vanguard.

Avatāra (अवतार). Sanskrit / n. / ʌ.vʌ.tɑːʀʌ / uh-vuh-tar-uh. The incarnation or embodiment of a deity in human or animal form. Lit. descent.

Avos (авось). Russian / particle / ɐ'vosʲ / ah-*voss*. Maybe, what if; faith, trust, hope in luck, serendipity, destiny, fate.

Azart (азарт). Russian / n. / ɐ'zaːrt / ah-*zarrt*. Heat, excitement, ardour, fervour.

B

Ba (bꜣ). Egyptian / n. / bæ / bah. Personality; everything that makes an individual unique; one of the three main constituents of the soul in Egyptian theology.

Béatitude. French / n. / beɪ'ætɪtjuːd / bay-*at*-it-ude. Supreme happiness; a state of blessedness.

Bhakti (भक्ति). Sanskrit / n. / bʰʌʜk.tiː / bhahk-tee. Fondness, attachment, homage, reverence.

Bhāvana (भावन). Sanskrit / n. / bʰhɑːwnɑː / bh-*hav*-nah. Cultivation, practice; meditation; application, development.

Bīja (बीज). Sanskrit / n. / biːdʒʌ / bee-juh. Seed(s); as per *bīja-niyāma*, the law of seeds, referring to causal patterns in the realm of organic phenomena.

Bildung. German / n. / ˈbɪl.dʊŋ / *bill*-doong. Education, formation, acculturation, cultivation, development.

Bildungsroman. German / n. / ˈbɪl.dʊŋs ʁo.maːn / *bill*-doongs roe-mahn. A coming-of-age story; a narrative of education or formation.

Boketto (ぼけっと). Japanese / adv. / bəʊ.kɛt.təʊ / boh-ket-toh. Vacantly, idly; e.g., gazing absently into the distance (without thought or sense of self).

Bon vivant. French / n. / bɔ̃ vivã / boh-vih-voh. Someone who enjoys and appreciates the good life.

Brahman (ब्रह्मन्). Sanskrit / n. / ˈbrɑːˌmən / *brah*-mun. The transcendent and immanent absolute reality; the supreme spirit that continually brings existence into being.

Brahma-vihārā (ब्रह्मविहारा). Sanskrit / n. / ˈbrɑːˌmə vɪˈhɑːrə / *brah*-muh vi-*har*-ruh. Qualities Buddhist practitioners are encouraged to cultivate. Lit. abode or dwelling of Brahma (the god of creation in Hindu theology).

Bricolage. French / n. / bʀi.kɔ.laʒ / brih-koh-laazge. DIY; a makeshift job; construction of something using whatever comes to hand.

Buddha (बुद्ध). Sanskrit / n. / bʊˈdːʰə / bd-*dha*. An awakened, enlightened being.

Budō (武道). Japanese / n. / buːdəʊ / boo-doh. Martial arts. Lit. the art or way of war.

C

Cafuné. Portuguese / n. / ˌka.fu.ˈnɛ / cah-foo-*neh*. The act of tenderly running fingers through a loved one's hair.

Camarada. Spanish / n. / kamaˈraða / cah-mah-*rah*-dtha. Pal, friend; basis for the term 'comrade'. Lit. roommate.

Carpe diem. Latin / exclamation / ˌkɑːrpeɪ ˈdaɪem / kar-pay *dey*-em. Make the most of the present moment or opportunity. Lit. seize the day.

Catvāri āryasatyāni (चत्वारिआर्यसत्यानि). Sanskrit / n. / kʌtˈwaːɹi ˌaːjʌˈsʌtˈjaːnɪ / cat-*vwah*-ree ah-yuh-suht-*yah*-nee. Buddhism's four Noble Truths. Lit. truths of the noble ones.

Chadō (茶道). Japanese / n. / ʧɑːdəʊ / chah-doh. The art of tea.

Chán (禪). Chinese / n. / tʃæːn / chan. Concentrated attention or absorption; the Chinese adaptation of *dhyāna*.

Charmolypi (χαρμολύπη). Greek / n. / sɑːməʊˈlɪ.piː / sar-mo-lih-pee. Sweet or 'joy-making' sorrow; mourning joy; happiness and sadness intermingled.

Chiaroscuro. Italian / n. / kjarosˈkuro / kyar-oss-*kour*-oh. Contrasts of light and dark/shade (usually pertaining to art).

Ching (經). Chinese / *n.* / ʧɪŋ / ching / aka jīng. Rule, norm; plan; classic, great book; scripture.

Chōros (χῶρος). Greek / n. / ˈkʰɔːrɒs / *khor*-ross. A place; usually denotes the quality of the place.

Chrysalism. English (new) / n. / ˈkrɪs.ə.lɪsm / *kriss*-uh-lissm. The amniotic tranquillity of being indoors during a thunderstorm; coined by John Koenig.

Chutzpah. Yiddish / n. / ˈxʊts.pə / *khutz*-puh. Insolence, cheek, audacity; nerve, effrontery, guts; may be used pejoratively.

Citta (चित्त). Sanskrit / n. / tʃɪ.dæ / chih-dtha. Mind and heart (combined); consciousness, awareness.

Cocaigne. French / n. / kɒ.kaɲ / kok-ang / aka Cockaigne (English). A mythical land of ease and plenty (etymology uncertain).

Coitus. Latin / n. / ˈkɔɪ.təs / *koy*-tss. Attraction; magnetic force; sexual union. Lit. coming, meeting, uniting together.

Compadre. Spanish / n. / kəmˈpɑːdreɪ / kom-*pah*-drray. Godfather; a term of respect and friendship for a man. Lit. co-fathers.

Concordia discors. Latin / n. / konˈkor.di.a ˈdis.kors / kon-*kor*-dee-ah *diss*-kors. Harmony (*concordia*) from discord (*discors*); discordant harmony; the principle that conflicts or oppositions can create harmony.

Connaisseur. French / n., adj. / kɔ.nɛ.sœʀ / koh-nay-sir. Expert; borrowed as 'connoisseur' in English. Lit. one who knows.

Cornu copiae. Latin / n. / kɔːnuː kəʊ.piːə / kor-noo koh-pee-uh. A symbol of nourishment and abundance, often a horn-shaped container filled with produce. Lit. horn of plenty.

Coup de foudre. French / n. / ku də ˈfudrə / coo-duh-*foo*-druh. Sudden and powerful love at first sight. Lit. a lightning bolt.

Craic. Gaelic / n. / kræk / crack. Fun, revelry, good times.

Cynefin. Welsh / n. / ˈkʌ.nɨ.vɪn / *kun*-uh-vin. Haunt, habitat; a place where one was born and/or feels at home.

D

Dada. French / n. / da.da / da-da. Avant-garde art movement that rejected logic and rationality as well as modern conventions, aesthetics and ideologies. Lit. hobby-horse; or meaningless babble.

Dadirri. Ngangiwumirr / n. / dəˈdɪ.ri / duh-*dir*-rree. A deep, spiritual act of reflective and respectful listening.

Daggfrisk. Swedish / n., adj. / dæːg.frɪsk / daag-frisk. The pure, clean feeling one might have from waking refreshed at sunrise. Lit. dew fresh.

Daímōn (δαίμον). Greek / n. / ˈðɛ.mɔn / *dthe*-mohn. A divine power that drives/guides human actions; a manifestation or channelling of divine power.

Dān tián (丹田). Chinese / n. / dæn.tiːɛn / dan tee-en. Places in the body that are believed to be significant in the flow of *qi*; focal points for meditative exercises. Lit. energy centre.

Dasein. German / v., n. / ˈdaːzaɪn / dah-zine. Martin Heidegger's term for a human being, capturing the notion that people always already exist in a context. Lit. being here/there.

Das Man. German / n. / das man / dass man. People, anyone; one. Lit. they-self or the they.

Datsuzoku (脱俗). Japanese / n. / dæt.su:zəʊ.kuː / dat-soo-zoh-koo. Unworldliness, saintliness; freedom from habit, escape from routine and the conventional. Lit. shedding or removing (*datsu*) worldliness or mundanity (*zoku*).

Dēmētēr (Δημήτηρ). Greek / name / dɨˈmiːtər / deh-*mee*-tuh. In Greek mythology, the goddess of grain, harvest, agriculture, fertility; known as Ceres in Roman mythology.

Dēmokratíā (δημοκρατία). Greek / n. / ðɪ.mo.kraˈti.a / thi-moh-kra-*tee*-ah. Force, power (*krátos*) of the people, citizens (*dêmos*).

Denkmal. German / n. / ˈdɛŋk.maːl / denk-maal. Monument, memorial. Lit. think-sign.

Desbundar. Portuguese / v. / dʒizbũˈdar / dez-bun-*dar*. Exceeding one's limits; shedding one's inhibitions (e.g., when having fun).

Desenrascanço. Portuguese / n. / ˌdɨ.zẽĵ.ʁɐʃˈkɐ̃.sʊ / *deh*-zen-hass-*can*-so. Artful disentanglement (e.g., from trouble); an improvised solution.

Dewachen (བདེ་བ་ཅན་). Tibetan / name / diːwə.ʧən / dee-wuh-chuhn / aka Sukhāvatī (Sanskrit). A celestial 'Pure Land' in certain schools of Buddhism. Lit. Land of Pure Bliss.

Dhárma (धर्म). Sanskrit / n. / ˈd̪ʱɑːmə / dhar-muh. Law; what is established; principles of the universe; guidelines for action; teachings (often specifically the Buddha's teachings).

Dhármacakrá (धर्मचक्र). Sanskrit / n. / ˈd̪ʱɑːmə.ʧʌk.ɽʌ / dhar-muh-chuk-ruh. A way of conceptualising, representing and teaching the dhárma. Lit. wheel of dhárma.

Dhvani (ध्वनि). Sanskrit / n. / dʰ.vʌ.nɪ / dh-vuh-nih. Sound, echo; hint, allusion; used in aesthetics and art appreciation to refer to allusion and implied or hidden meaning.

Dhyāna (ध्यान). Sanskrit / n. / ˌdh'jɑːnæ / dh-yaa-na. Intense, concentrated attention and absorption; cultivated and valued states of mind (which can be ordered in a developmental sequence).

Dionysus (Διόνυσος). Greek / name / ðió.ni.sos / dthe-oh-nee-soss. Greek god of wine, madness, frenzy, theatre and ecstasy; known as Bacchus in Roman mythology.

Disegno. Italian / n. / diˈsɛn.yɔ / dee-sen-yo. Fine-art drawing; the formal discipline required to represent the ideal form of an object in the visual arts.

Dǫkkálfar. Old Norse / n. / dɒk.æl.fɑː / dok-al-far. Dark elves (in Norse mythology); spirit beings who live within or under the earth.

Doxa (δόξα). Greek / n. / ˈdok.sä / dok-sah. Common belief, popular opinion; behaviour or practice in worship; glory.

Dṛṣṭi (दृष्टि). Sanskrit / n. / dʰrʃ.tʰɪ / dsh-thih. View, gaze, sight; as per samyak-dṛṣṭi, of the Buddhist Noble Eightfold Path.

Druptap (སྒྲུབ་ཐབས་). Tibetan / n. / drʌp tʰæp / drup-tap / aka sgrub thabs, sādhanā (Sanskrit). Exertion towards a spiritual goal; advanced meditation practices. Lit. means of accomplishing something.

Duende. Spanish / n. / ˈdwe̞n.de̞ / de-wen-deh. A heightened state of emotion, spirit and passion, often associated with visual art, music or dance.

Duḥkha (दुःख). Sanskrit / n. / ˈdʊ.kʰə / duh-kuh. Dissatisfaction, discomfort; suffering.

E

Ego. Latin / n. / ˈɛ.ɡɔ / *eh*-go. I, me, we; used by translators of Freud to represent the German *Ich*, referring to the construct of self.

Ehrenmal. German / n. / ˈeːrən.maːl / eer-en-maal. Monument or memorial to honour something or someone. Lit. honour-sign.

Eidólon (εἴδωλον). Greek / n. / ˈaɪ.ðo.lon / *eye*-dtho-lon. Image, representation, reflection; phantom; idol.

Eigentlichkeit. German / n. / ˈaignt.lɪç.haɪt / iy-gnt-leesh-kiyt. Ownedness, being owned, being one's own; often rendered as 'authenticity'.

Eigenwillig. German / adj. / ˈaign.vɪlɪç / i-gn-vill-isch. To have a will of one's own; behaving in a manner that reflects one's own personality.

Èit. Scottish Gaelic / n. / aɪt / iyt. Quartz crystals placed in streams so that they shine and sparkle in the moonlight.

Ékstasis (ἔκστασις). Greek / n. / ékˈstaːsis / ek-*stah*-sis. The state of being or standing outside oneself; trance, displacement; ecstasy, rapture.

Enkidu. Akkadian / name / ɛn.kiːduː / en-kee-doo. A wild, mythological figure, emblematic of nature, in the *Epic of Gilgamesh*; friend of the main protagonist, his death teaches Gilgamesh about mortality. Lit. creation of Enki (a Sumerian god).

En plein air. French / n., adj. / ã plɛn ɛʀ / ohn-plen-ayrr. Outdoors; in the open air.

Enraonar. Catalan / v. / en.ra.oˈna / en-ra-oh-*nha*. To discuss in a civilised, reasoned manner.

Enthousiasmos (ἐνθουσιασμός). Greek / n. / en.θu.si.asˈmos / en-thoo-sias-*mous*. The state of being inspired, possessed or driven by a divine being or force.

Epithymía (ἐπιθυμία). Greek / n. / e.pi.θyˈmi.a / ep-e-thy-*mee*-ah. Desire; sexual passion.

Erfolgserlebnis. German / n. / ɜːˈfɒlks.ɜːliːb.nɪs / er-*folks*-er-leeb-niss. A feeling of success; a sense of achievement. Lit. success experience.

Érōs (ἔρως). Greek / n., name / ˈe.rɔːs / *eh*-ross. Desire; passionate love; the god of love and desire in Greek mythology; known as Cupid in Roman mythology.

L'esprit de l'escalier. French / phrase / lɛsˈpʀi də lɛsˈkal.je /

less-*prree*-duh-less-*kal*-ee-ay. A witty and/or incisive rejoinder that comes to mind shortly after an interaction. Lit. staircase wit.

Et (את). Hebrew / particle / ɑːt / aht. A structural word that indicates the direct object of a sentence; its two letters – *aleph* (א) and *tav* (ת) – are also the first and last letters of the Hebrew alphabet, so it can imply the beginning and the end of something.

Eudaimonia (εὐδαιμονία). Greek / n. / juːdɨˈmoʊ.nɪə / yoo-de-*moe*-nee-uh. Being infused with divine grace; fulfilment, flourishing. Lit. benefitting from the agency of a good or beautiful (*eu*) spirit (*daimon*).

Eunoia (εὔνοια). Greek / n. / juːˈnɔɪ.ɑ / yoo-*noi*-ya. Good or beautiful thinking.

Euphoría (εὐφορία). Greek / n. / ju.pʰo.ríːa / yoo-for-ree-ah. Intense excitement or joy. Lit. being of good bearing.

F

Fernweh. German / n. / ˈfɪɜːn.veː / *fiern*-vay. Longing for the unknown; yearning for distant places. Lit. far pain.

Fiero. Italian / n. / ˈfjɛːɹo / fee-*yeah*-ro. Pride and satisfaction in one's achievements; especially deployed as a loanword when implying that this satisfaction has been earned.

Fiesta. Spanish / n. / fɪˈɛstə / fee-*ess*-tuh. Party; celebration.

Fika. Swedish / n. / fiːkæ / fee-kah. A coffee break; derived from *kaffe* (coffee).

Flânerie. French / n. / flɑn.ri / flon-ree. Leisurely or aimless strolling. *Flâneur* (n.): one who strolls. *Flâner* (v.): to stroll.

Folkelig. Danish / adj. / fɒlˈkɪ.liː / foll-*ki*-lee. Folkish; belonging to the people; democratic national spirit or sentiment; having broad popular appeal.

Freier Einfall. German / n. / ˈfraɪɐ ˈeɪn.fʌl / frhyer ain-ful. Free, spontaneous (*freier*) association, invasion, idea (*Einfall*); original German term for the Freudian technique of free association.

Frimousse. French / n. / fʀi.mus / frree-moose. A sweet or cute little face.

Frisson. French / n. / fʀisõ / frree-soh. A thrill; shiver; a combination of fear and excitement.

Fukinsei (不均整). Japanese / n. / fuˈkɪn.seɪ / foo-*kin*-say. Natural and spontaneous asymmetry or irregularity.

Fuubutsushi (風物詩). Japanese / n. / fu.bu.tsu.ʃi / foo-boo-tsoo-shi. 'Scenery poetry'; phenomena that evoke or prompt thoughts of a particular season.

G

Gaia (Γαῖα). Greek / name / 'γɛ.a / *kheh*-uh. Earth; in Greek mythology, the primordial Mother Earth.

Ganzheit. German / n. / 'gænz.haɪt / *ganz*-hite. Unity; integrated whole; undivided completeness; total and complete.

Geborgenheit. German / n. / gə'bɔʁ.gn̩.haɪt / guh-*bor*-gn-hite. Feeling protected and safe from harm.

Gedenkstätte. German / n. / gə'dɛŋk.ʃtɛtə / guh-dengk-shtet-uh. Memory, reflection; memorial, shrine. Lit. place of remembrance.

Gelassenheit. German / n. / gə'lasn̩.haɪt / geh-*lah*-sen-hiyt. Self-surrender, abandonment; yielding to God's will; serenity, calmness.

Gemilut hasadim (סֵיְדָסֵח תּוּלִיְמַג). Hebrew / n. / gɛ.mi'luːt ʜæ.sæ'diːm / geh-mee-*loot* hah-sah-*deem*. Acts of loving-kindness.

Gemütlichkeit. German / n. / gə'myːt.lɪç.kaɪt / guh-*moot*-lish-kite. A feeling of comfort, cosiness, homeliness. *Gemütlich* (adj.): cosy, homely, comfortable.

Gestalt. German / n. / gə'ʃtalt / guh-*shtalt*. An overall pattern or configuration; the notion that the whole is greater or other than the sum of its parts.

Geworfenheit. German / n. / gə'vɔːfən.haɪt / guh-*vor*-fuhn-hite. Thrownness; the condition, characteristic of human existence, of being thrown into contexts not of one's choosing.

Gigil. Tagalog / n. / 'gʰiː.gɪlː / *ghih*-gill. The irresistible urge to pinch or squeeze someone because they are loved or cherished.

Gnōmōn (γνώμων). Greek / n. / 'noʊmɒn / noh-mon. The vertical shadow-caster on a sundial. Lit. one who knows.

Gnôsis (γνῶσις). Greek / n. / g'nəʊ.sɪs / gnoe-sis. Knowledge; often implying secret or esoteric wisdom.

Gōng fu (功夫). Chinese / n. / gɒŋ.fuː / gong-foo. Acquisition of a skill, particularly after an investment of time and effort; now usually used specifically in reference to martial arts. Lit. work or achievement.

Gourmand. French / n. / ɡuʀmɑ̃ / goor-mohn. A person who appreciates and/or consumes good food and drink; often connotes greed
or gluttony.

Gourmet. French / n. / ɡuʀ.mɛ / goor-mehy. A person who appreciates and/or is knowledgable about good food and drink; more
refined implications than *gourmand*.

Gula. Spanish / n. / ˈɡuːlæ / *goo*-lah. Gluttony, greed; indulgence;
eating simply for the taste (i.e., not to satisfy hunger).

Gümüş servi. Turkish / n. / ɡə.muːʃ seə.vi / guh-moosh ser-vee / aka
serv-i sîmîn (original phrasing). The shining white glimmer of
moonlight on water. Lit. silver cypress tree.

Guru (गुरु). Sanskrit / n. / ɡʊ.ɾʊ / goo-roo. A religious or spiritual
teacher, guide, master; a revered person.

H

Hachnasat orchim (מיחרוא תסנכה). Hebrew / n. / ɦax.na.ʃat ɔːxɪm /
hakh-nash-at orh-khim. Welcoming or bringing in guests;
offering hospitality and respect to strangers.

Haiku (俳句). Japanese / n. / hai.ku: / hai-koo. A form of Japanese
poetry, usually seventeen syllables in length (with lines of five,
seven and five syllables), usually involves sudden juxtapositions
of ideas or images, especially relating to natural (e.g., seasonal)
phenomena.

Háidēs (Ἀδης). Greek / name / haˌjˈdɛːs / har-dees. In Greek mythology, both the underworld itself and the god of the underworld,
death, the dead, and wealth; deity known as Pluto in Roman
mythology.

Hallelujah (הַיְוּלְלָה). Hebrew / n., exclamation / ˌhæ.liˈluːjə / ha-
leh-*loo*-yuh. God be praised; an expression of worship or
rejoicing.

Han (한). Korean / n. / hæn / han. Sorrow, resentment, regret; possibly
with a sense of patiently waiting for redemption.

Harmonía (ἁρμονία). Greek / n. / ɑːmaʊˈniːjə / ah-moh-nee-yuh.
Concordance, union, agreement (e.g., of sounds).

Hatha (हठ). Sanskrit / n., adj. / hʌ.θə / huh-thuh. Branch of yoga
that focuses on the practice of *āsana* (postures) and *vinyāsa*
(dynamic transitions). Lit. force, effort, exertion.

Haute cuisine. French / n. / ˈo kɥizin / *oh*-kwee-zeen. Fine dining, especially involving rare and/or expensive ingredients, eaten in exclusive establishments. Lit. high cooking.

Heimlich. German / adj. / ˈhaɪm.lɪç / *hime*-lisch. Pertaining to the home; comfortable, familiar, known; secretive, clandestine.

Herrliche Gefühle. German / n. / ˈhɛrlɪç gəˈfyːl / *hair*-leesh guh-*foool*. Glorious, lovely, gorgeous (*herrliche*) feelings, sentiments (*Gefühle*); associated with Goethe, who described these as forces that 'give us life'.

Hiraeth. Welsh / n. / hira.ɪθ / heerr-ithe. Nostalgic, wistful longing for one's homeland; pertains to Wales specifically.

Hózhǫ. Navaho / n. / hɔ̃.ʒɔ̃ / hoh-zho. Peace, balance, beauty, harmony.

Hubris (ὕβρις). Greek / n. / hý.bris / hoo-briss. Extreme pride, arrogance or overconfidence; especially associated with behaviour that challenges or defies the gods.

Hugfanginn. Icelandic / adj. / ˈhuːfʌŋ.gɪn / hoo-fun-gin. To be enchanted or fascinated by someone or something. Lit. mind-captured.

Hygge. Danish/Norwegian / n. / ˈhʊːgə / hhoo-guh. A deep sense of place, warmth, friendship, contentment. *Hyggelig* (adj.): enjoyable, warm, friendly, pleasant.

I

Ib. Egyptian / n. / ɪb / ib. Heart (physical and metaphysical); the seat of emotion, thought, will and intention; a constituent of the soul in Egyptian theology.

Id. Latin / n. / ɪd / id. It or that; used by translators of Freud to represent the German *Es*, referring to instinctual drives.

Ikigai (生き甲斐). Japanese / n. / iːki.gɑi / ee-kee-gaee. A reason for being; meaning, purpose in life. Lit. life result, worth, use or benefit.

Iktsuarpok. Inuit / n. / ɪk.ˈt͡ʃuɑːpɒk / ik-*tsua*-pok. Anticipation felt while waiting for another's arrival, often accompanied by frequent checks on their progress.

In sha' Allah (ﻥِﺍَءﺎَﻟﻟّﻪ). Arabic / exclamation / ˌɪn.ʃˈɑ.lə / in-*shall*-ah. God willing; a hopeful wish. Lit. may God wish it.

J

Janteloven. Danish/Norwegian / n. / ˈjan.də̩loʊʔən / *yan*-deh-*low*-ven. Rules that discourage individualism; coined by Aksel Sandemose in the novel *A Fugitive Crosses His Tracks*. Lit. laws of Jante.

Jeong (정). Korean / n. / tɕ͡ʌŋ / chung. Deep affection, affinity, connectedness.

Jñāna (ज्ञान). Sanskrit / n. / ˌgnˈjɑːˌnæ / gn-*yaa*-na. Knowledge, especially experiential forms of apprehension (e.g., acquired through meditation); the total experience of an object; clear awareness.

Joie de vivre. French / n. / ˌʒwɑː də ˈviːvrə / *jwa*-de-*vee*-vruh. Zest for life; exuberance, ebullience; the knack of knowing how to live. Lit. joy of living.

Jouissance. French / n. / ʒˈwi.sɑ̃s / szh-*wee*-sonse. Physical or intellectual pleasure; delight, ecstasy; an orgasm.

Jūdō (柔道). Japanese / n. / dʒuːdəʊ / joo-doh. Martial art in which the aim is to subdue or immobilise an opponent (e.g., by pinning them to the floor). Lit. gentle way.

K

Ka (kꜣ). Egyptian / n. / kæ / kah. Vital essence; that which separates a living being from a dead one; one of the three main constituents of the soul in Egyptian theology.

Kairos (καιρός). Greek / n. / kɛˈros / keh-*ross*. The most opportune, ideal, supreme moment for decision or action; the right way, amount, moment.

Kāmesu micchācāra (कामेसुमिच्छाचारा). Sanskrit / n. / kɑːmeɪ.sʊ mɪk.hɑːʧɑːrʌ / kar-may-soo mik-har-char-uh. Unwholesome sexual or sensual behaviour or misconduct; proscribed by the third of Buddhism's Five Precepts.

Kanso (簡素). Japanese / n. / ˈkæn.sɒ / *kan*-soh. Simple, plain; elegant simplicity or a pleasing absence of clutter in works of art.

Kanyininpa. Pintupi / n. / ˌkæn.jɪnˈɪn.pə / *kan*-yin-*in*-puh. A protective, nurturing relationship between the provider and the recipient of care. Lit. holding.

Karma (कर्म). Sanskrit / n. / ˈkaːma / *kar*-muh. A theory or principle of causality, particularly with respect to ethical behaviour. Lit. action, work, deed.

Karmānta (कर्मान्त). Sanskrit / n. / kʌ.mɑːn.tʌ / kuh-marn-tuh. Action, management; administration; as per *samyak-karmānta* (i.e., right action), of the Buddhist Noble Eightfold Path.

Karuṇā (करुणा). Sanskrit / n. / kæ.rʉˈŋɑː / ka-roo-*nar*. Empathy, compassion; identifying with the other's suffering.

Kefi (κέφι). Greek / n. / ˈkeə.fi / *keh*-fee. Joy, passion, enthusiasm; high spirits; frenzy.

Kenopsia. English (new) / n. / kɛnˈɒp.si:ə / ken-*op*-see-uh. From the Greek roots *kenosis* (emptiness) and *opsia* (seeing); appraising the lack or absence of something (especially people); the strange eerieness of empty or abandoned places; coined by John Koenig.

Khaos (χάος). Greek / n. / xáos / khah-oss. Chaos; in Greek mythology, the void before the birth of the cosmos.

Kilig. Tagalog / n. / kɪˈliːg / kih-*leeg*. Sensation of butterflies in the stomach during interactions with a loved one or object of desire; exhilaration and elation, not necessarily romantic. Lit. shaking or trembling.

Kintsugi (金継ぎ). Japanese / n. / kɪn.tsʊ.gi / kin-tsu-gi. The art of repairing broken pottery using gold lacquer; metaphorically, rendering flaws and fault-lines beautiful and strong. Lit. golden joinery.

Klexos. English (new). n. / ˈklɛks.əʊs / *klek*-sohss. The art of dwelling on the past; coined by John Koenig.

Kōan (公案). Japanese / n. / ˈkəʊ.ɑn / koh-an. Principles of reality existing outside subjective opinion; an unanswerable question or riddle used in Zen to facilitate awakening. Lit. public record, official business.

Koinōnía (κοινωνία). Greek / n. / kɔɪˈnəʊ.nɪə / koy-*non*-ee-uh. Fellowship, communion; joint participation; connection, intimacy.

Koi no yokan (恋の予感). Japanese / n. / ˈkɔi.nɒ.jɒ.kæn / *ko*ee-nor-yo-kan. Premonition or presentiment of love; the conviction, on first meeting someone, that falling in love is inevitable.

Koko (考古). Japanese / n. / kɒ.kɒ / ko-ko. Weathered beauty; austere sublimity.

Komorebi (木漏れ日). Japanese / n. / kɒ.mɒˈɹe.bɪ / ko-mo-*reh*-bi. Dappled sunlight filtering through leaves. Lit. wood leaking sunlight.

Kosmos (κόσμος). Greek / n. / ˈkós.mos / *koss*-moss. The world or universe as a complex and orderly system.

Koyaanisqatsi. Hopi / n. / ˌkɔɪ.ɑːnɪsˈkɑːtsiː / koy-an-iss-*kah*-tsee. Nature out of balance; a dysfunctional state of affairs that calls for another way of living.

Kuài lè (快乐). Chinese / n. / ˌkwaɪˈlə: / kwy-*ler*. Pleasure, satisfaction; hedonic happiness. Lit. quick joy.

Kvell. Yiddish / v. / kvɛl / kvell. To feel strong and overt (expressed) pride and joy in someone else's success.

L

Lagom. Swedish / n. / ˈlɑːˌgɔm / *laar*-gom. Moderation; performing an action to precisely the right degree or amount.

Lakṣaṇa (लक्षण). Sanskrit / n. / ˈlʊk.ʃʊn.ə / *look*-shn-uh. Symptom, sign; quality, attribute; marks of conditioned existence.

Landvættir. Old Norse / n. / ˈlʌnt.vɛt.teə / *lunt*-veh-teear. In Norse mythology, land spirits, wights, sprites.

Lebenskrankheit. German / n. / leːbnsˈkʁaŋkˌhaɪt / lee-buns-*krank*-hite. Existential anomie; world-weariness; coined by Hermann Hesse to describe his own state of mind. Lit. life sickness.

Leggiadria. Italian / n. / l̩eddˈʒäˈd̠ɾ̠iːä / led-jah-*dree*-ah. Grace, loveliness, prettiness, elegance.

Lha'i rnal 'byor (ཀྱེའི་རྣལ་འབྱོར). Tibetan / n. / lə.hæiː rə.næl bəjɔː / luh-hah-ee ruh-nall buh-yor. Deity meditation, yoga; an advanced practice in which the meditator visualises interacting with or even becoming a deity.

Lǐ (理). Chinese / n. / liːi / lee-e. Law, order; rationality, reason; often used particularly with respect to the organic order found in nature (e.g., a flower as a systematic, cohesive organism).

Lǐ (禮). Chinese / n. / liːi / lee-e. Etiquette, decorum; ceremony, custom.

Līlā (लीला). Sanskrit / n. / liːlə / lee-luh. In Hinduism, reality as the outcome of creative divine play. Lit. game, play.

Ljósálfar. Old Norse / n. / ljouːs.æl.fɑː / lyoos-al-far. In Norse mythology, light elves who live in Álfheim.

Logos (λόγος). Greek / n. / ˈlo.ɣos / *loh*-yoss. Word, reason, plan; in theology, the principle of divine reason and creative order.

Ludus. Latin / n. / ˈluːdʊs / *loo*-dss. Playful or gameful forms of affection. Lit. game.

M

Maadoittuminen. Finnish / v. / ˈmɑːdoi̯.tuːmɪ.ɛn / mah-doi-too-min-en. Grounding, earthing; rooting oneself in nature.

Madhyama mārga (मध्यम मार्ग). Sanskrit / n. / ˈmʌdʰ.jʌ.mʌ ˈmʌɹːgʌ / mudh-yuh-muh mur-guh. The middle way or path; often used in reference to Buddhism.

Magari. Italian / adv. / maˈgɑːri / ma-gah-ree. Maybe, possibly; hopeful wish, wistful regret; in my dreams; if only.

Mahābhūta (महाभूत). Sanskrit / n. / mʌ.haːbʰuːtə / muh-har-bhoo-tuh. Great elements or forces; the dimensions or components that constitute the physical world – air, fire, water and earth.

Mahnmal. German / n. / ˈmaːnˌmaːl / marn-marl. Memorial or monument to a tragedy that serves as a warning against repeating it. Lit. warning sign.

Makários (μακάριος). Greek / n. / maˈkaːri.u / mah-kah-ree-oo. Blessed; happy.

Mamihlapinatapai. Yagán / n. / ˈmæ.mi.læ.pɪ.næ.tæˌpai / mah-me-lah-pee-nah-tah-pie. A look between people that expresses unspoken but mutual intent.

Manaakitanga. Māori / n. / ma.naːkɪ.tʌŋə / ma-nah-ki-tung-uh. Hospitality, kindness, generosity, support; respect and care for others.

Mandala (मण्डल). Sanskrit / n. / ˈmʌn.dʌ.lʌ / mun-duh-luh. A spiritual symbol, especially in Buddhism and Hinduism, usually geometric in form, representing the cosmos or aspects of it. Lit. circle.

Mångata. Swedish / n. / ˈmoːŋˌgɑːta / moo-on-gah-tah. The path of glimmering light that moonlight makes on water. Lit. moon (måne) road/path (gata).

Mania (μανία). Greek / n. / ma.nía / mah-nee-ah. Madness, frenzy, possession.

Mantra (मन्त्र). Sanskrit / n. / mʌn.trʌ / mun-truh. A meaningful word, phrase or sound that serves as an object of focus in meditation. Lit. mind tool.

Mārga (मार्ग). Sanskrit / n. / ˈmʌɹːgʌ / mur-guh. Path, road, way; often specifically a spiritual path (e.g., as per the fourth Noble Truth of Buddhism).

Mbuki-mvuki. Swahili / v. / mbuːkiː mvuːkiː / mm-boo-kee

mm-*voo*-kee. To shed clothes in order to dance; possible root of the phrase 'boogie-woogie'. Lit. to take off in flight (*mbuki*), to dance wildly (*mvuki*).

Melmastia (ملمستیا). Pashto / n. / mɛlˈmæs.tiʌ / mel-*mass*-tiah. Hospitality; the moral obligation to offer sanctuary and respect to all visitors.

Memento mori. Latin / n. / məˌmen.təʊ ˈmɔːri / meh-men-toh *moor*-ee. An object or symbol that serves as a reminder or warning of death and mortality.

Memento vivere. Latin / exclamation / məˌmentəʊ ˈvi.ve.re / meh-men-toh *vee*-ver-eh. Remember life; remember to live.

Mensch. Yiddish / n. / mɛntʃ / mentsh. A good human being in the fullest sense.

Meraki (μεράκι). Greek / n. / mɛˈræ.ki: / meh-*rrack*-ee. Ardour, especially for one's own actions and creations.

Meriggiare. Italian / v. / mɛ.rɪˈdʒeɑːrɪ / me-rri-*jah*-rri. To rest at noon, often in the shade.

Mésos (μέσος). Greek / n. / ˈme.sos / *meh*-soss. Mean, average; middle.

Mettā (मेत्री). Pāli / n. / ˈmɛt.tɑː / *met*-tah. Loving-kindness; benevolence.

Mitzvah (הַצְוָה). Hebrew / n. / ˈmɪts.və / *mitz*-vuh. Commandment; technically an action performed in fulfilment of religious duty but used colloquially in reference to all good deeds.

Mnemosyne (Μνημοσύνη). Greek / name / mnɛːmo.sýːnɛː / mnee-moh-sy-nee. In Greek mythology, the goddess (or personification) of memory; one of the Titans and mother of the Muses.

Mokṣa (मोक्ष). Sanskrit / n. / ˈmoːk.ʃə / *mohk*-shuh. Emancipation, liberation, release (particularly from *saṃsāra*).

Mono no aware (物の哀れ). Japanese / n. / mɒ.nɒ.nɒ.ʁ.wɐ.ɾeɪ / mo-no-no-uh-wah-ray. Pathos; appreciating the transience of the world and its beauty.

Morgenfrisk. Danish / adj. / ˈmɔːn.frɪsk / *morn*-frisk. Feeling rested after a good night's sleep. Lit. morning freshness.

Morkkis. Finnish / n. / mɔːks / morks. A moral or psychological hangover; post-hoc embarrassment or shame at one's drunken behaviour as well as dread or confusion about what one might have done.

Mot juste. French / n. / mo ʒyst / moh szhoost. Exactly the right word or phrasing. Lit. fair word.

Moûsai (Μοῦσαι). Greek / name / moˈːsaɪ / mooh-sai. In Greek mythology, the Muses; minor goddesses who were the divine inspiration for various branches of knowledge and the arts.

Mousiké (μουσική). Greek / n., adj. / moˈsi.kɛ̃ / moo-sih-keh. Art forms of the Muses, especially music and lyrical poetry; basis for 'music'. Lit. of the Muses.

Muditā (मुदिता). Sanskrit / n. / mʊ.dɪˈtʰɑː / moo-de-*tar*. Sympathetic, vicarious happiness.

Mudrā (मुद्रा). Sanskrit / n. / mʊ.dɹɑː / moo-drah. Physical gestures and postures; symbolic hand gestures, especially in Buddhist iconography. Lit. sign, token, seal.

Musāvādā (मुसावादा). Sanskrit / n. / mʊ.sɑːwɑːdɑː / moo-sah-vwah-dah. False speech, proscribed in the fourth of Buddhism's Five Precepts.

Mustérion (μυστήριον). Greek / n. / muːsˈteɪ.riːɒn / moos-*tay*-ree-on. Mystery, secret; a secret doctrine; a truth that requires initiation to experience or understand.

N

Naches. Yiddish / n. / ˈnʌ.xəs / *nuh*-khuz. Joyful pride in someone else's success (particularly someone we love or have a connection to).

Namaste (नमस्ते). Hindi / exclamation / nʌˈmæsteɪ / nuh-mah-stay. From the Sanskrit *namas* (bowing) *te* (to you); often interpreted in a spiritual context as 'I bow to the divine in you'.

Natura naturans. Latin / phrase / nəˌtjʊə.rə ˈnat.jʊr.anz / nuh-choor-rah *nah*-choor-anz. Nature as a creative force, process, or manifestation of the divine. Lit. nature naturing.

Nemesis (Νέμεσις). Greek / n., name / nɛ.mə.sɪs / neh-muh-sis. A process of justice and/or retribution, personified as a goddess in Greek mythology; a form of divine punishment against evil deeds, undeserved fortune and particularly *hubris* (arrogance towards the gods).

Nichtwollen. German / n. / nɪçtˈvɔlə / neekht-*voh*-ley. Non-willing, non-wishing, non-wanting.

Nirodha (निरोध). Sanskrit / n. / nɪ.rəʊd.hʌ / ni-rode-huh. Cessation; the third Noble Truth of Buddhism, which holds that *duḥkha* can be addressed by overcoming craving and attachment.

Nirvāṇa (निर्वाण). Sanskrit / n. / nɪə'wɑːnə / nir-*vwah*-nuh. Release from *saṃsâra*; ultimate happiness; total liberation from suffering. Lit. extinguished or blown out (as a flame).

Njuta. Swedish / v. / njuːta / nyoo-ta. To enjoy deeply; to appreciate profoundly.

O

Omega (Ωμέγα). Greek / n. / o'me.ɣa / oh-*mey*-kha. The last letter of the Greek alphabet (Ω, ω); can denote the end of a series or the conclusion of something.

Omoiyari (思いやり). Japanese / n. / o.moi.ja.ri / oh-moy-yah-rih. Altruistic sensitivity; an intuitive understanding of others' desires, feelings and thoughts; action resulting from this understanding.

Onsay. Boro / v. / 'ɒn.seɪ / *on*-say. To pretend to love.

Ö-pa-me (འོད་དཔག་མེད). Tibetan / name / əʊ.pɑːmeɪ / oh-par-may / aka Amitābha (Sanskrit). Celestial Buddha of Infinite Light and Goodness; creator of the 'Pure Land' (Sukhāvatī in Sanskrit).

Opia. English (new) / n. / 'əʊ.pɪə / *oh*-pee-ah. The ambiguous intensity of eye contact; coined by John Koenig.

Orgasmós (οργασμός). Greek / n. / ɔr.ɣa.'zmɔs / or-yaz-mos. Orgasm; climax; swelling, burgeoning; excitement.

Orka. Swedish / n. / 'ɔr̩ka / *orr*-kah. The requisite energy for a task; resilience, spiritedness.

Ouranus (Οὐρανός). Greek / n., name / oːra.nós / oo-rah-nohs. Sky; heaven; in Greek mythology, the god of the sky and heavens, son and/or husband of Gaia.

P

Paixnidi (Παιχνίδι). Greek / n. / pɛkʰ'niːdi / pekh-*nee*-dee. Playful or gameful forms of affection. Lit. game.

Panache. French / n. / pa.naʃ / pah-nash. Stylish, original or flamboyant self-confidence. Lit. plume (e.g., on a helmet).

Pāṇātipātā (पाणातिपाता). Sanskrit / v. / pɑːnaːtɪ.pɑːtaː / pah-nah-ti-pah-tah. To harm or kill living things; proscribed in the first of Buddhism's Five Precepts.

Pañcaśīlāni (पञ्चशीलानि). Sanskrit / n. / pʌn.ʧʌ ʃiːˈlɑːnɪ / pun-suh shee-*lah*-ni. The Five Precepts of Buddhism.

Pashtunwali (پښتونوالی). Pashto / n. / pʌʃ.tuːn.wɑːliː / puhsh-toon-wah-lee / aka Pakhtunwali. The ethical code of the Pashtun people. Lit. the way of the Pashtuns.

Passeggiata. Italian / n. / päs.sādˈjaːtä / pa-saj-yah-ta. A leisurely stroll.

Páthos (πάθος). Greek / n. / ˈpæ.θʊs / *pah*-thoss. Suffering; emotion; experience.

Paṭṭhāna (समृत्युपस्थान). Pāli / n. / pʌ.θɑːnʌ / puh-thah-nuh. Conditions; setting forth, going forward.

Persephónē (Περσεφόνη). Greek / name / pərˈsɛ.fə.ni / pur-she-feh-nee. In Greek mythology, queen of the underworld; daughter of Zeus and Dēmētēr; known as Proserpina in Roman mythology.

Pertu. Hungarian / n. / ˈpeə.ty / *pear*-too. Drinking or bonding ritual that signifies the establishment or maintenance of a friendship. Lit. by/for you.

Phi (φεῖ). Greek / n. / pʰeːˉ / fee / aka pheî. The twenty-first letter of the Greek alphabet; symbol for the golden ratio (1.618 . . .).

Philautia (φιλαυτία). Greek / n. / fɪˈlɔːtɪə / fi-*law*-tia. Self-love, encompassing self-respect, self-compassion and so on.

Philia (φιλία). Greek / n. / fiˈli.a / fi-*lee*-ya. Friendship; platonic love.

Phrónēsis (φρόνησις). Greek / n. / frʊˈniːsɪsˉ / froh-*nee*-siss. Practical wisdom; discernment; knowledge relating to determining ends and the means of attaining them.

Pneumatikós (πνευματικῶς). Greek / adj. / pnɛβ.mɑ.tiˈkos / pneu-mah-tee-*kose*. Spiritual; pertaining to the spirit; being with or of the spirit of God.

Polis (πόλις). Greek / n. / pó.lis / poh-liss. City-state; a body of citizens.

Poseidôn (Ποσειδῶν). Greek / name / po.se̯e.dɔ́ ɔn / por-seh-dorn. In Greek mythology, god of the ocean, earthquakes, storms and horses; known as Neptune in Roman mythology.

Prâgma (πρᾶγμα). Greek / n. / ˈprɑy.ma / *prayj*-mah. A deed or action; used to denote rational, sensible love.

Prajña (प्रज्ञ). Sanskrit / n. / prʌn.jaː / prun-yah. Wisdom and experiential insight.

Prāṇā (प्राण). Sanskrit / n. / prɑːnɑː / prah-nah. Air, wind; breath; spirit, life-force.

Pratītya-samutpāda (प्रतीत्यसमुत्पाद). Sanskrit / n. / praˈtiːt.jʌ sʌ.mʊtˈpɑːdʌ / pruh-*teet*-yuh suh-muut-*pah*-duh. Dependent origination; the law of conditionality.

Pretoogjes. Dutch / n. / prɛtˈoːx.jiːs / pret-*oh*-yeess. The twinkling eyes of someone who is engaging in benign humour or mischief. Lit. fun eyes.

Profanus. Latin / adj. / prɔˈfaːnʊs / proh-*far*-noos. Secular; origin of 'profane'. Lit. before (*pro*; i.e., outside) the temple (*fanus*).

Prōtógonos (Πρωτογόνος). Greek / n. / proˈto.ɣo.nos / pror-*tor*-khor-nors. In Greek mythology, the first generation of deities. Lit. first-born.

Q

Qì (氣). Chinese / n. / tɕʰiː / chee. Air, wind; breath; spirit, life-force.

Qì chang (氣場). Chinese / n. / tɕʰiː ʧæŋ / chee chang. Energy field (e.g., between or around multiple people).

Qì gōng (氣功). Chinese / n. / tɕʰiː gʊŋ / chee-gong. A practice of developing mastery over body and mind. Lit. breath work.

Quadratura. Italian / n. / kwad.raˈtu.ra / kwod-rah-*toor*-ah. Painting architectural details onto flat surfaces to create the impression of three-dimensional space. Lit. squaring, balancing.

Querencia. Spanish / n. / kɛˈɹɛn.sɪə / keh-*ren*-sia. A place where one feels secure and from which one draws strength.

Que será será. Spanish / exclamation / ke seˈra seˈra / keh seh-*rah* seh-*rah*. Acceptance of or resignation to fate. Lit. what will be will be.

R

Ramé. Balinese / n. / ɹɑːˈmeɪ / rah-*may*. A lively, boisterous social occasion.

Rasa (रस). Sanskrit / n. / rʌ.sə / ruh-suh. The emotional theme of an artwork and/or the feeling it evokes in the audience. Lit. juice, essence.

Reiki (霊気). Japanese / n. / ɹe̞ːkiː / ray-kee. A system of alternative medicine, usually credited to Mikao Usui, in which hands are placed on or close to the patient's body to direct the flow of *qì*. Lit. soul, spirit, miraculous, divine (*rei*) life-force (*ki*, aka *qì*).

Ren (rn). Egyptian / n. / rən / rn. Name (given at birth) that assured continued life for the person while it was spoken; a constituent of the soul in Egyptian theology.

Rén (仁). Chinese / n. / ɹɛn / ren. Humanity; benevolence; the positive feeling generated by altruistic behaviour.

Renaissance. French / n. / ʀ(ə).nɛ.sɑ̃s / ruh-nay-sohs. A period of European history between the thirteenth and seventeenth centuries, driven by the rediscovery of classical works and associated with great humanistic art and philosophy. Lit. rebirth or revival.

Resfeber. Swedish / n. / riːsˈfiːbər / reess-*fee*-burr. The sense of excitement and nervousness experienced by a traveller prior to undertaking a journey.

Riposo. Italian / n. / riˈpɔso/ rre-*poor*-soh. Rest, repose; a nap.

Ṛta (ऋतं). Sanskrit / n. / rə.tə / rh-t. Order, rule; truth; that which is properly or excellently joined; the principle of natural order that regulates and coordinates the operation of the universe.

Rūpa (रूप). Sanskrit / n. / ruːpə / roo-puh. Matter, body, material form; in Buddhism, the first *skandha*, which refers to the material body.

S

Sacer. Latin / adj. / ˈsaːtʃer / sar-cher. Sacred, holy, hallowed, consecrated; something set apart; origin of term 'sacred'.

Salām (مالس). Arabic / n. / saˈlaːm / sah-*lahm*. Peace, harmony, wholeness, prosperity, welfare, tranquillity; used as a salutation.

As-salāmu ʿalaykum (مكيلَعمالّسلا). Arabic / exclamation / asːaˈlaːmu ʕaˈlajkum / ah-sah-*lah*-mu kha-*lay*-koom. Standard greeting. Lit. peace be upon you.

Salon. French / n. / sa.lɔ̃ / sall-ohh. Cultural event or gathering, usually devoted to literature and art, often organised by a female host. Lit. lounge or sitting room.

Sama (عامَس). Arabic / n. / ˈsa.ma / *sah*-mah. Devout contemplation; worship, particularly in the Sufi tradition, often involving music, singing and dance. Lit. listening.

Samādhi (समाधि). Sanskrit / n. / sʌˈmaːdʰɪ / suh-*mah*-dee. Acquisition of integration, wholeness, truth; intense concentration or absorption; one-pointedness and unification in meditation.

Śamatha (शमथ). Sanskrit / n. / ʃʌ.mʌ.θʌ / shuh-muh-thuh. Slowing or calming down; one-pointed meditation (e.g., as a means to calm the mind). Lit. pacification, rest.

Saṃjñā (संज्ञा). Sanskrit / n. / sə̃.gnjaː / suhm-gnyah. Perception, cognition; in Buddhism, the third *skandha*.

Saṃkalpa (संकल्प). Sanskrit / n. / sũ.kʌl.pʌ / suhm.kul.puh. Resolve, determination; purpose, intention; as per *samyak-saṃkalpa*, of the Buddhist Noble Eightfold Path.

Saṃsāra (संसार). Sanskrit / n. / ˌsə̃ˈsɑːrə / suhm-*sah*-ruh. Cyclical, circuitous change; a theory of rebirth; the nature of conventional existence. Lit. wandering or world.

Saṃskāra (संस्कार). Sanskrit / n. / sə̃ˈskɑːrʌ / suhm-*skar*-uh. Mental volitional formations; karmic imprints; conditioned things; in Buddhism, the fourth *skandha*.

Samudaya (समुदाय). Sanskrit / n. / sʌ.mʊˈdaɪ.jʌ / suh-moo-*dye*-uh. Origin, cause; Buddhism's second Noble Truth, which identifies craving and attachment as the main cause of *duḥkha*.

Samyak (सम्यक). Sanskrit / n., adj. / sʌm.jʌk / sum-yuk. Right, correct; best.

Saṅgha (संघ). Pāli / n. / ˈsʌŋ.gʌ / sung-huh. A Buddhist community. Lit. assembly.

Sati (समृति). Pāli / n. / ˈsæ.tiː / *sah*-tee / aka smṛti (Sanskrit). Mindfulness or awareness of the present moment. Lit. recollection or remembrance.

Saudade. Portuguese / n. / sɐwˈða.ðɨ / sow-*dha*-dh. Melancholic longing; nostalgia; dreamy wistfulness.

Savoir être. French / n. / sav.waʀ.ɛtʀ / sav-wah-et-ruh. Knowing how to carry oneself; interpersonal skills. Lit. knowing how to be.

Savoir faire. French / n. / sav.waʀ.fɛʀ / sav-wah-fare. Life skills; social and practical know-how; the ability to behave in the best and most confident way in a variety of situations. Lit. knowing how to do.

Savoir vivre. French / n. / sav.waʀ.viv.ʀ / sav-wah-*veev*-ruh. Familiarity with norms and customs; refinement. Lit. knowing how to live.

Schnapsidee. German / n. / ʃnaps iˈdeː / *shnaps*-ee-*day*. A ridiculous plan, usually, though not necessarily, formulated while drunk; generally used pejoratively. Lit. liquor idea.

Sébomai (σέβομαι). Greek / v. / ˈsɛb.ɔm.aiː / *seb*-ohm-aaee. To revere, honour; to be in awe of.

Sehnsucht. German / n. / ˈzeɪnˌzuːxt / zeen-zukht. Life-longings;

intense desire for alternative paths and circumstances. Lit. addiction to longing.

Selah (הֶלָּס). Hebrew / n. / siːlɑː / see-lah. A pause for reflection; a musical interlude (e.g., in a psalm).

Sfumato. Italian / v., adj. / sfuˈma.to / sfoo-*mah*-toh. Derived from *fumo* ('to smoke'); to soften or shade into; to taper or fade out; a painting technique in which colours are subtly shaded into one another; vague, blurred, mellow.

Shabbat (תָּבַּשׁ). Hebrew / n. / ʃəˈbaːt / shuh-bart / aka šabbāṯ, Sabbath. From the verb *shavat,* meaning 'to rest or cease'; a day set aside each week for rest, abstinence and/or worship in various religious traditions.

Shalom (םוֹלָשׁ). Hebrew / n., exclamation / ʃɔːˈləʊm / shor-*lome.* Peace, harmony, wholeness, prosperity, welfare, tranquillity; used as a salutation.

Sheut (šwt). Egyptian / n. / ʃwɛt / shwet. Shadow, silhouette; the ever-present shadow of death; a constituent of the soul in Egyptian theology.

Shinrin-yoku (森林浴). Japanese / n. / ʃin.ɹiːjɒk.ə / shin-ree-yok-uh. Appreciating and harnessing the restorative power of nature. Lit. forest bathing.

Shizen (自然). Japanese / n. / ʃiːzɐ̃N / shee-zun. Naturalness; absence of pretence, contrivance or premeditation (e.g., in art).

Shù (恕). Chinese / n., v. / ʃuː / shoo. Forgiveness or to forgive; mercy; reciprocity.

Siddhārtha (सिद्धार्थ). Sanskrit / n. / sɪd.dɑːr.θʌ / sid-dar-thuh. One who has achieved an aim; the given name of the Buddha.

Siesta. Spanish / n. / sɪˈɛstə / see-*est*-uh. A short nap, usually taken in the early afternoon.

Ṣifr (رفص). Arabic / n. / sɪfr / sif-rr. Void; empty place; zero, cypher; possibly an adaptation of the Sanskrit *sūnya*; origin of 'zero' in English.

Śīla (शील). Sanskrit / n. / ʃiːlʌ / shee-luh. Morality, ethics, virtue; custom, practice; conduct; disposition, nature, tendency.

Simpatía. Spanish / n. / sim.paˈtiːæ / sim-pah-*tee*-ah. Accord and harmony within relationships and society generally.

Sirva vigad. Hungarian / v. / ʃiːrvɒ vigɒd / sheer-va vig-od. Taking one's pleasures tearfully in a melancholic intermingling of joy and sorrow. Lit. weeping (*sirva*) merrymaking (*vigad*).

Sisu. Finnish / n. / ˈsi.su / *si*-soo. Extraordinary determination and courage, especially in the face of adversity.

Sjövættir. Old Norse / n. / ˈsjø.vɛt.teə / *shyoor*-veh-teear. In Norse mythology, sea spirits, wights, sprites.

Skandha (स्कन्ध). Sanskrit / n. / ˈskʌn.dʌs / *skun*-duss. Aggregate, heap, grouping; used to describe the five elements that constitute the human being.

Smultronställe. Swedish / n. / smʊl.trɒnˈstɛl.ɛ / smool-tron-*stel*-eh. A quiet place where one goes to retreat or relax. Lit. a forest berry patch.

Sobremesa. Spanish / n. / so.breˈme.sa / soh-brreh-*may*-sah. Talking while sitting around the table after eating. Lit. over/on/above table.

Soirée. French / n. / swa.ʀe / swah-rray. A cultured evening party that usually centres on music or conversation.

Solivagant. Latin / n., adj. / səʊˈlɪ.və.gənt / so-*liv*-a-gnt. A lone wanderer; characterised by lone wandering.

Sophia (σοφία). Greek / n. / soˈfi.a / soh-*fee*-ya. Wisdom, knowledge.

Storgē (στοργή). Greek / n. / stoɹˈyə / store-*geh*. Familial love; care and affection, usually among relatives.

Substantia. Latin / n. / sʊpˈstan.ti.a / soop-stan-tee-ah. Essence, substance; material, contents; self-subsistence.

Sukha (सुख). Sanskrit / n. / ˈsʊ.kʰə / *suh*-kuh. Pleasure; ease; satisfactoriness; antonym of *duḥkha*.

Sukhāvatī (सुखावती). Sanskrit / n. / suːkɑːvʌti: / soo-kar-vuh-tee. A celestial 'Pure Land' in certain schools of Buddhism. Lit. Land of Pure Bliss.

Śūnyatā (शून्यता). Sanskrit / n. / ʃʊn.jʌˈtɑː / shoon-yuh-*tah*. Emptiness, boundlessness, boundarylessness; the idea that all phenomena arise due to the presence of certain conditions and have no intrinsic identity.

Superego. Latin (new) / n. / ˈsʊ.pɛr ˈɛ.gɔ / *su*-per eh-go. Used by translators of Freud to represent the original German *Über-Ich* (i.e., 'over-I' or 'above-I'), referring to internalised societal norms and values.

Surāmerayamajja pamādaṭṭhānā (सुरामेरयमज्ज पमादठ्ठाना). Sanskrit / n. / sʊˈrɑːmeɪ.rʌ.jʌ.mʌ.dʒʌː pʌ.mɑːdʌt.hɑːna: / soo-*rah*-may-ruh-yuh-muh-juh puh-mah-dut-hah-nuh. Intoxicating and/or unmindful states resulting from the consumption of alcohol and other drugs, proscribed by the fifth of Buddhism's Five Precepts.

Sutta (सूत्र). Pāli / n. / ˈsʊt.ə / *soo*-tuh / aka sūtra (Sanskrit). Teaching, rule, aphorism. Lit. thread, string.

Symposion (συμπόσιον). Greek / n. / sɪmˈpoʊ.si.ən / sim-*poe*-see-un. From *sympinein*, meaning 'to drink together'; a banquet and/or drinking party, accompanied by music and conversation (e.g., philosophical discussions).

T

Ta'ârof (تعارف). Persian / n. / t̪ʰɒːˈrof / thar-*rof.* Politeness; social intelligence (e.g., in exchanging hospitality and gifts).

Taarradhin (تراضٍ). Arabic / n. / ˈtæн.ræн.diːn / *takh*-rah-deen. A win–win; a solution or compromise in which both parties are satisfied.

Tai chi (太極). Chinese / n. / taɪ tɕʰiː / *ty*-chee / aka tài jí. A martial art involving slow, deliberate movements. Lit. supreme or ultimate force/energy.

Taizé. French / n. / ˈtɛ.zeɪ / *teh*-zay. Contemplative Christian worship practised by the ecumenical Taizé community in France, characterised by music and/or singing, interspersed with readings, prayers and silence.

Talkoot. Finnish / n. / ˈtal.koːt / *tahl*-koort. A collectively undertaken task; voluntary community work.

Tantra (तन्त्र). Sanskrit / n. / ˈtʌn.trə / *tun*-truh. Any systematic teaching, method or practice; more recently used to denote sexual–spiritual practices. Lit. weave or loom.

Tao (道). Chinese / n. / tʰaʊ / t/d-ao. Omnipotent and all-pervasive creative, generative power; path or way; the unfolding process of reality itself.

Tarab (طرب). Arabic / n. / ˈtɑːrəb / *tah*-rrb. Singing, chanting; musically induced ecstasy or enchantment.

Tat tvam asi (तत्त्वमसि). Sanskrit / phrase / tʌt.twʌm.æsiː / tut-twum-ah-see. A central expression of *ádvaita* philosophy, articulating the oneness of *ātman* and *Brahman*. Lit. Thou art That.

Te (德). Chinese / n. / tɜː / *ter* / aka dé. Virtue; morality; integrity; inner power.

Tempus fugit. Latin / phrase / ˈtɛm.pəs ˈfuːdʒɪt / *tem*-puss *foo*-jit. Time flies, flees, escapes.

Terroir. French / n. / teʀwaʀ / *tayr*-wahr. The natural ecosystem or environment in which a product is grown and the qualities imbued within the product as a result. Lit. earth or soil.

Tertulia. Spanish / n. / terˈtul.ja / terr-*tool*-ya. A social gathering or conversation, usually with literary or artistic overtones.

Þetta reddast. Icelandic / phrase / ˈθæ.tæ ˈrɛtːast / *tha*-ta *reht*-ust. Everything will work out OK; used especially in unpromising circumstances.

Thymós (θυμός). Greek / n. / θyˈmos / thoo-*moss*. Spiritedness; connotes flesh and blood.

Titânes (Τιτᾶνες). Greek / n. / ti.tan.ɛs / tih-tah-ness. In Greek mythology, the Titans, the second generation of deities.

Tjotjog. Javanese / v. / ʧəʊ.ʧəʊg / choh-chog. To fit; to harmonise in a relationship and with society at large.

Tonglen (གཏོང་ལེན). Tibetan / n. / tɒŋ.lɛn / tong-len. A meditation practice that involves 'breathing in' the suffering of others, transmuting it in one's heart, and 'breathing out' love. Lit. giving and taking, or sending and receiving.

Torschlusspanik. German / n. / ˈtɔːʃ.luːs.pæ.nɪk / *torsh*-looss-panik. Worry about diminishing life opportunities as one ages; acting hastily when time is running out. Lit. gate-closing panic.

Toska (тоска). Russian / n. / tʌˈskaː / tuh-*skah*. Longing, often for one's homeland; nostalgia, wistfulness.

Turangawaewae. Māori / n. / təˌrʌŋ.gəˈwaɪ.waɪ / tur-rang-uh-why-why. A place where one feels rooted, empowered and connected. Lit. a place to stand.

U

Ubuntu. Zulu/Xhosa / n. / ʊˈbuːn.tʊ / uu-*boon*-tuu. Kindness and benevolence to others in a spirit of common humanity.

Uitbuiken. Dutch / v. / ˈəʊt.bɜː.ɣən / *oat*-ber-ghen. To relax, sated, between courses or after a meal. Lit. outbellying.

Unbewusste. German / n., adj. / ʊn.bəˈvʊst / oon-buh-*voost*. Unconscious; used as a noun in psychoanalytic theory (*das Unbewusste*) to denote aspects of the mind that are inaccessible to conscious inspection.

Upaniṣads (उपनिषद्). Sanskrit / n. / ʊˈpə.nɻ.ʂəd̪ / oo-*puh*-nee-shuud. Foundational texts of what is now known as Hinduism; the concluding sections of the four *Védas*. Lit. sitting down near.

Upekkhā (उपेक्षा). Pāli / n. / u.pɛkʰˈʃaː / oo-pekk-ah. Equanimity, detachment; calmness, balance.

Utepils. Norwegian / n. / ˈuːtəˌpɪlz / oo-*tuh*-pilz. A beer that is enjoyed outside, especially in the sunshine. Lit. outdoor lager.

Utu (उतु). Sanskrit / n. / ʊtʊ / uu-tuu. Seasons, as per *utu-niyāma*, the law of the seasons: the regularity of environmental phenomena.

V

Vāc (वाचा). Sanskrit / n. / waːk / vwahk. Speech, voice; as per *samyak-vāc*, of the Buddhist Noble Eightfold Path.

Vættir. Old Norse / n. / vɛt.teə / veh-teear. In Norse mythology, nature spirits, wights, sprites.

Vajrayāna (वज्रयान). Sanskrit / n. / ˌvʌ.dʒrəˈjaːnə / vud-jruh-*yah*-nuh. An esoteric branch of Buddhism involving advanced (Tantric) teachings and practices. Lit. diamond or thunderbolt (*vajra*) path (*yāna*).

Vatnavættir. Old Norse / n. / vaht.nə.vɛt.teə / vaht-nuh-veh-teear. In Norse mythology, water spirits, wights, sprites.

Vedanā (वेदना). Sanskrit / n. / veɪ.dʌ.naː / vwey-duh-nar. Feeling tone; quality of a sensory object (pleasant, unpleasant or neutral); in Buddhism, the second *skandha*.

Vedānta (वेदांत). Sanskrit / n. / veɪ.dʌːn.tʌ / vey-duhn-tuh. The concluding sections of the four *Vēdas*. Lit. end of the *Vēdas*.

Vēdas (वेद). Sanskrit / n. / ˈveɪ.də / vway-duh. The foundational texts of what is now known as Hinduism. Lit. knowledge, wisdom.

Vidunder. Swedish / n. / viːˈdundə / vee-doon-duh. Miracle; prodigy; monster; any impressive or threatening entity that inspires awe.

Vijñāna (विज्ञान). Sanskrit / n. / vɪg.njaːnə / vwig-yah-nuh. Consciousness, mind; discernment; in Buddhism, the fifth *skandha*.

Vinyāsa (विन्यास). Sanskrit / n. / vɪnˈjaːsə / vwin-*yah*-suh. The dynamic movement between *āsana* in yoga; a form of yoga with a particular emphasis on movement between postures. Lit. to place or arrange in a special way.

Vipāka (विपाक). Sanskrit / n. / vɪˈpaːkʌ / vwih-*pah*-kuh. Ripening; the result, ripening or maturation of *karma*.

Vipassanā (विपश्यना). Pāli / n. / vɪ.pʌ.sʌ.naː / vwih-puh-suh-nah. Insight; clear seeing; cultivating awareness (e.g., of the nature of reality).

Vorfreude. German / n. / 'foːa̠ˌfʀɔɪ.də / *for*-fhroy-duh. Joyful anticipation derived from imagining future pleasure.

Vyāyāma (व्यायाम). Sanskrit / n. / vjɑːjɑː.mʌ / vyah-yah-muh. Effort;
exercise, training; as per *samyak-vyāyāma*, of the Buddhist
Noble Eightfold Path.

W

Wabi sabi (侘寂). Japanese / n. / ɰaːbi sɑːbɪ / wah-bee sah-bee.
Imperfect, weathered, aged, rustic beauty; the aesthetics of
impermanence and imperfection.

Waldeinsamkeit. German / n. / valt'ain.zaːm.kaɪt / valt-ayn-sam-
kite. The sensation of isolation experienced when alone in the
woods. Lit. forest solitude.

Wanderlust. German / n. / ˌvæn.dɛˈlʊst / *van*-deh-*loost*. Desire or pre-
dilection for travel and adventure. Lit. desire to hike or roam.

Weltanschauung. German / n. / 'vel.tæn.ʃaʊʊŋ / *vell*-tan-shao-ung.
An overarching worldview or philosophy of life.

Willkür. German / n. / 'vɪl.kyːɐ / *vill*-kuah. Following or obeying the
will; choosing to obey oneself; arbitrariness, capriciousness.

Wú wéi (無爲). Chinese / n. / wuː weɪ / woo way. Natural, spontaneous, effortless action; aligning with the *Tao*. Lit. non-action or
non-doing.

X

Xenia (ξενία). Greek / n. / x.sen.ía / kh-sen-ia. Guest friendship; the
importance of offering hospitality and respect to strangers.

Xìng fú (幸福). Chinese / n. / ɕɪŋ.fʊː / *shing*-fuu. Contentment; deep
happiness. Lit. fortunate blessing.

Y

YHVH (יְהֹוָה). Hebrew / n. / jɛ.həʊ.væ / yeh-hoh-vah / aka Yahweh.
The Hebrew name for God (usually held to be unpronounceable
and/or too sacred to be uttered).

Yīn yáng (陰陽). Chinese / n. / jiːn.jʌŋ / yin-yung. Holistic duality;
dialectical, co-dependent opposites. Lit. cloudy sun.

Yoga (योग). Sanskrit / v., n. / jəʊ.gʌ / yoh-guh. A psychophysical system of spiritual training and development. Lit. to yoke, add, join, unite, attach.

Yuán fèn (緣分). Chinese / n. / juɛnˈfɛn / yoo-en-*fen*. A relationship ordained by destiny; natural affinity or chemistry.

Yūgen (幽玄). Japanese / n. / ˈjuːgən / *yoo*-gn. Obscurity, cloudy impenetrability; unknowability, mystery; the unfathomable depths of existence.

Z

Zanshin (残心). Japanese / n. / zãˌn.ɕɪn / zan-shin. A state of relaxed mental alertness, especially in the face of danger or stress. Lit. remaining/enduring heart–mind.

Zen (禪). Japanese / n. / zɛ̃N / zun. Concentrated attention or absorption; the Japanese adaptation of *dhyāna*.

Zeus (Ζεύς). Greek / name / zɛ.us / zeh-oos. In Greek mythology, the god of sky, thunder, law, order, and justice; supreme deity of the Olympian gods. Known as Jupiter in Roman mythology.

Notes

In the process of researching and writing this book, I have consulted numerous published sources (mostly academic papers). These sources are acknowledged with a number at the relevant place in the text, which will enable you to delve deeper into any specific topic that interests you. However, in order to save space (and paper!), I have placed the corresponding details of the citations on my website at: www.drtimlomas.com/thehappinessdictionary

Index